973.926
Mazlish, Bruce, 1923-
    Jimmy Carter : a character portrait /
Bruce Mazlish and Edwin Diamond. New York
: Simon and Schuster,
288 p. ; 24 cm.
Includes bibliographic
index.
ISBN 0-671-22763-7   ;-7
    1. Carter, Jimmy, 1924
United States--Biograp
United States--Election--1976.   4. United
States--Politics and government--977- I.
Diamond, Edwin, joint author.
    E873
                            973.9260924   79-17093

COP   2

D1042090

General Research Corp.   1980

Jimmy Carter

A CHARACTER PORTRAIT

Bruce Mazlish and Edwin Diamond

SIMON AND SCHUSTER · NEW YORK

Lyrics for "Song for Woody" by Bob Dylan reprinted by permission of Ram's Horn Music, Cooper Station, New York.

Dylan Thomas: "The Hand That Signed the Paper," The Collected Poems of Dylan Thomas, copyright 1939 by New Directions Publishing Corporation; "A Refusal to Mourn the Death, by Fire, of a Child in London," The Collected Poems of Dylan Thomas, copyright 1945 by the Trustees for the copyrights of Dylan Thomas; "Do Not Go Gentle into That Good Night," The Collected Poems of Dylan Thomas, copyright 1952 by Dylan Thomas. Used by permission of New Directions and by permission of J. M. Dent & Sons, Ltd., and the Trustees for the copyrights of the late Dylan Thomas.

DESIGNED BY EVE METZ
MANUFACTURED IN THE UNITED STATES OF AMERICA

1 2 3 4 5 6 7 8 9 10

LIBRARY OF CONGRESS CATALOGING IN PUBLICATION DATA

MAZLISH, BRUCE, DATE.
  JIMMY CARTER : A CHARACTER PORTRAIT.

  INCLUDES BIBLIOGRAPHICAL REFERENCES AND INDEX.
  1. CARTER, JIMMY, DATE.   2. PRESIDENTS—UNITED STATES—
BIOGRAPHY.   3. PRESIDENTS—UNITED STATES—ELECTION—
1976.   4. UNITED STATES—POLITICS AND GOVERNMENT—1977–
1. DIAMOND, EDWIN, JOINT AUTHOR.
E873.M39   973.926'092'4 [B]   79-17093
ISBN 0-671-22763-7

Acknowledgments

While many men and women helped us in this study, the following deserve special thanks: Patrick Anderson, Peter Bourne, Pat Caddell, Orde Coombs, Ruth Daniloff, Adelina Diamond, William Greider, Anne Mazlish, T. MacNeil Simpson, Robert Whelan, Don Winter, and Walt Wurfel. Special thanks also go to our colleagues in the Department of Humanities and Department of Political Science at MIT.

We also wish to acknowledge the contributions of sources, friends and associates who were helpful in the following places:

—In Atlanta and Plains, Joe Cumming, Reverend Austin Ford, David Gambrell, Peggy and Charles Hicks, Jesse Hill, John Langford, John and Sue Mobley, John Moss and family, Tom Perry, Maxine Reese, Elizabeth Rindskopf, Mary Ann Thomas, Jan Williams, Virginia and Frank Williams;

—In Cambridge and New York, Joe Barnard, Steve Brill, Walter Dean Burnham, Pamela Ealls, Clay Felker, Doris Kearns, Edward Kosner, David Laventhol, Chris Lydon, Richard Neustadt, Jonathan Moore, Tom Morgan, George McMillan, Richard Reeves, Hunter S. Thompson;

—In Washington, Susan Battles, Ann Compton, Franna Diamond, Nicholas Daniloff, John Deardourff, Sam Donaldson, Mel Elfin, Andrew Glass, Tim Kraft, Jon Margolis, Susan McIlhenny, Charles Morgan, Martin Nolan, Allen Otten, Robert Shogan, Curtis Wilkie, James Wooten.

The preparation and editing of this study also benefited from many skillful hands, but especially those of the following: Loraine Bennett, Annette Borenstein, Marjorie Lucker, Theodora Oppel, and Ann Rourke.

5

JIMMY CARTER

Special thanks must also go to our editor at Simon and Schuster, Alice Mayhew.

Finally, of course, the opinions and conclusions offered here are solely those of the authors.

BRUCE MAZLISH
EDWIN DIAMOND

CONTENTS

1
The Figure in the Tapestry

JIMMY CARTER has been the most "open" of men, and of presidents. He has presented himself to us in the most familiar of modes, as Jimmy and not James Earl Carter, Jr., made public his intimate thoughts and feelings, granted interviews on all subjects to all kinds of questioners (often telling them more than they had actually asked to hear). Yet, more than halfway through his first term, people were still saying that President Jimmy Carter seemed "remote" and "difficult to comprehend." While new presidents are always a little mysterious, Arthur Schlesinger, Jr., noted, Jimmy Carter "seems more mysterious than most." In *The New Yorker*, a correspondent wrote of her puzzlement and the sense of "a distance" between Carter and her which had to do not with political positions, but rather, "with feeling unsure about what he is like as a person—what fires his spirit, what dampens it, what frightens him, what moves him, what goes through his head and his heart when he is grappling with this issue and that. There is something about Jimmy Carter which makes him opaque to me. I feel as though I were looking at the wrong side of a tapestry."

For many of us, Jimmy Carter also is a troubling figure. He created high expectations as a campaigner; once in office, he didn't appear to deliver on his promises. By the summer of 1979, his

9

service as President was widely described as a "failure." Even James Fallows, who had served as Jimmy Carter's chief speechwriter during his first two years in office, has referred to Carter's "passionless" presidency. Public opinion polls were showing he couldn't be elected President against Gerald Ford if the election had been held in, say, August 1978 rather than November 1976; Democratic voters were telling the surveyors as early as 1978 that they preferred the "exciting" Senator Edward M. Kennedy over the "uninspiring" Jimmy Carter as their nominee in 1980. The Camp David summit and his dramatic trip to Jerusalem and Cairo to engage in personal diplomacy helped reverse that trend. His success in bringing together President Sadat and Prime Minister Begin to achieve a framework of peace put to rest, at least temporarily, the charges of "failure." But a few weeks later his ratings dropped again as domestic concerns, mainly inflation, eclipsed his foreign policy success. By late July 1979, even after his energy speeches and cabinet shake-up, his job rating was the lowest since Harry Truman's.

Disappointed by Carter's perceived "passionless," lackluster leadership, especially in domestic matters, and still unable to get a fix on him, people have been left with feelings of annoyance, anger, and, at times, anxiety: what we don't understand, threatens us. Unfamiliarity, perversely, also has bred something akin to contempt for Jimmy Carter. Many people not only feel unsure about what he is like as a person and a President but also are not interested in finding out about him in any serious way. He is judged "boring." Even his religious convictions, which are so central to his life and Presidency, have been dismissed as phony or suspect.

Jimmy Carter in some ways has "failed." But his Presidency cannot be dismissed as a failure. Those who pronounced the Carter Administration a failure based on the record of the first three years need only ask themselves what Ford's record or Senator Kennedy's record would be at that point if either man had been serving instead of Carter. Carter's troubles, to a certain extent, involve more than his unimpressiveness, or "phoniness," and more than the public's level of boredom or suspiciousness. Post-Vietnam, post-Watergate, post–civil rights movement, no single overriding crisis rivets public or press attention. Instead of one issue, we face what seems like a complex, growing, and perhaps intractable number of mixed issues, such as persistent stagflation. We want our leaders to do something about our problems, at the same time distrusting these leaders, and demanding less rather than more government. Since solutions appear to create additional, and worse, problems, large numbers of citizens simply wish to turn off politics and the President entirely. But Jimmy Carter remains, as Lyndon Johnson would say, the only President we've got. And those who have written the obituary for his second-term chances in 1980 ought to remember the political wisdom that holds "You can't beat somebody with nobody."

Jimmy Carter, we will argue, is not opaque, or unimpressive, or boring. While his Presidency may come across as passionless, he himself embraces, contains, powerful emotions. He is a complex, contradictory personality. Most of us, of course, are complex; Jimmy Carter, however, is *more* complex and full of contradictions, one of the reasons he reached the Presidency in the first place—and one of the reasons his Presidency in late 1979 seemed to be stumbling. Part of his contradictory complexity is an openness that has contributed to "The Mystery of Jimmy Carter," rather than resolving it. Jimmy Carter freely offers himself for his portrait, but he doesn't sit still. Or, more accurately, Jimmy Carter has so many *sides* that, in any given situation at any given time, one or another contrary side may appear. Critic Michael Novak, writing in the Washington *Star*, can fault Carter for being a rationalist who sees facts and relations abstractly, while the *New Yorker* writer worries that Carter may be too much of an emotionalist, ready to abandon himself to his feelings. Both are right in their judgments, just as the public is correct when it sees him as a liberal on some issues and a conservative on others.

II

THIS STUDY of Jimmy Carter is frankly interpretive. Our aim is to increase understanding of his character, and thus his Presidency, to find what fires his spirit and what dampens it. We have no intention of trying to make people "like" him or "dislike" him; nor is it important for our work whether or not we like or dislike him, either. We do not aim to change anyone's opinions of specific

Carter policies, though we hope that people who disagree—or agree—with him on the Middle East, energy, or defense policy will at least have a better insight into how he came to those policies.

An interpretive study does not mean a partisan study. If anything, it means trying to be more careful and impartial than usual, and paying conscious attention to unconscious biases in us and, perhaps, in our readers. John Dollard in *Caste and Class in a Southern Town* spoke of the difficulty of being respectful of the people he interviewed, yet faithfully reporting what they said: "People seem to feel that objectivity is equivalent to hostility and that one is either for them or against them." We have tried to be neither for nor against Jimmy Carter.

We believe, however, that the widespread misapprehensions existing about him among many people often reflect unreasoned biases. Southern, pietistic, low-key, Carter *does* appear different —and limited—to many people. Not too long ago, many people refused to put Richard Nixon under real scrutiny until the Watergate disclosures made it impossible to deny any longer the evidence of his character; in their support of Nixon, they didn't want to see anything bad in him. Today, others refuse to understand or scrutinize Carter; in their anger or disappointment, they don't want to see anything good in him. With Carter, too many people are in fact looking at the wrong side of the tapestry, in part because he shifts around, but also because of their own limited perspectives. The reasons for this reaction to Jimmy Carter become a part of any interpretive account, and an understanding of the "real" Jimmy Carter involves real understanding of ourselves as well.

III

HOW CAN WE BE SURE that we have achieved true understanding of Jimmy Carter? After all, we know that politicians tend to be actors, and that they project artful public images with the help of elaborate publicity machines (which also attempt to smother unfavorable impressions). Yet, while all of us wear disguises of sorts, there are limits to the best iconography, whether self-made or media-created. Jimmy Carter himself has declared that it is "almost impossible for a public figure to disguise his character or views." As he said to us during an interview, "Your basic motivations are fixed by the time you are an adult." (He also added, "Obviously you learn and your attitudes can change.") Character, then, is knowable.

This does not mean we have "scientific" knowledge—a kind of mathematical formula, or set of abstractions—to explain a person. Nor does it mean we have a novelist's knowledge and are able to reconstruct precise dialogue and mental processes ("As he pondered the neutron bomb decision, President Carter calmly thought of . . ."). We don't believe we can do that, either. But it is possible to get inside another person, and know him or her, by a combination of fact-gathering, reporting, research, interviewing, analysis, and interpretation. We have sought to decipher the "meaning" inherent in the events of Jimmy Carter's life, not only to describe them. Ours is a collaboration between an historian and a journalist; where other books on Jimmy Carter have stopped, we have tried to begin by asking our kinds of questions and aiming for a middle register between an anecdotal narrative and a detached analysis.

This analysis involves, to a certain extent, the kind of "knowing," as opposed to "knowledge," that many of us experience all the time. We say of a friend, or a public figure, "Oh, yes, I understand why he did . . . It's in character." Asked to explain, we might go into his or her background, and then say, "You see, that behavior seems only natural." The nineteenth-century romantics called this knowledge "on the pulse"—we *feel* we know, based on our own experience and on "life."

Hamilton Jordan, President Carter's chief assistant and closest political adviser, has a superior kind of "personal knowledge" of Jimmy Carter. "I understand him, and I understand when he does certain things," Jordan told us. "I understand what it is in his background that's causing him to do things. If I enumerated—and again, I'd think about this a lot if I had a chance to put it down on paper—it's the rural South . . . It's the influence of the church. It's growing up in the depression . . . It's the military experience and engineering experience, and it's coming back to Plains and starting with nothing and being successful as a small businessman. It's exposure to politics. It's being a Democratic President, who's not performing as a Democratic President is supposed to." Jordan

13

added that, of course, there's also his mother and father. "But it's difficult to relate it all, one to the other."

IV

JORDAN PROVIDES a good starting point for this interpretive biography: an account relating the major themes of Jimmy Carter's life "one to the other." Some of the themes in his life are familiar ones. "I am a Southerner and an American," Jimmy Carter announced in his autobiography, *Why Not the Best?* Carter is a typical Southerner in placing that identity first, before his larger nationality. (Not many of us say, "I am a New Englander and an American," or, "I am a Californian and an American.") The person, Jimmy Carter, like many other Southerners, carries the "burden of Southern history." In the South, William Faulkner wrote, "the past is not dead. It is not even past."

Another heritage is Jimmy Carter's religion. His conversion experience and the evangelical character of the Southern Baptist faith are well known by now; less appreciated is the influence on Carter of the theologian Reinhold Niebuhr. Even less understood is the pervasive way Carter's religious experiences—Sunday after Sunday, for years, he prepared his Bible classes like a preacher—have shaped the style and spirit of his leadership. The theme of religious belief runs from his earliest years right through to the Presidency. Those who expected him to thump the Bible or to evoke God's name from the Oval Office were looking for the wrong signs; but to ignore or underestimate Jimmy Carter's religious experiences is to forgo any serious understanding of him or his Presidency.

Similarly, the President, Jimmy Carter, cannot be understood without a comprehension of some of the burdens of the present and the weight of contemporary politics. Pressures on the Presidency from the Congress, the courts, and the press historically have limited the incumbent's efforts to lead the country in the direction of his own vision. In the late 1970s, however, after forty years of growth at the expense of other institutions, the powers of the Presidency came under special challenges. Party loyalties have broken down. A strong and undisciplined Congress has asserted imperious claims of its own. As long ago as 1968, Walter Lippmann wrote that the country needed "deflationary" policies: leaders who would reduce political promises, cut down on overseas commitments (at that time Vietnam; today it could be South Korea or Africa), offer competence rather than charismatic glamour. Yet, at the same time people demand a "strong" leader; and the contending demands create a pressure chamber for any President, including Jimmy Carter.

It is against the background of these well-documented public histories that our story unfolds. Our major themes will be personal, but public as well, keeping the social and political histories always in view. Jimmy Carter's character has to be aligned with the circumstances of his inheritance as well as the circumstances he inherited when he became President.

V

OF THESE MAJOR PERSONAL THEMES, some appear in Jimmy Carter's earliest years, and reoccur throughout his life; each involves complex pressures. A first theme concerns Carter's feelings of *belonging and being apart*, in his family, in the company of men, and in society in general. In Jimmy Carter, the outsider's needs conflict with the insider's needs. To some extent, of course, this tension exists in all of us. Immanuel Kant described the "unsocial sociability" of man, his drive to enter the state of society while retaining his isolation and autonomy.

A second theme concerns Carter's need to *measure up and to win*, the efforts of a shy, timid, undersized boy to be the tough, successful "little man" his father demanded. His father was the biggest man in Jimmy Carter's life, and a voice whose injunctions he still heeds.

A third theme concerns Carter's *power of thinking and acting positively*. Jimmy Carter's successes have come in part through his incredible self-confidence—his belief in his goodness and in his abilities to succeed—which makes defeat simply unacceptable. In his inner life, self-confidence helps Carter put out the enormous energies necessary for winning. In the life of politics and the outer world, however, a good will and a strong will may not be enough for "winning." Complex political problems do not succumb so simply to positive thinking.

A fourth theme involves *control*. First and foremost, he controls his emotions. In his own words, "I doubt that anyone has ever seen me livid . . . I really cannot recall a time when I lost control of myself or even lost control of my temper." Secondly, he controls carefully what he allows people to see of himself. Different people see different sides of Jimmy Carter and come away with different impressions, not just because of their own political perspective. Carter *wills* it that way. Representative Elliott Levitas, a Congressman from Atlanta, first observed Carter when the two men served in the Georgia state legislature in the 1960s. Carter, says Levitas, "reveals only that aspect of himself that is directly relevant to the person he is with." While Jimmy Carter may pour out one side of himself—as he did, for example, in his interviews with *Playboy* magazine—the other "sides" are held tightly in control. Still his deep anger sometimes finds release in the frequently observed Carter sarcasm. A fifth theme involves Carter's special view of leadership. His character and experiences, particularly as a Baptist lay preacher, a submarine officer and an anti-politics politician, have shaped his conception of what a leader does. He believes in the goodness of the People, and that the good leader must principally summon the People to do the best within them. While this notion is not unfamiliar—Carter acknowledges he learned this interpretation of history from Leo Tolstoy—Carter has had great difficulty translating what he sees as the People's needs into national policy.

The final theme, running deepest in his character, can be described as the *fusion of contradictions*. The ambiguities that could tear another person apart are held together in Jimmy Carter. He is a Southerner who spent most of his life escaping from the South. He talks of the land and the Old South with its agrarian values— and embraces the business ethic of the New South. He is both a liberal and a conservative; he wanted to rid the South of its racial incubus, yet was sympathetic to white Southerners. He attacks oil companies for greediness—but then decontrols natural gas prices to encourage their self-interested search for new sources. In person, he is both shy and extremely self-confident, "soft" yet steely. He is a national "leader" who never learned the art of leading large numbers of people.

The ways in which Carter fuses contradictions and exerts control over conflicting, tearing elements are fascinating to us, both as students of politics and personality and as citizens of Carter's America. Because warring forces clash in him with greater intensity than in most of us, his balancing task is harder. Because he is *the* President, the stakes involved in how Carter governs—himself and the country—are higher for all of us.

2
Family

JIMMY CARTER WAS, first of all, part of and apart from the family of James Earl and Lillian Carter. Family played, and continues to play, a major role in Jimmy Carter's life, as it does for all of us. But for him, family had a special intensity. In his own family, he learned a pattern of relationships that persists today in his White House "family."

His original family joined both white and black: mammies raised him, and his earliest playmates were black. In his mind, he belonged, felt unity, with a "family" that included his black playmates and his black mammies, as well as his parents and sisters and brother. In an idyllic account of his childhood, Jimmy Carter describes how he and his playmates—almost all black—would hunt, fish, swim, float on rafts, wrestle, and fight, existing together in the most intimate and constant ways. The unity parted, however, in school and in church. His black friends went to the black school and the black church; the segregated white schools and churches were in Plains. His family pulled apart as black and white separated under the pressure of Southern racial beliefs. Carter, or at least a side of him, came to resent that pressure. As an adult, Carter confronted that resentment—belatedly, his critics would say. But they have not allowed for his wish, deep-seated in all of us, to undo the separateness in order to reunite the original "family" as he recalled it, or wished it to be. Carter's special version of this wish, which he has imposed on the experiences of his childhood, becomes a reality for him. Out of this "reality" he finds identities with both the oppressed and those who have the authority to impose oppression.

Carter's concept of family still animates his political intentions today. It is a word often evoked in his speeches and conversations. By his own repeated testimony, he wants his service in the Presidency to be remembered as an administration that, as he said in his Inaugural Address, had "strengthened the American family, which is the basis of our society." During the campaign he would say frequently, "I come from a good family and I want you all to be part of my family." At times he stretched the idea of "family" to include everyone everywhere. When he attended the ceremonies marking the opening of the new Children's Hospital National Medical Center in Washington in March 1977, he said he hoped the new facility would set a standard for care and love for children that will "permeate the consciousness of parents and nurses and doctors throughout our system and perhaps even through the world."

Carter's idea of family extends from his own family in Plains, Georgia, to the ends of the earth, to the family of man and nations. The continuous tension between belonging and being apart within these families creates one of the contradictions in Carter that he just barely manages to keep from flying apart. The outward signs of this inner tension in Carter can be seen, for example, in his alternating appearance of warmth and iciness, of emotionalism and rationalism—behavior that leaves many people puzzled and uneasy.

While it would be hard to find a political figure who would run *against* "family," its special meaning for Jimmy Carter goes beyond the normal manufactured rhetoric of campaign speeches and dedication ceremonies. In Jimmy Carter's picture of the world a vivid, indeed dominant, image is that of his own loving, caring, close, united, extended, encompassing family. Yet, not everyone even in his own family remembers it quite that way. Jimmy Carter's memories of his immediate family are sometimes different from the memories of other members of his family, his sisters, his brother, and his mother. Sometimes, too, his own remembered accounts clash one with the other.

Carter sometimes remembers his childhood as sunny. He presents us with an idyllic picture of a Huck Finn boyhood, fishing, hunting, running in the woods. Yet sometimes Jimmy Carter's own remembrances of his childhood sound tinged with a certain resentment and defiance, at odds with the major themes of love and caring. "I worked hard when I was a little child, but I'm proud of it," he once said. "I lived in an isolated area when I was a little child, but I'm proud of it."

Carter, in fact, keeps coming back to memories of how "hard" his early life had been. He once said that his "favorite book of all time" is *Let Us Now Praise Famous Men*, "because of the analysis of the way I lived. That was the way I grew up." The book, a social documentary with text by the poet and writer James Agee and photographs by Walker Evans, describes the bleak "unimagined existence" of the family of George Gudger, a white Alabama "one-mule half-cropper," or sharecropper, and two other poor white tenant farmers, the Richetts and the Woods. The families raise cotton out of the unyielding land—a job "by which one stays alive and in which one's life is made a cheated ruin." Jimmy Carter's autobiographical words and his remembrances to interviewers were offered up in the context of a political campaign, when it is absolutely necessary for all candidates to control carefully their public words and images. Carter, understandably, wanted to present himself as a presidential candidate who knew the value of hard work; he didn't want to sound like the richest kid in town. Still, the Carters may have been among the most substantial families in the area. How could young Jimmy Carter be well off and yet feel poor? The task of finding the real child, and the man, within the edited images of memory and political iconography, can be enormously complex. How Jimmy Carter experienced reality counts as much as "actual events." In his memory, childhood embraced both happiness and a harshness more emotional than physical.

II

THE CARTERS of Sumter County were not just a family—they were a Southern, white, rural, middle-class family. In the South, the English traveler Francis Butler Simkins once wrote, the family was traditionally the core of society: "within its bounds everything worthwhile took place." Just as slavery and its aftermath helped create a distinct *Southern* history, so too did that "peculiar institution" help create a distinct *Southern* family. Like so much else in the South, the family bears the burden of white-black relationships. Black men farmed for white landowners, who in turn cared for their Negroes after a fashion; black women raised white children (and cooked, sewed, and cleaned house for their families); white men often slept with the black women who "belonged" to them, during slave times and after.

These relationships form part of that special sense of belonging together and yet being separate in the rural South, and in Jimmy Carter's own life. White "needs"—for mammies, for household workers, for mistresses—imposed a special burden on both white and Negro families, blurring the otherwise rigid caste line between the races.

In the South, for young white children of Jimmy Carter's time, white mothers merged almost imperceptibly with black mothers. Care, food, love, attention—in a word, nurturance—came as often from the black "helper mother" as from the white natural mother. So did discipline. Jimmy Carter and his brother and sisters were hardly unique in having a black mother.

Actually, Jimmy Carter had a succession of black mothers. Annie Mae Jones, an ample woman (larger for example than Lillian Carter), came when Jimmy Carter was six or seven. Mrs. Jones recalled for one interviewer how often Lillian Carter, a registered nurse, was away from home, taking care of the sick of Sumter County: "Miz Lillian, she nursed day and night. She was just like a doctor. If anyone got sick on the place, she'd be right there. I did practically everything because she would be on night duty. She'd leave in the evening and she wouldn't be back until the next morning. She'd come in and she'd have to go to bed and go to sleep. And be ready to go to work the next night. And I knew what to do. And I'd say, well, I'll stay with the children—cook, feed them. If they had to go to school, I'd get them off. I was right there every day. Sure was."

The absent—or "distancing"—mother can make life seem hard for some children (though many other children don't feel abandoned or unloved in such situations). In Jimmy Carter's case, he had black "mammies" at his side, and he even sounds proud of his mother's work outside the house. As he recalled, "My mother is a registered nurse, and during my formative years she worked constantly, primarily on private duty either at the nearby hospital or in patients' homes. She typically worked on nursing duty twelve hours per day, or twenty hours per day for which she was paid a magnificent six dollars, and during her off-duty hours she had to perform the normal functions of a mother and a housekeeper. She served as a community doctor for our neighbors and for us, and was extremely compassionate towards all those who were afflicted with any sort of illness." Lillian Carter, before her son, had learned to live apart and together.

III

JIMMY CARTER'S FAMILY was not just Southern and white; it was southwestern Georgia rural, one of only two white families surrounded by about twenty black families in Archery, a collection of houses two miles from Plains. Family necessarily played a more central role than usual. There was a little else to compete with it, few, if any, alternate sources of influence in childhood, certainly in the preschool years. Jimmy Carter's best friend until he was almost fourteen was A. B. Davis, a black boy. The sort of segregation that occurs in cities and small towns, even in Plains, where whites and blacks live apart, was unknown in Archery. The boys could be close, but had to be separate: Jimmy had to go first, to be the pitcher, to lead—"to star," in Davis' own words.

Being a Carter meant also being in a family in a social setting. The Carters were modest, respectable, strong, hardworking yeomen, not upper-class "plantation whites," but not "trash" either. The yeoman knows where everyone's family stands, or has fallen, in the community. It matters that you are the son of Mr. James Earl Carter, a prospering merchant-farmer of Sumter County; that you come from perhaps one of the two leading families around Plains (the Williamses were the other); that you are related, kin, to half the families in the area. This, too, is what family meant growing up in Plains.

IV

FAMILY ALSO MEANT an extended web of relations and, in the largest sense, ties to the past, to generations that envelop the family in both myth and history. The family line is the carrier not only of physiological characteristics—we all are aware of traits that repeat themselves through generations: a particular way of walking, the setting of a jawbone, the cast of an eye—but equally of psychological traits: a manner, a temper, the presence of a pronounced shyness or an imperious will. Generations generate character as well as physiognomy. The Carter clan can trace its ancestry back to Thomas Carter, Jr., who came to Virginia around 1635, some fifteen years after the Pilgrims arrived in Massachusetts aboard the *Mayflower*. For about 180 years ancestors on both sides of Jimmy Carter's family have flourished in Georgia and, in the last hundred years or so, specifically around Plains.

The Carters owned slaves, when they could afford them, just like their neighbors. When James Carter died in 1858, he left 303 acres that sold for $1200. His Negroes were more valuable: the county records show that Green sold for $1106; Solomon, $1261; Frank, $1200; Titus, $900; Mary and Joe, mother and child, $1125.

To defend the Southern way of life, Carters fought in the Confederate Army. None apparently rose above the rank of private. (On his mother's side, one Gordy died in the war, while another fought in the state militia.) Recent generations of Carters, and Jimmy Carter in particular, never defended the peculiar institution of the South, or glorified the war, or even referred to the illustrious Confederate cause. As far as can be determined, Jimmy Carter and his family have taken their stand outside the mystique of the Old South, free of nostalgic attachment to the days of slavery and dashing Confederate uniforms.

Though the Civil War was no longer refought in postwar days by the Carter line, another heritage of violence appears through the family history. Violence, we know, recurs as a theme in Southern life and literature, most memorably in the novels of William Faulkner. Violence flows from many elements in the South—the

23

land wrenched from the Indians; the slaves held, ultimately, by the threat of force; the struggle for property in times of limited wealth; the frontier society, where men hunted and owned guns, as casually as they owned hats or shoes (long after the frontier had ceased to exist).

Memories of those times still live within many Southerners. Griffin Bell, Carter's friend and first Attorney General, chose to talk to us not about abstract justice or the affairs of his department but about the injustices done to the Creek Indians of Georgia over 150 years ago. He spoke of the white man's expropriation of 4.7 million acres of Indian land lying between the Flint and Chattahoochee rivers. Joining in the rush to settle these lands, an earlier James Carter, and his brother Jesse, moved to Talbot County in southwestern Georgia, and eventually prospered as cotton planters.

Since James Carter's time, three generations of Carters have been involved in cases of manslaughter and violent quarrels over property. Around 1841, James Carter's son Wiley shot another white man in a quarrel over a slave. Wiley Carter was acquitted on the grounds of self-defense. His son, Littleberry Walker Carter, who had served in the Civil War, died under mysterious but violent circumstances. Apparently Littleberry Walker Carter was killed in a drunken row with his partner over the proceeds of a flying jenny they owned and operated. Littleberry Walker's son, Billy, also died violently in 1903. A farmer and the owner of three sawmills, he was shot to death in a dispute over the ownership of an ordinary office desk.

One of Billy's sons was William Alton Carter, who saw the shooting. He was fifteen then. After the killing Alton became, in his words, "kind of the head of the family from then on." Alton's brother was James Earl Carter, Jimmy's father. Alton started working in 1905 in a general store in Plains; through the years, he became known as Uncle Buddy; eventually he and his son, Hugh Carter, Sr., came to own the store together, until Uncle Buddy's death in January 1978. Hugh claims to operate the world's largest worm farm, and also serves as a state senator. His son, Hugh, Jr., was put in charge of reducing expenses at the Carter White House, and earned the nickname "Cousin Cheap."

For two generations or more, then, the Carter heritage is that of the successful, industrious, busy farmers and shopkeepers.

They are not rich or famous, but they are substantial people of the middle class. Religion is a strong, but not dominating, force in their lives. It is the land and business that call forth their major energies, with the two connected through sawmills, the industrial outgrowth of the basic crops. The strand of violence seems to fit oddly with these middle-class qualities. Yet it is there—even discounting Littleberry Walker Carter's murder, even seeing the other Carters as the aggrieved and innocent parties.

V

THE CARTER LINE is one half of Jimmy Carter's inheritance. Another side of him comes from his mother's family, the Gordys. Peter Gordy, Jimmy Carter's great-great-grandfather, came from Maryland to Georgia sometime around 1803. His grandson, James Thomas Gordy, went off to fight for the Confederacy in 1864. James's son, James Jackson, known as "Jim Jack," was Jimmy Carter's grandfather on his mother's side. He made a profound impression on both his daughter Lillian and her son. Photographs show that even at sixty he was a fine-looking man, over six feet tall, weighing 190 pounds, with pale blue eyes, graying hair, and a dashing mustache.

Jim Jack is the parent that his daughter Lillian remembers vividly as friendly and outgoing. "My father was a very compassionate person," she once said. "My father loved everybody." She says she remembers her father's many black friends. "My feelings toward blacks are from him," Lillian Carter remarked.

Jim Jack's life was the life of politics, which was for white men only at the time. His daughter describes him as "the best, biggest politician in this part of the world. He kept up with politics so closely that he could tell you—almost within five votes—what the people who were running would get in the next election. And so he was very popular." Jim Jack had been a farmer and a school teacher, and served as a postmaster during four presidential administrations. According to Jimmy Carter, this required "nimble political footwork because at that time there was no civil service system. To the winners went the spoils."

Jim Jack was an avid supporter of the populist leader Tom

Watson; one of Jim Jack's sons was named after Watson, and Jim Jack served as Watson's Third District campaign manager when he ran for Congress. Tom Watson's populism spanned many years and took on a number of shapes, one of which, toward the end of his life, was rabid racism. Jim Jack, despite his "numerous" black friends, remained loyal to Watson until the end.

Jim Jack Gordy never ran for office himself, but he was deeply involved in politics and in the patronage system by which the Democratic Party of Georgia took care of its supporters. He had also served for a long time in Richland as chairman of the board of education and used that post to get patronage jobs for the deserving in schools and colleges. At the end of Gordy's own career, the spoils system took care of him, and he was given a doorkeeper's job at the state capitol.

The Gordy heritage passes on new attributes to Jimmy Carter, while reinforcing others. Like the Carters, the Gordys started out as farmers, not businessmen. But their "business," increasingly, became politics. On both sides, the Gordys and the Carters are energetic and ambitious. They are solid citizens and generally unremarkable—until the last generation, and the union of James Earl Carter and Bessie Lillian Gordy.

3

Mr. Earl

IN ALMOST ALL THE ACCOUNTS of the parents of Jimmy
Carter published before and during the presidential campaign, the
press interviewers and political analysts assigned clear roles to
James Earl Carter, Sr., and Lillian Gordy Carter. The stories described the mother as the "liberal" counterweight to the "conservative" father in the life of Jimmy Carter. James Earl Carter, Sr.,
the austere landowner and merchant, represented ambition and
authority. Miss Lillian, the nurse, was the "caring" side of Jimmy
Carter, devoted to helping the poor and the weak; Miss Lillian
stood for nurturance and warmth. Jimmy Carter had said as much
himself in *Why Not the Best?* If the childhood years were in some
ways harsh for Jimmy Carter, it most likely was his father's doing;
if childhood was radiant and bright, then it must have been because
of the love generated by his mother. If Jimmy Carter, the man and
the President, showed great drive and discipline, then it came from
his hard-headed businessman father; if he worked for human rights
and social justice, then these values flowed from his compassionate
mother. Life and behavior, however, may seldom be that simple.

James Earl Carter, Sr., like his older son after him, was a
complex, often contradictory figure. Exuding strength, he was
timid; hardworking, yet fun-loving; ambitious, yet satisfied. In
public, he appeared hard; in private, he was compassionate. Above
all, he was there, looming larger than life in the memories of his
children. While Lillian Carter was away nursing, James Earl was

at home shaping his children's lives, imposing his perfectionist demands on them. He was a caring parent—perhaps too caring. It was James Earl who set seemingly impossible standards of performance for his children, especially Jimmy; he taught them always to play to win, and even to win out over him.

In his stocky figure, he embodied authority. He provided the punishments, the whippings, that remain so vivid in his children's minds. His was the voice of command that established their feelings toward all later authority. For Jimmy Carter this meant that, faced with authority, one obeyed, even if resentful inside. He would not openly rebel against his father's punishment, or Navy hazings, or legislative rebuffs from the Congress, but endure and go his own way. He would also identify with authority and, in authority himself, impose the same perfectionist demands as did James Earl Carter, Sr., but on himself, not on his staff. Only when his Presidency seemed lost, in mid 1979, did he demand better performance, and then in a schoolmasterish way—with evaluation forms.

James Earl Carter, Sr., clearly cannot be summed up in a simple phrase. Most accounts portray him in simple terms, and invariably as a racist. Jimmy Carter's own account in his autobiography contributes to this portrait. By exaggerating his father's racism, Jimmy Carter looks good in contrast, a progressive hero. The fact is, Earl Carter was a more complicated man, and hard to nail down with stock labels, as befits a father in this emotion-laden relationship. Earl's effect on his son Jimmy, as well as on his other children, was profound. Outwardly a typical Southerner, in their memories he possessed almost God-like qualities.

II

JIMMY CARTER IS effusive in his praise of his father's business abilities. James Earl Carter, Sr., was, Jimmy Carter writes in *Why Not the Best?* an "extremely competent" farmer and merchant, "always probing for innovative business techniques or enterprises." But though Jimmy Carter is very detailed about many aspects of his family, he offers no explanation of exactly how James Earl Carter, Sr., started out in the business world. He tells us that his father went through the tenth grade of the Riverside Academy in Gainesville, Georgia, "the most advanced education of any Carter man since our family moved to Georgia." In World War I, he joined the U.S. Army and served as a first lieutenant. One result was a high esteem for the service academies, which he passed on to his son. Earl, however, was no saber rattler. He had not seen combat; according to Jimmy Carter, he had "extremely bad eyesight" and was assigned to the Quartermaster Corps.

Lieutenant Carter returned to Plains after the war. His mustering-out pay apparently helped him start a few ventures. Like many another speculator, he leased land, planted a crop, and hoped for—gambled on—a good yield and a good market price. Some ventures paid off; others didn't. But quite clearly, by the testimony of his bride-to-be and others, he made an impression as a go-getter around town.

James Earl Carter, Sr., met Lillian Gordy in 1921. She was a nurse in training at the local private hospital, the Wise Sanitorium, run by three brothers of the Wise family. At the time she was also seeing another young man named George Tanner. Her employer, Dr. Sam Wise, intervened. "I don't like you going out with him [Tanner]," she says he told her. "I'll tell you who I would like you to go out with. It's Earl Carter. He's a boy that has more ambition than anybody in this town, and he's going to be worth a lot someday."

When James Earl Carter married Lillian Gordy in 1923, he was earning a hundred dollars a month; he had planted an Irish potato crop to pay for their honeymoon. "The potatoes didn't do so well," Lillian Carter recalls, and the honeymoon trip was postponed. Still, her husband's financial standing in the community was high enough for him to qualify for a loan; according to Lillian Carter, her husband bought his first farm on credit. The farm did well, he repaid the loan, and he bought a second and then a third farm. After that, Lillian Carter says, "We never had anything on credit. Everything—we paid cash for everything."

James Earl Carter also did some land speculation, buying and selling pieces of farm property; he also began lending money to other Sumter County residents so they could buy property, and he held their personal notes. According to Uncle Buddy, who marveled at his brother's business sense, there were perhaps 600 white

29

farmers in the area, and most of them came to James Earl to borrow money or get credit at one time or another. James Earl's own holdings grew to encompass 4000 acres, farmed by 200 black tenant sharecroppers, who called him "Mr. Earl." He also opened an office in Plains and became a commodities broker, buying peanut futures on contract from local farmers and selling to an oil mill. Later, he began selling seeds and fertilizer from the office, which became Carter's Warehouse.

The farm he bought on credit was located in Archery near the railroad refueling stop. Shortly after his marriage, he had also opened a store next to the Archery house. When Jimmy Carter was a young boy, the store sold overalls for a dollar a pair, work shoes for a dollar and a half, and the Carters' own farm products, such as syrup, side meat, lard, cured hams, stuffed sausage, and wool blankets. Though Jimmy Carter doesn't say so directly, most of the customers were black, Mr. Earl's tenant sharecroppers.

At one point, too, James Earl Carter began selling insurance policies from his warehouse office in Plains. As Uncle Buddy remarked about his younger brother's enterprising ways, "He was just a wizard, if you want to know the truth." He was kind to everybody, Uncle Buddy added, except those who owed him money.

III

BY THE TIME his first child, James Earl Carter, Jr., was born in 1924, Mr. Earl was on his way to helping run the affairs of Sumter County, along with the other settled white landlords. He served on the county board of education, and in 1952 he won election as state representative from Sumter County to the Georgia legislature.

If James Earl Carter was "innovative" in business, then he was, again in Jimmy Carter's words, "conservative" in politics. By some accounts, he was a Republican for a time; his son Billy Carter recalls how his father was opposed to Franklin Delano Roosevelt in the early 1930s, a position that brought James Earl Carter, Sr., into heated arguments with his father-in-law, Jim Jack Gordy.

Most of all, James Earl Carter, Sr., was a "Talmadge Man," first for "Old Gene" Talmadge, who was governor of Georgia 1933–37 and 1941–43, and then for Old Gene's son Herman, who took over when his father died, in the old dynasty way of Southern politics. During the Talmadge years, Georgia political power rested on the effective disfranchisement of black citizens, through intimidation and poll taxes, and the almost equally effective disfranchisement of urban citizens, through the county-unit system.

Old Gene Talmadge stands as one of the great demagogues and race baiters of the twentieth century. He was a tall, lean figure, usually stumping the crossroads towns in shirt sleeves, and his horn-rimmed spectacles and red galluses became his trademark. His appearance was mostly a bit of stage business. Talmadge wore $250 suits and owned the finest limousine made in his time; he would get to the edge of a small town and change into old work trousers held up by red galluses, walk into the town, actually stand on a tree stump, and go into an oration about how "evil nigger folk is trying to take over and kill all the white people." Then, when the crowd had gone home, he would get back into his $250 suit, climb into his limousine, laugh about what fools he had made of those "stupid red-necks," and ride to the next town. Historian George Tindall called him "the successor of Tom Watson." Talmadge, he wrote, "flaunted a populistic rhetoric against the railroads, monopolies, and Wall Street, and championed the virtues of work, thrift, individualism, and piety." He also pitched his racist appeal to small-town merchants and the independent farmers, in addition to the red-neck and the wool hat vote.

As governor, Talmadge acted on his populist rhetoric, lowering property levies, reducing telephone, railroad, gas, and power rates, and endorsing protective tariffs. But, in a pattern typical of the old Georgia politics, he also acted in a way to appeal to the business establishment. He slashed state expenditures, starved public services, and left a surplus in the state treasury. What he took from the Georgia Power Company, for example, in rate reductions, he gave back in property tax cuts. From the beginning, Talmadge attacked the New Deal and its policies of relief for the poor and minimum wages for workers. He was against the Agricultural Adjustment Administration (AAA). The New Deal, he declared, was all "downright Communism an' plain damn-foolishness."

His son Herman continued in the pattern when he took over in 1947. His racist oratory won him votes outside Fulton County (Atlanta), but his regressive tax program gained him the approval of the Atlanta business elite. Herman Talmadge also spent more on education than in the previous history of the state, built new highways, sought to attract new industry, and allocated funds for mental health and agricultural research during his governorship. In 1956, Talmadge was elected to the U.S. Senate. The years of the 1950s were a time of material improvement for many Georgians, and for no one more so than Herman Talmadge. When his wife, Betty, sued him for divorce in 1977, she placed his assets at $2.5 million, including the value of his plantation, Lovejoy.

The Talmadge mixture of populist rhetoric and a "business-like" administration—and personal enrichment—made a potent combination in Georgia politics, and it was a lesson not lost on the next generation of office seekers. Race, however, became a shifting ingredient in the mix. The county-unit system was overturned in 1962 by the Supreme Court, and blacks began voting in significant numbers from the mid-1960s on.

IV

STATE REPRESENTATIVE JAMES EARL CARTER, SR., may have been a Talmadge man until he died of cancer in 1953, but, his widow and his children claim, he was never a racist. Though he may have believed in white supremacy, he never joined the KKK or the White Citizens' Council, Lillian Carter has said. The way Lillian Carter now sees it, the terms "segregationist" and "integrationist" just didn't exist then. "There was no such thing as a liberal then," Lillian Carter said to us; everyone believed in the Southern "way of life." Lillian Carter may have cared for blacks, as a nurse and a Christian woman, while Mr. Earl may have been opposed to any "race mixing," including allowing blacks to enter his front door for social visits (as opposed to entering as housekeepers and cooks). But Mr. Earl always supported her, paid for the medicines she used, and made her liberal good works possible. His older brother, William Alton—Uncle Buddy—may have been, and still was until he died, a segregationist; but her husband, Lillian Carter said, was exactly the opposite of Alton. "I never did hear Earl say n-i-g-g-e-r. I don't even say it. I can't even say it. I hate it."

Jimmy Carter's memories are more complex than his mother's. Passages in *Why Not the Best?* show father and son with different attitudes about blacks; they have their first, and last, "racial argument"—Jimmy Carter's term—when he is twenty-seven and home on leave from the Navy, and agree never to discuss race again.

But Jimmy Carter softened with time and came to share his mother's belief that Mr. Earl was a man of his times and would have changed as the times changed. When Jimmy Carter became governor of Georgia, a new library at Georgia Southwestern College in Americus was dedicated in memory of James Earl Carter, Sr. The program notes recalled him as a man "dedicated to the ideal that all young people should have an education, and to that end he sponsored the construction of an adequate modern building for Negroes several years before equal opportunity became a major social issue." The notes serve as a reminder of the mocking definition of a pre–civil rights movement white "moderate"—someone who believed the separate facilities of the black school ought to be as good as those of the white school.

V

THESE WERE SOME of the remembered accounts of the public Mr. Earl. The private Mr. Earl appears, again in the memory of his widow and children, to be a contradictory figure. First of all, he was perceived, especially by his children, as a "big" man, a powerful man. Ruth Carter Stapleton, the third-born child, has described her father as a man of "prominence" whose "influence touched everyone." He reluctantly played the role, Mrs. Stapleton says, of "rural royalty." At Christmastime, he "took more time to talk to friends and employees . . . it became a tradition for many of his friends to stop by and pay their respects to Daddy." Family photographs of Mr. Earl, however, show a decidedly unregal figure, a short jowly man with thinning hair, stubby fingers, and eyeglasses.

His stoutness apparently created an air of solidity. Even in

1953, as he was beginning to die from cancer, he impressed his nephew Hugh Carter, Jr., who was paging for him in the legislature, as a "big man." The drop from his middle-age weight of around 200 pounds to 110 in the last year of his life was a wrenching sight for all around him, and especially for Jimmy Carter, returning from the Navy, and long absences from Plains, to be with his father.

Along with the perception of James Earl Carter's strength in the life of his children was the perception of his authority. His children draw a picture of a stern, punishing father. It was, of course, the 1920s and the 1930s, when parents of the middle class whipped their children perhaps more frequently than today. A Southern patriarchal father would be expected to be strict. His child-raising views were direct: children had to work and they had to mind. When his children fell short of his expectations in some way, James Earl Carter's response could be swift and explosive. An odd note of the Carter violence seems almost to erupt in Earl's treatment of his children. In *Why Not the Best?* Carter writes that his father "was a stern disciplinarian and punished me severely when I misbehaved. From the time I was four years old until I was fifteen years old, he whipped me six times, and I've never forgotten any of those impressive experiences." While it may seem extraordinary for someone to remember, forty years later, the exact number of whippings over the course of eleven years, it can make sense when we realize that what is trivial for a grown-up is momentous for young children, magnified beyond "real reality" in their "psychic reality."

Still, not all the Carter children have the same intensity of recollection. Gloria Carter Spann, the second-born child, says she lost count of her "spankings" (not "whippings"). One time, she told us, "Ruth and I had a fight in the bathroom over the washcloth . . . and Daddy took his belt off and came . . . both of us, with mother in between . . . and got about two licks; I still carry the scar." This last was said with a smile. Another time: "But the worst lickin' we ever got, Mother bought us new Shirley Temple dresses and we went uptown and had a mud fight, and when we got home with these new Shirley Temple dresses all muddy with red mud all over, both of us got whipped."

Mr. Earl spoke to his children with the voice of authority. As

34

Gloria Spann explained, "I don't know how many talkings-to Jimmy got. I got plenty of lectures. Some lectures ended by punishments 'worse than death.' Restrictions for two weeks, for example. As we got older, Jimmy couldn't have the car. I couldn't have a date. It was just awful." Once, sitting on a swing on her porch in Plains in the summer of her fiftieth year, she re-created a scene from her childhood more than four decades before: "When Daddy went out there and sat on that swing, he would call, 'GLORIA.' Oh, I thought, what have I done now?"

Interviewers frequently prompted the Carters to recall episodes of "color" from their childhood; but even allowing for these proddings, Mr. Earl clearly remains a strong memory twenty-five years after his death. Three times a day he was home for meals, in the manner of farm men. He was a constant visible example of hard work himself; he had his children, especially Jimmy, working alongside him. Jimmy Carter remembered getting up at four A.M., along with the sharecroppers, during the fieldwork season. As a small boy, he carried water to the croppers from a nearby spring so they could keep working. The croppers and little Jimmy worked until sundown, with time off for breakfast and for dinner—and "brief breaks to let the mules rest." Mr. Earl paid his croppers $1.25 a day for the men, seventy-five cents for the women, and twenty-five cents for the children. The work was heavy all year round, Jimmy Carter remembered: "My daddy saw to that, with his widely diversified farm industries."

While Jimmy Carter set down the work schedule in his recollections, others remember less rigorous times. Ruth Carter Stapleton has frequently described growing up in the "overly protective environment" of Mr. Earl's house, where she "never had to wash a dish or launder underwear." Gloria Carter Spann remembers what she calls her father's habit of "directed recreation": "Daddy felt our time should be occupied all the time. We had a bicycle, a trapeze under the tree, a tennis court. We had a horse to ride and a pond to fish in. He enjoyed these as much as we did." Ruth Carter Stapleton recalls hunting, fishing, and target practice with her father: "I was an eight-year-old sharpshooter," who constantly tried to please her father by hitting the bull's-eye as often as she could.

These views, divergent from Jimmy's, point ahead to his "political" exaggerations and mismemories, so vividly displayed in his 1976 campaign and his Presidency. He seems compelled to project his inner feelings—his emotional reality—outward as a description of events and external reality. He does not "lie"; but he shapes the world according to a "deeper" truth, his own needs.

Mr. Earl wanted results even when he or his children played. He pitched on the Plains all-white baseball team—the same position Jimmy Carter played in the Secret Service–press games four decades later—and he used to take on his son on the Carter tennis court between the Archery house and the roadside store. According to Jimmy Carter, the father always beat his little son at tennis, using "a wicked sliced ball which barely bounced on the relatively soft dirt court."

As Gloria Carter Spann remembers, all the children were compelled by their father to try to beat him. Talking about her brother Jimmy Carter's intense desire to win, and his dislike of being a loser, she said, "That's something I think he got from Daddy. Daddy liked cards, and he always taught us to play to win. Even when we were little, we had to play against him to win." In sports as well as work, Mr. Earl looked for results.

Still another side of James Earl Carter, Sr., somewhat at odds with the image of his striving and his austerity, appears in the recollections of his family; this is the image of the "fun-loving" husband and the parent who, as Jimmy Carter wrote, "loved to have a good time, and enjoyed parties much more than my mother." "My daddy worked hard and was a meticulous planner like me," Jimmy Carter said to us, "but he was an exuberant man. He had an enjoyable life, like my brother Billy. If you know my brother Billy, then you have taken a major step toward knowing my father."

Billy Carter himself, when we recounted to him what his brother had said, agreed that "I am a lot more like my father than Jimmy was. . . . It's on account of my outlook," he explained. "I do not say my father didn't have to push, because he did. But he made an extremely good living and everything else, which I do, too. I don't have the push that Jimmy has. You know, to succeed at everything he tries. . . . It does not bother me to lose a softball game; it drives him crazy. I won't say our daddy didn't have that push, but he was kind of like me; he was satisfied with what he was

36

doing, instead of wanting to keep going, and going and going and going. I like to get involved in the state legislature and things like that, local politics, but I don't like to gallop with it. I enjoy life. I would rather do nothing more than sit around and drink beer with 'em; I get along with everybody. I enjoy life. I am doing exactly what I want to do. My father was kind of the same way. He did what he wanted to do.''

The Carter daughters have similar memories. Ruth Stapleton has recalled the "annual Elks Children's Christmas Party" that, she said, her father inaugurated back in the 1930s on the large rolling lawn in front of the Americus Elks Club, for all the white farm children who lived in Sumter County. James Earl Carter, Sr., liked to dance, too, with his wife and also with his two young daughters, to the popular music of the swing era. Gloria Spann remembered dancing "the two-step and whatever it was then. He was a good dancer. He had all the latest records: Tommy Dorsey, Benny Goodman, Artie Shaw. He liked to work hard, but he liked to dance, go out and have a good time.''

James Earl Carter had met Lillian Gordy at a dance. After their marriage, "they had their own dates on Saturday night," Gloria Spann recalls. "When we were young, they'd go out. They had fun together." Though he taught Sunday school and read a chapter of the Bible each night to his family, James Earl Carter, Sr., was not straitlaced, at least not in his daughter Gloria's recollections. The Carters, mother and father, would also have a regular bourbon nightcap after Bible reading, though the children didn't know that, Lillian Carter says.

Some of the apparent contradictions in these remembered accounts may be no more than the perspectives of different observers, recalling different times. Jimmy Carter's memories are of the stern taskmaster and the aggressive businessman; for his first-born, Mr. Earl had the highest expectations. "Daddy always wanted Jimmy to go straight to the top," Gloria Spann says. "No matter how well Jimmy did, Daddy always said he could always do better." For the two middle children, the daughters, the memories are of another, later period when they were older, and when their father was older and more successful. With prosperity and age, parents often mellow; they let younger children have privileges that the older ones had to wait for longer. Parents become more permissive, and often more tender and open in their affection. Also, as a boy, Jimmy Carter's relations with his father, particularly in the matter of discipline and authority, would naturally be different from those of his sisters. For the younger son, Billy, born in 1937, his father had by then become in fact "Mr. Earl," a kind of rural royalty, entitled to enjoy the bounty of his business acumen. All the memories may be "true," as accurate as family memories may be.

VI

BUT THERE IS at least one side of James Earl Carter, Sr., that nowhere appears in *Why Not the Best?* or, as far as can be determined, in any of the numerous interviews that Jimmy Carter has given since he became a figure of national prominence. According to Gloria Spann, their father was "a very timid man," so shy that he could not discuss it with anybody. His timidity, she said, caused him to hide his good deeds and his emotions. Gloria Spann likened her father to a character in a book by Lloyd Douglas: "You know the man in the novel *Magnificent Obsession* who did things for people provided they would never tell anybody he had done it? My father lived like that. One of the families in town was just destitute one Christmas. The town got up a basket. He ordered a silk dress sent to the mother of the family anonymously. I said, 'Daddy, why did you do that?' He said, 'She has no money, she has no food. But she's getting food, she's being looked after. But never in her life has she had a silk dress.' "

She also remembered a time when she was working in her father's office in the late 1940s. She kept track of the "peanut tickets"—the records of orders in his brokerage operation in the Carter Warehouse. As she told us: There were "secrets between me and my Daddy. . . . My Daddy kept candy in his office drawer and every afternoon when the kids left school, they came by and each one of them came in to speak to my Daddy and get a piece of candy. Well, all the kids knew him and they loved him and they weren't a bit afraid to come in. Now I've heard some people say he was a very stern man, but I've never seen a child afraid of my Daddy."

Not only was the stern Mr. Earl unwilling, or unable, to be known in his good deeds; he also tried to avoid any public demonstration of his personal feelings. Again, according to Gloria Spann, they were at work, father and daughter, in the office. Her father saw a black man being helped out of a car. "Daddy went out there and he got him in a firm grip and said, 'Jack, this is Mr. Earl. Come here, I want to show you something.' So he brought him in, and the man was blind. Daddy put his arm around him and he took him and he said, 'I want you to put your hand out, and I want you to feel this wheel [where seeds were sorted]. I want you to feel everything about this office, so when you come back here you'll know how to get in and out.' I saw the tears in Daddy's eyes, you know, as he was showing Jack everything about the new office, just as if it was the most important thing. It was a man who had done business with Daddy over the years, and a dynamite blast had blinded him, and this was his first time out. I had never seen my Daddy just virtually embrace a man before."

Jimmy Carter, on his account, had never seen that side of his father. He had left home at the age of seventeen and had not seen his father at all, except during brief visits in Annapolis and a few home leaves in Plains, until his father's death in 1953. During these few visits, they quarreled, Jimmy Carter says, at least once over race. Jimmy Carter felt, it seems, that he had gone beyond his father, and was emancipated—superior to the older man's racial attitudes. In the radiant light of his own righteousness he was unable to notice, then, the ambiguities of his father's behavior. He could only see his father in black and white.

In 1953, all the Carter children gathered in Plains to be at their father's side when he died. On the day their father died, Jimmy Carter and his sister Ruth began to notify people around Plains. "We started out early in the morning," she says. "We went to black and white." To their surprise they found out, talking to the family's friends, that their father had supplemented the income of many families of both races or helped pay for college expenses. Jimmy, we are told, was visibly shaken by this knowledge. Ruth Carter Stapleton says it was "one of the few times I ever saw Jimmy cry. . . . He began to review his life," she remembers. He told her, "I want to be a man like my father."

In Jimmy Carter's own account, as his father lay dying, hundreds of people came to speak to Carter, Sr. "It was obvious that he meant much to them, and it caused me to compare my prospective life with his. . . . I began to think about the relative significance of his life and mine. He was an integral part of the community, and had a wide range of varied but interrelated interests and responsibilities. He was his own boss."

James Earl Carter, Sr., died in July 1953. In November, his son Jimmy resigned from the Navy and returned to Plains. He had decided, he had told his sister Ruth, to become a man like his father. In part, he did; but there was also much more—and perhaps less—in Jimmy Carter as well.

4

The Legend of Lillian

FEW PEOPLE, men or women, young or old, have captured public attention as stunningly as Lillian Gordy Carter did in the spring and summer of 1976, during her son Jimmy's presidential campaign. At the age of seventy-eight, she became one of the most instantly recognizable, and quotable, people in America. "The Nation's Grandmother," a Washington *Post* article called her; she was "a legend," in the admiring words of one weekly magazine writer.

Still, for all this high visibility and acclaim, Lillian Gordy Carter is a relatively neutral or unremarked figure in the recollections of her son Jimmy as well as in the interviews given by her other children. James Earl Carter, Sr., comes alive in the Carter children's memories; he is a tangible *physical* presence—Mr. Earl. Lillian Carter is more remarkable by her absence. She is away from home, sometimes for days at a time, occupied with nursing duties among the black families who sharecrop the Carter land, or she remains unobtrusive in the background, reading one or another book.

It was only natural that Jimmy Carter should try to give a fuller account of his dead father than of the very much alive Miss Lillian. The celebrated woman known as Miss Lillian has been able to speak for herself. Her "irrepressible" zest for life, her presence on speakers' platforms and at baseball games, her well-known "outspokenness" ("What goes down with [her] comes up," her sister, Mrs. Emily Dolvin, once announced) more than made up for the somewhat evanescent role assigned her in *Why Not the Best?* In a way, it seems that she has spent the latter part of her life "making up" the role she played earlier as mother and wife, as well as making up the role she has played in her eighth decade. Lillian Carter has become "a legend," although perhaps not in the sense intended by her many admirers.

If Earl Carter was a complex person, Lillian seems less contradictory; but her view of her husband is itself complicated. Her relation to him and her role in the family seem to be different at different times. She obviously loved him, but she also seems to be ready to apologize for some of his actions of which she disapproves and to feel herself morally superior to him. If she was perceived by her children as less omnipresent and omnipotent than James Earl Carter, Sr., her shaping role in their lives was nevertheless great. She was the culture bearer in the house. She also offered them religious inspiration—the message of "natural Christianity," not that of the segregated church. Her use of prayer taught them a form of positive thinking, a lesson her son Jimmy particularly mastered.

In the later years of her life, she joined the Peace Corps, and came at last to deal with the racial problem in the way she had long desired: by finally ending for herself, psychologically, the separation of the races and merging with blacks. In her own life, Lillian Carter dramatizes the theme of belonging and being apart.

II

SHE WAS BORN Bessie Lillian Gordy in 1898. When she served in the Peace Corps in 1966, she told other corps people to call her "Lily." Miss—or "Miz"—Lillian seems to be a media invention. Bessie Lillian Gordy was one of eight blood brothers and sisters in the family of Jim Jack and Mary Ida Nicholson Gordy. The Gordys also adopted and raised the children of the mother's sister, who had died and left them orphaned. Jim Jack's mother also lived with them. "With thirteen of us around the table for supper, we had to learn that we couldn't always have an extra slice of bread just because we wanted it. Someone else might have a greater need," Lillian Carter remembered. It was a "nice, happy . . . very close family," she adds, though "we fought like cats and dogs."

According to Lillian Carter, a frequent visitor to the Gordy house was William D. Johnson, the bishop of the black African Methodist Episcopal Church. Bishop Johnson and Jim Jack, a white Methodist, used to talk about the Bible. "This was strange for the turn of the century," Lillian Carter recalls, "my father being so friendly toward them." It was also an unusual standard of behavior for Deep South whites thirty years later, in the house of James Earl Carter and Lillian Carter. Jimmy Carter tells the story of how one of the bishop's sons, Alvan Johnson, was treated in Mr. Earl's home. Johnson, writes Jimmy Carter, "became a very good friend of us children and my mother. He was the only black man who habitually came to our front door. Whenever we heard that Alvan was back home for a visit, there was a slight nervousness around our house. We would wait in some combination of anticipation and trepidation until we finally heard the knock on our front door. My daddy would leave and pretend it wasn't happening while my mother received Alvan in the front living room to discuss his educational progress and his experiences in New England [where he was going to school]. For this was one of the accepted proprieties of the segregated South which Alvan violated. Even when Bishop Johnson came to see my father, he would park in front of the store and send one of his drivers to the back door to inform my daddy that he would like to see him, and Daddy would go out to meet the Bishop in the yard."

Lillian Carter's memories of Alvan Johnson differ somewhat from her son's. Her recollection is of a specific visit. It seems that one Sunday she had picked up Alvan's mother, the bishop's wife, and brought her back to the house so that Mrs. Johnson could talk to her son up North on the telephone—the Carters had the only phone in the area at the time. When Alvan Johnson returned to Plains a few months later, he came by to thank Mrs. Carter and give her "a big box of candy." In her memory, her husband spoke to Johnson at the front door and only left the room so that she and the young man could talk: "It wasn't a slap in the face, and it wasn't the fact that he was a segregationist . . . there was no such thing as segregation; it was the way of the world, which was a terrible way. . . . I know in my heart that had Earl lived through the desegregation, he would have felt just exactly like I do. I just hate for anything to be said about him being unkind, 'cause he wasn't.''

Whatever version is "factual"—just one visit or habitual visits, politeness or rudeness—in Carter's memory his mother appears as a friend of blacks and his father as a man who followed the "accepted proprieties." In much the same way, while Jimmy Carter talks about how hard his mother worked at her nursing career, and about how long she was away at her duties, Lillian Carter says that it really wasn't a career, that she "never depended on nursing for any kind of living or anything . . . other than just pin money," and that she quite happily gave up her duties for the life of housewife and homemaker. As she tells it, she was more a nursing volunteer aide than anything else. She says nothing of long hours, or absences. She and Dr. Sam Wise "had this little deal . . . if he had somebody who came into the hospital and was unable to pay, he would do it for nothing if I would nurse [that patient] through the critical part for nothing." Since the black sharecroppers were earning a dollar a day—less for the women—there were many patients who received free care from Lillian Carter. ("They couldn't afford to have a doctor like the white people could.") She even helped deliver babies for the sharecroppers. Her husband, for his part, paid for all the "outside expenses"—the medicines, the medical supplies—when she took care of "his" field hands and their families.

The "absences" of Lillian Carter that Jimmy Carter remembers may not have been actual physical departures as much as emotional absences. Lillian Carter had her second child, Gloria, just two years after Jimmy Carter was born, and a new baby's needs can create in a small child a sense of "absence" of the mother around the house. Also, by her own description, Lillian Carter was something of a self-absorbed young woman; she preferred reading and being alone to visiting with friends. She has frequently acknowledged that she had no close women acquaintances—probably not too surprising, given the fact that the Carters were one of the two white families around Archery. The image of the lively, gregarious, zestful Miss Lillian came much later in her life.

She rather than Mr. Earl appears to be the "austere" figure when Jimmy Carter was growing up. Books were her passion then; she has spoken of having "orgies of reading." "Although my father seldom read a book," Jimmy Carter reports, "my mother was an avid reader." Lillian Carter read at table, and so did her children: "They watched me read and they naturally wanted to read." Reading, in Gloria Carter Spann's words, could be used as an "excuse for not doing other things" by the Carter children. Their mother would ask them to do something, be told they were reading, and end up doing it herself. At birthdays and Christmas, she gave books as gifts to her children. Her favorites were Russian novels. She also read autobiographies and biographies. She liked especially Dostoevsky. In contrast, Jimmy Carter's fiction favorite was Tolstoy's *War and Peace*. Faulkner was her other great favorite, and she has given all his works to her son Jimmy. Books remained important to her throughout her life; writing home from the Peace Corps in India, in her seventies, she pleads with her family to send her novels.

During the 1976 campaign, Lillian Carter impressed interviewers with her independence, Christian integrity, and old-fashioned plain talk. These qualities were usually set in the context of her "liberal" stands on civil rights and the cause of black people. Andrew Young, who first met Lillian Carter in the 1960s, declared that he had learned from her that the difference between Southern liberals and Northern liberals is "the difference between partnership and paternalism." Orde Coombs, an urbane black writer, was similarly taken by her. "She is the out-of-place doyenne of Plains, Georgia," he wrote. "A woman who has been ahead of her time and still *is* in her hometown, but who has suddenly found that the times have caught up with her, that now she can get off her chest all she ever wanted to during the past 50 years among people who could not stand her eccentricities, her deviations from normal racist behavior." Lillian Carter remembered that she was "never one to be running in and out of people's homes. Small-town people can sometimes be afraid of independent minds."

Coombs came away thinking of her as a heroine out of Faulkner, someone in the mold of the Southern white aristocratic lady in *Light in August* who defends a black man. But Lillian Carter herself acknowledges a less heroic account of her "independence" as a younger woman. Her husband was the strong one in the family; he was the boss, she says. Raised as a Methodist, she even became a Baptist when she married because Earl was a Baptist. He also controlled the money and gave her an allowance for shopping: "He was the head of the family and I never did anything that he didn't want me to do. If I did, I had to apologize—or I was in trouble. I've apologized to him many a time when I felt like it was his fault." To keep the peace and the harmony in the family, Mr. Earl may have routinely punished the children, either physically, by his words, or, in Lillian Carter's recollections, "by taking some of [their] pleasures away." Lillian Carter says she hated punishing her children: "If I had my life to live over, I never would hit another child a lick." Once, she remembered, "I hit *at* Ruth one time and fell to the floor with a kidney stone attack!" Mostly she saw herself as the peacekeeper: "I stood between the children and Earl a lot of times. But I don't know of a better father in the world than he was about trying to keep [them] happy."

By all testimony, Mr. Earl's wife was quiet, dutiful, the dependent partner in a traditional small-town marriage. While Mr. Earl was alive, her departures from the accepted behavior of southwestern Georgia were confined to her nursing work and to certain social amenities like receiving the box of candy from Alvan Johnson and attending the funerals of members of the black tenant families who worked the Carter farms. Since her husband would decline to accompany her, she would take her little son Jimmy along to the services.

Whatever her "zest" for life in her younger years, it was principally lived through books. She let her husband sweep up the children in the orbit of his busy activities; when he would take his teenage daughter Ruth dancing at the Elks Club in Americus, she would stay at home with her work or her reading. She allowed her housekeepers to run home and hearth; she wasn't keen on housework. When the media were intent on discovering "Miss Lillian" during the 1976 campaign, various reporters, savoring her down-home aura, asked her about her favorite dishes. She told the food editor of the Macon *Telegraph-News*—and others—"I don't have any recipes and I despise cooking."

When Lillian Carter's husband died, she was, in her own words, full of pain and distress. Back then, she felt bitterness at "every woman who had a husband." She felt a deep unchristian anger at her husband's family, and particularly at his older brother, William Alton—Uncle Buddy. In 1953, her three older children were married and had their own children; she saw herself alone, except for sixteen-year-old Billy at home. She had never taken an interest or active role in her husband's many business enterprises; his commodities deals and land speculations were another world for her. She urgently needed "the support of an adult," she recalls, but Uncle Buddy "never once asked if there was anything he could do to help." After that indifference at the time of her new widowhood, they hardly spoke to each other ever again (and not, as generally assumed, because of his segregationist ways).

The death of a husband of thirty years was a shattering experience. Twenty-three years later, when we talked to her, she was still attempting to understand the experience, and had read Lynne Caine's *Widow,* a popular seller of the mid-1970s. Son Jimmy had come back from the Navy, and together they owned Mr. Earl's businesses, but she had no role in them. For two years Lillian Carter was in a kind of limbo as Jimmy Carter took charge of the business in the same way her husband had been in charge. She baby-sat with her grandchildren, fished, raked pine straw, and chopped in her garden—and felt "unhappy" and "bored." ("Boredom," she recalled, "is one of the worst sins of all.") After two years, she resolved that the "best thing was to find something to get away from Plains to do." One of her sisters was a housemother for a fraternity at Auburn University in Alabama. Lillian Carter applied for a similar job and was accepted; in 1955 she became housemother of the Kappa Alpha fraternity. Her son Jimmy gave her a new Cadillac, "so they wouldn't think I was poor," and she drove off to Auburn. She stayed for seven and a half years, advising the Kappa Alphas on their love lives, lending them her car when they needed one, and returning home occasionally to Plains.

Lillian Carter left her Kappa Alpha "family" and returned to Plains in 1962. For a time, it was as if she had never been away. The "best" white women of Plains had a club of their own, called the "Stitch 'n' Chat"; they would meet at a member's house, have refreshments, sew, and exchange news and gossip. Lillian Carter was one of the original members, but the old boredom set in again.

She took to leaving meetings early, even though she knew that "if I leave, they'll probably talk about . . . some little thing that I've done."

She gave the townspeople a big story to chat and chew upon when she worked for Lyndon Johnson in his race against Barry Goldwater in 1964, the year Georgia went Republican. Johnson favored desegregation, making him a traitor to the South. Lillian Carter was viewed in much the same way. She was co-chairman of the Johnson campaign office in Americus; her major responsibility was handing out brochures. But, she recalls, "low, bad white fellows" would make threatening phone calls, and the children of some of her supposed friends—the good people of Sumter County —would wait for her and taunt her when she left the Johnson office at night. They would, she said, "throw things like a tomato or rotten orange or something to hit my car. And I was called a n-i-g-g-e-r l-o-v-e-r."

Lillian Carter, together with her son Jimmy, also created a stir in the same year when they voted, almost alone, at a Plains Baptist Church meeting in favor of allowing blacks to attend church services. One of the complaints of some of her white neighbors about Miss Lillian was not that she was an "integrationist" ("She didn't want them in the church any more than we did") but that she wanted to "show up" others, because she thought she was "better than anyone else." Lillian Carter liked to say and do certain things, it was claimed, more because it rubbed people the wrong way rather than because she thought someday it would be considered right. Perhaps it was the active assertion of the quiet superiority she felt as a reader and person of large mind. Later, others would see the same trait in her oldest son. At times it seemed as if her life in Plains had become a status game, enduring snubs and, she remembered, holding her head a little higher and "snubbing them back."

Her depressing loneliness was brightened mainly by her grandchildren. She ran errands for them, took care of them when their mothers were away, as the black Rachels and Annie Maes had done for her. She no longer had a titular role in the family business; her son Billy had bought out her half interest. She watched a great amount of television, as older people often do: soap operas, talk shows, sports, including wrestling. Her sons were prospering in business; Jimmy Carter had become a community leader—and a state senator. Even her daughter-in-law Rosalynn, Jimmy's wife, had learned bookkeeping and was an active part of the warehouse business operations.

Lillian Carter *did* feel she was better than her widow's circumstances. One night early in 1966, while watching the *Late Show* on television in her home in Plains, Lillian Carter saw a public service announcement asking for Peace Corps volunteers. When the announcer said, "Age is no barrier," Mrs. Carter, who would be sixty-eight that August, took it, she says, "as a challenge," wrote for an application, and put her life in order so that she could "join up." On her application she stressed her qualifications as a registered nurse and asked to serve in India.

It was a highly dramatic move, as well as a dramatic choice of assignment. There seems, indeed, to have been some kind of "acting" going on on Lillian Carter's part. When she told her children of her idea, expecting them to try to dissuade her, Jimmy Carter said, as she told us, " 'Mother, you've always been for the underdog and I think that would suit you fine. Where do you want to go?' And I said, 'I put in my application'—I was mad with him though because he didn't tell me I couldn't go—'I wanted a warm country, I wanted a black country—a dark country and a warm climate.' And he said, 'What does that mean?' I said, 'I want to go to India.' Well, then . . . I came home and called Ruth; she's my sweet one, and I knew she would stop me. And I said, 'Ruth, I'm going to join the Peace Corps and I asked to go to India.' She said, 'Mother, let me get my globe.' So she got her globe and she says, 'Oh, Mother, that's a perfect place to go. You know, Bombay has always sounded to me like Arabian Nights, and I want to see you over there.' So you see, I had to go to keep from losing face."

She was going about as far from Plains as she could get (just as her son Jimmy had done when he joined the Navy to see the world). Her separation, however, was only to find another place like the one she had come from: "a black country." In India, Lillian Carter tried to deal with the same problem of being apart and belonging that she had known in her native Georgia.

Lillian Carter left for her Peace Corps training in September 1966. She was attending language classes at the University of Chicago on September 14, 1966, the day Carter ran third to Ellis Arnall and Lester Maddox in the Georgia Democratic primary for governor.

A young, Peace Corps white couple, Larry and Sandy Brown, sought out Lillian Carter on the first day of registration; Larry Brown's father had been a fundamentalist minister. His mother was a Southerner, and he himself had lived in the South as a child as his father moved from one ministry to another. When the Browns exchanged introductions with her, she told them, "My name is Lillian Carter, but call me Lily." Larry Brown was curious to learn why she had signed up for the Peace Corps. She told him, that first day, "I like black people. . . . I couldn't do enough for them in the United States and that's why I wanted to join." Her statement, Brown informed us, "was like a red flag to me . . . it made me very suspicious of her." Brown felt unsure about whether "Lily Carter" was something of a phony, given to making outrageous statements that would shock people, or whether she was a "white Southern lady out of the old school." He wavered between the two views, while finding her an engaging, delightful, alive personality.

Later, when they visited her in her billet outside Bombay, they would listen, in Brown's words, "to her tales of Plains, which we didn't believe." The "tales" included the stories of the integration battle at the Plains Baptist Church and of her friendship with various black leaders, such as Andrew Young. When Lillian Carter told the Browns about her "black friends," Larry Brown recalls, it wasn't so much that he didn't believe her as that he thought she was "deluding" herself. Her ability to recast the past in a certain way, Brown said, was something he could well understand, remembering his own family. "She dramatized everything," Brown explained, "and that's a very Southern thing."

Less sympathetic observers, particularly non-Southerners, upon meeting Miss Lillian, see mainly the self-dramatizing actress rather than the Southern lady of a certain station. One interviewer described her as "Ethel Barrymore, Greta Garbo, and Bishop Fulton Sheen rolled into one." The Browns, however, retain their affection for Lily Carter, and continued to see her during her son's campaign and after he became President. After returning from India, Larry Brown became director of the Massachusetts Advocacy Center, a children's rights group, and learned that, in reality,

Lillian Carter did know black leaders such as Andrew Young and was able to enlist their help in some projects of concern to Brown.

One other young man came to know Lily Carter during her three months in Chicago. As part of the screening process to determine the fitness of Peace Corps volunteers for overseas duty, she met with a psychiatrist for regular weekly interviews. In her own words: "They didn't have one in Americus and I never needed one. So every week it got to the point where they tried to find out why, and it seemed that I was hard to understand, and finally one day I had been there over two months then and had gone there every week, and he said to me, 'I just simply can't understand'— what they were doing was examining me to see if I was psychiatric —psychic—if I was able to stand the terrible things that I was going to face in India. And he said, 'Mrs. Carter, I can't seem to find out why [you want to go].' It depended on him whether I could go or not . . . [so I told him] I want to be in a warm dark continent with dark people. And I said that was the reason that I wanted to go; there was a frustration I had had living in the South . . . and I hadn't been able to do anything there . . . so I needed to get to this and I knew this was the climax of the whole . . . and I went, and I was fulfilled. Everything I did—that's in the Bible, too—was brought back to me a hundredfold. Everything I did for them came back to me. I lived every day with the black race and to me they were like they were Negroes; they were just like our blacks here, except that they couldn't understand our problem—there they couldn't understand, but they understood me. It was the most fulfilling time of my life."

The Chicago psychiatrist also provided a kind of therapy for Lily Carter, as well as insights into her most private thoughts. In one of her letters home about her Peace Corps training experience, she described how, at first, "I thought I just had to get along with everybody, always agree with everything, and never feel any animosity. Then, one of the psychiatrists said, 'Get mad—have a natural anger—cuss somebody out—throw something!' That eased my mind, because then I felt free to just be ME!" Later, in India, she wrote, "Well, I got mad today and exploded! . . . I've just let myself be pushed around too much, and I had to stop it. I'm feeling so low—getting mad always makes me feel sick." In her first "life time," anger was something that had to be controlled, even though it was something "natural," almost physical. Everyone in Mr. Earl's house had to master control of anger. During the campaign, when interviewers pressed Lillian Carter for details about her older son, she would tell them about the throb in the vein of Jimmy Carter's temple, the one telltale sign that he was angry, and making every effort to contain his anger. Later, during his travails with Congress over energy, his sympathizers wished he could "let go." But even at his lowest point in the polls, he held in his feelings.

When the Peace Corps experience was well behind her, Lillian Carter says she confided some of her feelings to her son Jimmy. It was during the presidential campaign, after a benefit reception. Harry Belafonte and Andrew Young had both been present, and Miss Lillian had been introduced to the singer by Young. She had enjoyed herself—"I had a ball"—and when she saw her son Jimmy, she said, "Jimmy, I wish I were black."

"Mother, why?" he replied.

"Jimmy, I don't know. I just do."

Later, she offered an explanation that put her wishes "to be black" in the social context of Plains and related these same desires to her personal life and her need to resolve her feelings of belonging and being apart: "In saying that, I felt like I could fight my battles better if I were black. I think it's because I just purely loved the black and I had had such a difficult time—not that bad, because I can just stay here [Plains] and I don't have to see anybody, but a difficult time when I'm in a conversation with somebody—at my club, for instance—and I hear of little things, and I speak up right quick, you know, and then they hate me. But I just figured if I were black, how I would like to get out and fight a battle that is never ending. . . . I don't think it matters the color of the skin . . . it just so happens that I happen to be born white, but I think I've lived out of my element."

In India, where she saw Indians as American blacks, Lillian Carter had found her element. After two years of Peace Corps service, she returned to the United States, worn down, badly underweight, a stranger in her native land. At the Atlanta airport, she experienced intense culture shock. Almost in a state of hallucination, she saw the blacks around her in the airport lounge as Indians. Momentarily, the separation of the races had finally been overcome for her.

III

CULTURE IN AN EARLIER AMERICA, and certainly in the South, tended to be "women's work." Georgia Supreme Court Justice William Gunter, one of Jimmy Carter's friends since the mid-1960s, has a small-town background similar to Carter's. In the rural South, he explained to us, most men had to scrape for a living and had no time for books or the social amenities. Literature and the graces belonged to the mother or maiden aunts or school-marms. A white Christian woman of a certain standing could help blacks and the afflicted; a white male of the yeoman class would be "vulnerable" in society for the same actions.

The care of culture, of the family, and of the "childlike" Negro often went together for women. In Faulkner's *Intruder in the Dust*, a black character says, "If you got something outside the common run that's got to be done and can't wait, don't waste your time on the menfolks; they works on what your uncle calls the rules and the cases. Get the womens and children at it; they works on the circumstances."

"Subservient" though women may have appeared in the forms and rules of an older, segregationist, male-dominated rural America, in reality women exerted—*knew* they had—a certain superiority in the circumstances. Women could bend or break the rules in the cause of Christianity or compassion. If men dominated the family by physical strength, the women ruled through moral rectitude. Lillian Carter says of her son Jimmy, "I taught him everything he knew, even about the birds and the bees; everything, he would come to me. His father was a busy man. . . . He had great aspirations for them; well, he wanted more than anything was for them to get a good education. I had a degree as a nurse, but my husband didn't go to college, and I just think it was daily teaching." Similarly, a note of high-minded superiority echoes in Lillian Carter's explanation of why her husband was a segregationist: "He didn't know anything; he was taught—these people are taught from their mother's and father's segregation."

Serious "believing" religion was woman's work, too, as it

often is in American homes. True Christianity, if not the church, treats all persons as equal; read one way, the scriptures could inspire opposition to segregation. For Lillian Carter, to be "religious" was not the same as being a "churchgoer": "I can't understand people in my church going and praying . . . I don't do that . . . and pretend to be such a Christian and have this attitude towards the blacks."

Prayer in church is a formality, but private prayer for Lillian Carter is central to being a "natural born Christian": "Prayer can just get you anywhere you want to go." In the mysterious ways of religion, prayer gave her strength, comfort, a feeling of being in touch with God, who would support her—as it has millions of believers. God couldn't be asked for unchristian acts, like success; she didn't pray for Jimmy Carter to win in the Maryland primary. But she could pray for her son to do God's will in a Christian fashion. God could be evoked for family: "With fourteen-fifteen grandchildren, one great-grandchild, and driving along, going to Americus to buy groceries, I'll think of some little instance and I'll quickly say a prayer. You know: 'Let 'em be happy, let 'em manage'—things like that."

Culture and religion—books and God—sustained the mature Lillian Carter in her separate existence. Perhaps she always had her own private world, perhaps aloofness came with the death of her husband. Through direct daily conversations with God, through prayer, and because of her immersion in her own life, Lillian Carter was able to go her own way. "I am my own person," she once said, "and I am a lone person. I like to be alone a lot. . . . I have people who come to visit me and I visit them, but it's not a sincere, close thing." She loves people in general, but no person individually. The "lone person" in a constricted society extracts some benefits; he or she can take unpopular positions. The loner is often less vulnerable to public criticism: "One value I taught my children is never—Do the best you can with what you have and don't worry about criticism." As President, Jimmy Carter could echo his mother and say, "This is not an office which can be conducted on the basis of looking for approbation." Like her, he felt secure in his superiority, even when his abilities came under attack.

The morally superior individual may often sound self-righteous, even melodramatic. "Putting on airs" and exaggeration are part of Southern lore. Jimmy Carter's press secretary, Jody Powell, would explain to skeptics concerned about some specific claim the candidate had made: "If a south Georgia farmer has a mule, it's the best damned mule that ever existed." All the remembered accounts of the several lives of Lillian Carter—the "closest," "happiest" family, the "scores" of black friends and visitors, the "selfless" caring, the triumph over "nasty" snubs—have to be viewed in this light. We have already suggested that Jimmy Carter falls into exaggerations and falsehoods out of a need to impose his inner reality on the external world. Now we can see that, for both Jimmy Carter and his mother, such claims may occur also out of the conscious Christian desire to see the best in people. On a conscious level, it is a Christian attitude. On another level, it may reflect a desire to see the best in ourselves, as well. We wish to be good and to do the right thing. And we end up believing that we have done it. The end result is that all the Carter family, but especially the mother and older son, came across to many people as incurably stagey.

IV

"EVERY MAN IS an exception," Jimmy Carter quotes the philosopher Kierkegaard in *Why Not the Best?* The mother and father of James Earl Carter, Jr., gave him a distinct heritage, physical and emotional, as each set of parents does for each of us. But "exceptional" as each of us may be, most lives trace certain familiar, general patterns. In this sense, the man Jimmy Carter is no exception.

Mr. Earl was omnipresent; he saw that his intentions for his family were carried out. "Uncultured" and business-oriented, he nevertheless usurped some of the "mothering" roles in the Carter family, for his son Jimmy in particular. His paternal presence and the anticipation of his punishments are as tangible in Jimmy Carter's memories as the red clay fields of southwestern Georgia. He is, in short, a father of a familiar kind, if we can believe the textbooks—a father who stirs a mixture of admiration, fear, and feelings of rivalry in some of his children.

The psychologist Erik Erikson, in his classic interpretive biography of Martin Luther, *Young Man Luther,* describes how the heavy hand of moralistic paternalism can squeeze out, in a young child, the "small and highly satisfying delinquencies" of life, like daydreaming and other spontaneous, undirected activities—or make children feel guilty and inferior when they enjoy these "delinquencies." One practical result can be a child like young Martin Luther: "someone with a precocious conscience, a precocious self-steering and eventually an obsessive mixture of obedience and rebelliousness." Such children, if they survive, may offer a kind of moral leadership later in life, as religious reformers or Presidents.

The death of James Earl Carter, Sr.—as the deaths of strong husbands and always-present fathers often are—became an event of wrenching proportions for every member of his family. His death ended Lillian Carter's way of life as a mother, a homemaker, and wife. As many widows do, she created a new life for herself. Her daughter Gloria Spann says, "She had the courage and the good health to go ahead and keep on walking in a marvelous direction." Her eventual final destination proved to be the woman, larger than life, known as Miss Lillian, the President's mother. In the process, the figure of James Earl Carter, Sr., became overshadowed.

The reality is that both parents "shaped" Jimmy Carter, just as most of us are influenced by both mother and father. Jimmy Carter saw himself as an exception; we can now see that it was the special personalities of James Earl Carter/Mr. Earl and Earl's wife/Lily/Miss Lillian that combined to produce even more special personalities in their sons and daughters.

5

Gloria, Ruth, and Billy

BILLY CARTER once told a television interviewer, "I got one sister who's a Holy Roller preacher. Another wears a helmet and rides a motorcycle. And my brother thinks he's going to be President. So that makes me the only sane one in the family." In an interview with us, he gave a different assessment of his brother, his sisters, and himself. "The trouble is," he said, "we are all too much alike."

Brothers and sisters, of course, influence and shape one another, just as they are shaped by their parents, the common influence. While the Carter brothers and sisters are individuals in their own right, they share characteristics. Jimmy Carter's sisters and brother illustrate different aspects of his character, and the different ways of responding to the family and social setting in which he grew up. Their stories also illuminate some of the "hardness" of life and the tensions within the outwardly "loving" Carter family. They show ways of responding to being part of the Carter family, and growing up in Plains, Georgia.

Most important, their stories also illustrate certain characteristics that Jimmy Carter has fused together in his own personality. In their characters we can see in "pure" form different roads that Jimmy Carter could have taken: Gloria, who never fulfilled her bright promise; Ruth, who turned to honest fraudulence; and Billy, who battled his private frustrations and aggressions to the point of public drunkenness and disorder.

II

GLORIA CARTER, by all accounts, was the most outgoing and talented of the Carter children; now, in early middle age, she is the most withdrawn, content to be, she says, a "homebody." She was born in 1926; Jimmy was just twenty months old when she came home from the hospital. Both Gloria and Jimmy Carter remember how, as children, they often tangled, as do many brothers and sisters who are close in age. Their rivalry was complicated by Jimmy's undersized frame. As he tells it, "Gloria was younger than I, but larger during our growing years." Photographs of the Carter family show two blue-eyed, fair-haired children, one slight, the other sturdy. On Gloria Carter's first day of public school, she remembers, her brother Jimmy "asked me not to tell anybody I was his sister because I didn't talk right; I had been raised out there in the country around the black children and I talked like they did. And he was grown then, third grade, and I was still a baby."

Around the house, the two children still tangled. One time Gloria threw a wrench at Jimmy, and, he says, he "retaliated by shooting her in the rear with a B.B. gun." The rest of the day, whenever Gloria heard a loud noise, like the sound of a car, she began crying.

Most of the brother-sister rivalries between Gloria and Jimmy took less dramatic turns. What Jimmy Carter may have lacked in size by comparison to his sister, in his growing years, he made up for with a kind of Huckleberry Finn guile. He would pay Gloria five cents to pick peanuts for him to ease his chores; then he would persuade her to plant the nickel in a flower bed in order to grow a "money tree." Gloria invested a lot of her nickels in the flower bed before she caught on to the fact that her brother was digging them up.

He had other country-boy tricks. Once, Gloria Carter remembers, when he was ten and she was eight, they went by the Seaboard Railroad line to Alabama to visit an aunt. "Jimmy was to look after me and I was to do whatever he said. When we got to

Columbus, Georgia, the train stopped; so Jimmy got out of the train—off the train—to walk outside, and I didn't see him. And the train started off, and I started crying; I was miserable, just miserable. I didn't know what to do. It had left Jimmy in Columbus and he was gone forever, and it was miles down the track before he popped up in the seat in front of me. . . . He was mischievous."

Gloria and Jimmy soon had another rival in the house with the birth of Ruth Carter in 1929. While Jimmy Carter had his own room in the clapboard house behind their father's general store in Archery, Gloria and Ruth shared a room.

Gloria Carter's childhood nickname was "Go Go," suggesting her strong, active, energetic nature. John Pope, a friend of the Carter family since childhood, once called Gloria Carter the "prettiest and sexiest girl in all of Sumter County." She was an excellent student, but still felt the pressure from her father to do more: "We were always encouraged to do better than we did. Even if you got 97 per cent on a test, he wanted to know why you didn't make 100 per cent. If you got a B, you were sentenced to dig ditches. He was never happy with our grades." When she did less than A in one course, a friend, Virginia Williams, recalls, "She flung a fit . . . she tore her report card."

Nevertheless, in the rural South of the 1930s, parents—and society—put limits on what even the brightest and most aggressive girls could learn, and do. Young white ladies were to be neat, well-mannered, and well-behaved—to look and talk "nice." The concerns of the world—land, sex, money, politics—belonged to men, and boys becoming men. Business matters were the preserve of Mr. Earl, and she says, "My father never discussed finances or his personal business with us, never." The Carters still had their housekeepers and maids to care for them, to wash, to cook, to clean. Mr. Earl's son Jimmy had regular jobs to do after school, and he was paid to do them; Mr. Earl's daughters, Gloria and Ruth, instead received an allowance. As Gloria Carter explains it, "Jimmy was given chores to teach him how to make a living, and to give him a responsibility. . . ."

In her teens, Gloria Carter longed to be out of high school, out of Plains, away from her parents—not unlike her brothers and her sister and generations of American sixteen-, seventeen-, and eighteen-year-olds in cities as well as small towns. "I signed up for college the day I graduated from high school," she says. She also smoked her first cigarette that week.

Gloria Carter went off to Georgia Southwestern State; she studied journalism and was active on the newspaper, and in dramatics and basketball. The year was 1945. Servicemen in Army browns and Navy blues came home on furlough, danced at college mixers, sipped punch at church socials. Gloria Carter met an Air Force enlisted man named Everett "Soapy" Hardy, who had worked as a soda jerk in Americus before entering the service. She and Hardy ran off to be married in December 1945. Their romance faded, as the Hardys moved from one Air Force base to another. In 1949, Gloria Carter left Hardy, taking their two-year-old son, Willie, with her. When she arrived by bus in Plains, her son in her arms, her "luggage" consisted of one dress in a brown paper bag. The boy's nickname was "Toady."

Toady has been described as a handsome boy with nice manners who could suddenly turn ugly. He got into trouble, as some boys do, breaking into a store, stealing cars. He was sent to various psychiatrists, taken out of public school in Plains, dispatched to a military academy, and finally sent to a special school for emotionally disturbed children—all, it seems, to no avail. In 1978, at thirty years of age, he was in jail on the West Coast for armed robbery committed while under the influence of drugs. He is an acknowledged homosexual.

Despite her troubles with Toady, Gloria Carter began to build a new life in Plains. She attended business school, became a farm tax expert, and kept books for eighteen different farms around Plains, working long hours. She was meeting the demands for hard work and high performance that her father had made, but she was still unhappy.

Gloria Carter married a second time, this time "a man very much like my father." The marriage took place, she tells us, a week before her father died. Her new husband was Walter Spann, who lived about twelve miles down the road. As Gloria Carter describes him, "He's a farmer, he worries about the weather, and he's outside every night to see if it's going to rain." Like Mr. Earl, he is at home for three meals a day; the Spanns' house in Plains had been owned by James Earl Carter, Sr., who rented it out. Walter Spann, like Mr. Earl, is a conservative and a Republican.

III

IN 1960, at the age of thirty-four, Gloria Spann experienced a religious conversion. She was feeling overwhelmed by guilt and by the realization that she had "absolutely no control" over young Toady. She also faced openly the realization that she really did not like the long hours of bookkeeping and the demands of her job. Mr. Earl's daughter did not like to work, and she blamed her father for the pressure he had put on her to work. All she wanted, she said, was to be a farmer's wife and "not worry about anything except if it rained." Having confronted her thoughts about her child, and her own childhood, she "fell absolutely in love with Jesus. I made a total commitment." Gloria Carter Spann had until then regarded herself as "self-centered. . . . I thought I could handle everything myself." Now she threw herself upon God. A prayer retreat a few weeks later—where Gloria "cried and cried and cried"—confirmed her new way. The result was a kind of freedom: "I don't worry about anything at all. I know God will answer all my prayers even if I don't always see the manifestation of the answer. Yes, I have problems, but I know they always turn out for the best. . . . I began to realize that God is nothing but love, and I'm his favorite child." She then connected this love to her husband, Walter: "I finally admitted to myself that I loved Walter more than anything. And since all love comes from God, there was nothing wrong with devoting my life to him. So I became a full-time housewife. I became absolutely free to be exactly what I am. I didn't have to feel intimidated any more by trying to be perfect, trying to make myself an example so others would have nothing to criticize."

For all the change in her life that this experience caused, she hesitates to say she has been "born again"; on the spectrum of religious intensity, Gloria Carter Spann told us, she lines up "medium right" compared to her brother Jimmy and her sister Ruth. Gloria Spann had solved her own problems, after great pain; unlike her brother Jimmy and her sister Ruth she was not driven to solve other people's problems as well. A significant rival to Jimmy Carter in childhood, she fades from his life—and from public attention—as she abandons the highly competitive family field of battle and retreats to her own home and husband.

IV

RUTH CARTER was born in 1929. She looks like a little princess in Carter family photographs—fairer skin, curlier and blonder hair, bluer eyes, a more angelic look than any of the others. She is the one sitting in housekeeper Annie Mae's lap as the older children group around her. Her father called her "Whoop De Do," a name that suggests images of excitement and effervescence. Everyone agreed she was his favorite; he taught her how to shoot target rifles and how to dance. He took her as his "date" to the Elks Club. She excelled at play, in sports, in school, all effortlessly. Her brother Jimmy tended to take her side in the small skirmishes between Ruth and her sister Gloria. Jimmy and Ruth, everyone said, were closer than the others; she was the one who introduced him to her best friend, Rosalynn Smith, the girl he decided to marry after their first date. No wonder blonde, beautiful Ruth Carter, growing up in the 1930s in Sumter County, Georgia, felt she belonged to a kind of rural royalty.

When in 1946 she went away to Georgia State College for Women, she hardly studied; but marriage and children, rather than grades and a career, were the target of many young ladies in the postwar years. Ruth Carter achieved both; in 1949 she married a tall young veterinarian named Robert Stapleton and moved to Fayetteville, North Carolina. Two sons and two daughters were born between 1951 and 1959. The Stapletons also acquired a cabin retreat in the woods outside Fayetteville and later a vacation home in Portugal.

It was a storybook life, with each page full of love—except that Ruth Carter Stapleton in early middle age rewrote most of the pages. She offered instead a grim story of a childhood of too much attention and not enough love.

Like Jimmy Carter, Ruth Carter Stapleton has written a kind of autobiography. Her book *The Gift of Inner Healing* deals in part with growing up in the house of Mr. Earl and Lillian Carter. But where Jimmy Carter narrates events in a flat, spare engineer's prose, understating all feelings, Ruth Carter Stapleton skips over events and presents instead explicit, highly personal emotions.

Ruth Carter Stapleton believed herself to be happy and loved until, she writes, she married. Then she became aware of what she calls "my feelings of rejection," feelings of having been rejected by her mother, and also of starting to reject, to be resentful of, her mother and her father:

> My father had loved me very deeply, but his way of expressing that love was not altogether healthy. He had given me everything I had ever wanted. "Ruth," he used to tell me, "you are the most wonderful person in the world."
> I had been raised to believe that I was God's gift to the world, the most beautiful child ever born. I was led to believe that I was the most gifted of persons. I grew up thinking I was the queen of the universe.

While her father "overindulged and spoiled" her, the ways of rural southwestern Georgia also reinforced the illusions he fostered. "At home I had played with the black children on the farm," Ruth Carter Stapleton says. "I never knew until I became an adult that there had been an unwritten law, spawned by centuries of prejudice, that the white children must be allowed to win all the time. So every game I ever played throughout my entire childhood I won. I was best at kick the can, fastest in any race, and I always caught my friends immediately at hide-and-seek. I grew up believing that I was the most loved person in the world." She adds: "To fall short of number one in any area of life registered as unbearable failure."

The adoration flowed exclusively from her father. Ruth Carter Stapleton did not believe that her mother loved her. She says carefully that Lillian Carter "didn't overindulge me. That made me feel rejected, even though I now realize she was just treating me normally." It is hardly uncommon for mothers and daughters to be rivals for the attention of the husband-father. Ruth Carter Stapleton admits that she was a "flirtatious, spoiled Southern belle who thrived on being loved."

The "demanding adult relationships of marriage" that so unnerved and overwhelmed Ruth Carter Stapleton as a young woman were tied to familiar marital struggles. She was not "organized" as a young wife, or devoted to domestic chores; and in this respect, Ruth Carter Stapleton was like her mother, Lillian. Young married life, she has since said, was "just babies, doctors, bottles and diapers." Her sole "intellectual" interest then was Henry David Thoreau's *Walden:* "Everything Thoreau says hits something deep within me. From the time I was sixteen years old I kept some of his material with me most of the time. Many times I slept with it under my pillow just in case I woke up in the night, just to read and read. In those early days of having all my babies . . . Thoreau was like blood in my veins."

The Stapleton marriage tottered. They had moved to Fayetteville, some 450 miles away from Plains, so that she couldn't run home to her family every time they squabbled. Even in Fayetteville, however, there was a Carter cousin with whom her husband worked as a vet. She was, she recalls, totally unable to make decisions. "I constantly fell into states of depression and anxiety which led to hypertension. I couldn't have described my feelings in such clinical terms; I just wanted to scream." She was twenty-nine years old.

Her emotional state was one that is not unknown to countless thousands of other young women who believe that too many pregnancies have come too fast. Ruth Carter Stapleton's anger at her husband has been shared by other young mothers. He had not been present at the births of their two sons—once because he had the flu, the other time because he overslept—and she "hated" him for his absences. Still, he scraped together enough money to build for her a "Walden" retreat—a cabin on the edge of a lake some ten miles from Fayetteville.

Perhaps, she decided, there was an intellectual way out of her severe depression. She resolved to go back to college to complete the education she had broken off in her junior year for marriage. Ruth Carter Stapleton majored in English and religion. It was, she later said, "the hardest thing I ever did in my life. I was convinced I would fail. I knew I couldn't pass an examination; but in the end I made eighties in everything." She received a master's degree in teaching and got a job in a Fayetteville high school teaching English.

On her lunch hour, she took a Bible class at nearby Fort Bragg, the big Army base that was a staging area during the Vietnam war. The high school job did not last long. She was fired for teaching religion or, as she said, counseling students with their problems instead of helping them with English. The principal had told her she had the choice of "teaching" or "preaching."

By chance, she got an opportunity to preach openly. The chaplain who led the noon Bible class at Fort Bragg went off to Vietnam, and she took over. For the next several years she taught Bible classes in the Fayetteville area. People heard of her Monday night prayer meetings, and came to her for help with their problems. Ruth Carter Stapleton remembers that for seven years "I was very religious. . . . I lost contact with everything that was of the world. . . . I withdrew from every group, my husband's social life. All I did was pray, read the Bible and speak."

Still, she remained unhappy. Ruth Carter Stapleton had taken the paths of the intellect, of a new mid-life career, of prayer and ascetic religion—and she had not escaped the demons she felt pursuing her. She sought psychiatric help, and she says that failed her, too. But shortly thereafter a miracle of sorts took place; she experienced what she calls "physical healing."

As with many miraculous cures, several accounts of the episode exist. Lillian Carter's version describes a case of post-partum blues that lingered for over a decade: "She became very depressed after the last child was born; not seriously, but too much for her. The pediatrician who was tending the child advised her to go into psychiatry, which she did. . . . She went into psychoanalysis, one of those groups. She loved it. . . . and I think in eight months or something like that she was out of there."

In an interview with Jessamyn West, Stapleton had given a guarded version of what she called "the greatest emotional crisis in my life. . . . My father's indulging love. His effort to protect me from all obstacles almost crippled me after I left home." Elsewhere, she speaks of having suffered since she was sixteen from a "crippling" ailment that grew progressively "worse and worse."

Her affliction reached a breaking point in what was either a car accident or a suicide attempt. In her book *The Gift of Inner Healing,* the first sentence reads, "RUTH. YOU WANTED TO DIE." One day in 1966 she was driving to the Fayetteville airport. She had invited a man, a psychologist and spiritual leader, to speak at the retreat she was having for her Bible class. On the way to the airport to pick him up, she says, "I jumped from my car when my brakes failed. After that I was much bandaged because of the accident. I went to the meeting and sat with my bandaged leg on a chair." After the meeting, she says, the speaker came to her house and sat next to her in a small room lined with her religious books.

As she tells it: " 'Ruth,' he asked, 'what's hurting you so badly that you would want to take your life?' I had never told *anyone* the experience that had hurt me so. It was so minuscule to have caused the pain I had experienced. But as we sat there, he dug out bit by bit my relationship with my father and mother. And at last my little secret—which basically was no more than an error in the definition of love, but which had come to control my whole life, giving me my unrealistic feelings of rejection—was laid bare and accepted."

This extraordinary session had extraordinary consequences for three people. Ruth Stapleton says she is no longer "crippled." Her husband, Robert Stapleton, also had what she calls "an instantaneous miraculous healing." For a long time he had to wear braces on his feet: "He had not been, at the time I began my work, a Christian; afterward he became one. One day he prayed, asking God to heal his feet; and from that moment on there has been no pain, no need for braces." Finally, Ruth Carter Stapleton's older brother, Jimmy Carter, received counseling from his sister during his own crippling depression in the fall of 1966, after his defeat in the Georgia gubernatorial primary. Jimmy Carter, as we will show, traces his own born-again experience from the period of a walk in the woods with his sister Ruth. Her healing techniques developed as she pursued her ministry. In 1966, from both their accounts, there was no miraculous cure; rather, the intensity of their special brother-sister relationship illuminated the moment.

In her counseling sessions and in the intimate recitals of her "inner healing" workshops, Stapleton refers to her own feelings of anger, of pride, of hatred, and of sexual conflict. She herself radiates sexuality. In one workshop, she described how her own inner healing took place. "You see," she told an audience of perhaps 2000 people, "my Daddy wanted a boy . . . and all during my childhood I tried to be that boy. I was Daddy's eight-year-old sharpshooter. 'Watch Ruth shoot a rifle,' he would say." Then, after inner healing, "I didn't have to hit the bull's-eye any more. . . . I didn't have to try to be a boy any more . . . at last I could polish my nails. . . . I didn't have to wear pants suits. . . . I saw Jesus touch my Daddy . . . and my Daddy giving up the boy. And I could rejoice."

Those who have sat through inner healing workshops aren't sure what to call her, or her work. She is not a Holy Roller; she doesn't get down on her knees or muss one strand of her frosted blond hair. She is not a preacher or a minister. She thinks the term "faith healer" was used by people seeking to hurt her brother's presidential campaign. "Jesus does the healing," she says.

For those who are "imperfect," she offers "faith-imagination therapy." She has people relive troublesome "traumatic episodes," to re-enact the event in their fantasies. She then asks them to bring Jesus, or the Holy Spirit, into the imaginary scene. Jesus is the intermediary who brings about a new outcome. Ruth Stapleton blends psychological insights with religious insights. She analyzes dreams, uses the power of suggestibility, and deals mainly with sexual problems, many involving homosexuals seeking help. At the core of her work is the assumption that we must all return to the little child within us.

Her book gives case studies: Mary Anne, whose marriage she saved; Jeff, who had trouble relating to women; and Jody, who came to her because he was troubled about his homosexuality. She "diagnosed" that he needed to identify with a father figure during his childhood; she leads Jody back through his memories to the time he was six years old, sitting in his mother's kitchen. "Now the doorbell rings. Go to the door and open it," Stapleton directs. "Who's going to be there?" asks the grown-up Jody, a bit frightened. Answers Stapleton: "Jesus is going to be there. He's got a baseball bat and glove with him. He wants you to play ball with him." Thus, writes Stapleton, "through the prayer of faith-imagination I slowly, verbally took six-year-old Jody through an entire ball game," with both Jesus and Jody going up to bat. In later sessions, she helped Jody create a new and more supportive "memory bank." As a result, she says, he gave up his homosexual habits.

Since Jesus does the healing, she says she only sits by the person, works to get at the basis of the pain, and then, "through guided meditation," tries to help the person find the healing. Still, she does make use of well-known principles of psychology and of religion, even combining the vocabulary of the two: for example, she has described her technique as probing "the subconscious depths with the scalpel of the Holy Spirit." Whatever the extent and value of her own therapy, she quite clearly learned enough about psychotherapy to apply later to the healing of others.

For herself, however, psychotherapy was not enough; she needed to tie it to religious feelings, to fuse psychology and Christianity. Not surprisingly, her work has been challenged by both trained psychotherapists and by mainstream clergy, whose criticism ranges from the argument that there is no biblical basis for her work to the charge that she is practicing therapy without a license. While these complaints may be justified, her defenders point out that her work falls well within the Christian evangelical tradition of "miraculous healings" and sudden conversions.

V

RUTH CARTER STAPLETON'S successful conversion, of herself and others, has paid off handsomely. Her efforts have been rewarded financially (though much of the money she receives goes to her "mission"). Behold, Inc. is the organization she set up in 1972 to handle the income from her work, her books and her audio tapes, her lecture fees and other related activities. According to the marketing director of her publishers, her first book, *The Gift of Inner Healing* ($4.95), sold 300,000 copies through January 1, 1978. The audio cassettes sell for $14.95. In 1975, Ruth Carter Stapleton conducted inner healing workshops in some seventy-five American cities; during the campaign, her efforts on behalf of her brother cut into the inner healing workshops, but in 1977 and 1978 she was busier than ever. She ran a series of workshops called "Behold, New York," "Behold, San Francisco," and so on. She established a thirty-acre retreat, Holovita Ranch, near Dallas, Texas. ("It provides a place where people may come for the healing of the whole person, body, mind, and spirit.") Then came trips to Scandinavia, Britain, Germany, Japan, Australia, and, as she says, "on and on and on." Ruth Carter Stapleton is still her father's daughter. If he were alive, Mr. Earl, even by his most perfectionist standards, would have to agree that she has hit the bulls'-eyes of impressive, difficult targets.

Billy Carter had said of his brother and sisters that they were all too much alike. Ruth and Gloria both experienced difficult marriages. Both remember the voice of their father and his stern demands—as well as his excessive love. Both suffered severe depression and sought psychiatric assistance. Both found solace, and then cure, in religion, becoming born-again Christians. Gloria Spann's new life took the form of a homemaker's role in Plains, devoting her time and energy to her husband. Ruth Stapleton's new life took her far from Plains, constantly traveling in pursuit of her ministry. Their lives of depression, healing, religion, and eventual success represent one of the legacies of the family heritage of James Earl and Lillian Carter.

VI

BILLY CARTER describes himself as the most "normal" of the Carters. It is probably true that he is like many of the adult men of Plains, in views and behavior. He called himself the "token redneck" of the Carter campaign in 1976. Bemused reporters wrote that he was a "good old boy"—the hunting, drinking, relaxed Southern country man, and he played up to that role. "Yes, sir, I'm a real Southern boy," he would say. "I got a red neck, white socks, and Blue Ribbon beer." He became so popular that he hired an agent to handle requests for his presence on the lecture and publicity circuits. When the agent took over in 1976, Billy Carter began charging $5000 or more for an appearance at events such as the Pole Climbing World Championship in Lexington, Kentucky, a baseball "nickel beer" night in Cleveland, assorted business meetings, beauty contests, belly-whopping diving exhibits, and freckle-counting competitions. He lent his name to a new drink, "Billy's Beer," bottled in Kentucky. In the good-old-boy tradition, he said yes to everything but "serious" invitations, turning down requests to speak at Tulane Law School and the University of Georgia, among other places.

Good old boys also were supposed to be segregationists rather than racists. They go along with the new ways of the New South, but just barely; one supposed attribute is not to care too much about politics at all. Billy Carter seemed to fit the image. He appears to be the Carter who was least eager—to put it evenly—for integration and the Carter least concerned with appearing to be a great friend and helper of the poor, the black, and the needy. Except for casting votes for Lyndon Johnson—and Jimmy Carter —he tells people he has been a Republican.

Billy Carter has a book of sorts on the market, too. Ruth Stapleton managed, with the help of a ghostwriter, to produce *Brother Billy*. One of the stories she recounts is about the time, during "a heated moment" in Jimmy Carter's race for governor, when Billy Carter ripped a telephone from a wall and threw it out into the front yard. Others have noticed, and remarked upon, the "relaxed" Billy Carter's capacity for sudden rage and violence. In Plains during the 1976 presidential campaign, a gasoline explosion threatened Billy Carter's Amoco service station across the street from Carter's Warehouse, where Billy Carter managed the family's multimillion-dollar-a-year agribusiness; Billy Carter had to be physically restrained from running into the danger area, and he tried to punch photographers who were taking his picture. Tears in his eyes, Billy Carter yelled—spectacularly and inaccurately— "It's all I have." The damage to the gas station turned out to be slight.

Powerful emotions always seem to be close to the surface of Billy Carter. In many ways, he is, still, Mr. Earl's son, and his pointed joke about being the only "sane" one in the family may be aimed as much at himself as at his brother and sisters.

VII

WHEN BILLY CARTER was born in 1936, his brother, Jimmy, was twelve years old; his younger sister, Ruth, seven. He has, in his recollections, no memories of hard times or, on the other hand, of a particularly close family life. His childhood was reasonably happy, he says, "because I was so much younger, I was almost like an only child." He has no clear memories of his brother, nor has he any strong memories of his father's discipline. Mr. Earl, perhaps, had softened by the time Billy Carter was growing up. Billy Carter does remember two or three whippings from his father. One time he and his black friend Bishop stole and ate some green pears, and lied about it. Mr. Earl whipped both boys. Even the mellowing Mr. Earl did not abide boys who told lies.

Billy Carter shares an important memory with his brother; he also remembers being a "timid" child. Like the other Carter children, his playmates growing up in Archery were mostly black. His constant playmate was very dark skinned; Billy Carter himself had fair skin and fine blond hair, so blond it was almost white. The two boys, Billy and his friend, were called "Day" and "Night." But Billy Carter takes pains to explain that "I never had any close friends . . . still don't." He makes an emphatic distinction between having friends and having a "close friend." He has a good friend now, in middle age, named Virge. "I went to school with him," he told us. "We really weren't close friends until later on. . . . Virge probably got an IQ of seventy-five . . . but he'd do anything in the world for me, and I would for him. And we really didn't get close until the last eight or nine years." His brother, Jimmy Carter, Billy Carter says, "is the same way with friends."

Mr. Earl had his own nickname for Billy Carter; his youngest son was called "Head." Billy Carter explains that from the time he was six years old until high school his hair was cropped in the briefest of brush cuts. His father was the barber. At school in Plains, Billy Carter was an indifferent student, unlike his brother and sisters. Once his father was called to the school because of a U—for unsatisfactory—that Billy Carter had received in deportment on his report card. "My father told me, 'One more U, and I'm going to whip you.' I set a world's record for praying, but it didn't work." He received four U's on his next report card and was whipped.

Billy Carter was fifteen when his father first became ill in 1952. Jimmy Carter was a naval officer up North in New York, learning about nuclear reactors; Billy Carter all but dropped out of high school to care for his father. "I drove for him all that time, and also stayed with him that last year he lived. . . . He really started getting sick in '52 and real sick in 1953. It was just a gradual thing. I don't suppose they knew much about cancer. . . . He went from about 200 pounds down to about 110 pounds before they realized what was wrong.''

After his father's death, Billy Carter at sixteen could have become the man in the family; but he could not take charge of his father's businesses. His older brother, Jimmy Carter, had decided to come back from the Navy and take over. Jimmy Carter, the brother that Billy Carter scarcely knew existed, a stranger actually, was in charge.

Billy Carter let his hair grow out just a bit. He discovered girls, beer, and cars like most sixteen-year-olds. If his normal feelings caused some conflicts with the strictures of his church, then he would jettison the church. In Plains, then and now, he says, the hypocrites pray on Sundays and raise hell the next Saturday night. He wouldn't be a hypocrite; he stopped going to church services on Sunday.

In 1955, two years after the death of his father and the return of his brother, Billy Carter left Plains. He took a customary Southern route, joining the military, in his case the U.S. Marines. He got out of Plains the first day it was possible. ''I actually joined the day I was eighteen. I quit school, lacking two months of graduating from high school, and then they talked me into going back to school. . . . But then I graduated one night and at four o'clock the next morning, I was on the way to Parris Island.'' The ''they'' who made him wait, he said, were his mother and his brother—the new authority figure and head of the household.

Billy Carter wanted to marry one of his Plains High classmates, sixteen-year-old Sybil Spires. Lillian Carter and Jimmy Carter opposed those plans, too, arguing the couple were too young to be married. Billy Carter didn't accept their arguments. He saw himself much like everyone else. In *Mary Hartman, Mary Hartman,* the television soap-opera satire, one of the characters is asked why she married so young. She replies, ''Well, I grew up in Ohio and there wasn't that much else to do.'' Billy Carter's comment was ''I guess that's about the way it was here.'' Billy Carter and Sybil Spires were married in the summer of 1955, as soon as he finished his basic training.

The Marines had a special appeal for Billy Carter. ''I guess I joined the Marine Corps because I always heard they were bad asses, and I wanted to be a bad ass. I never did quite make it.'' To be "bad ass" meant that "in boot camp one Marine can take care of ten Air Force people. I found out that two Marines couldn't take care of seven, right after I got out of boot camp . . . because I tried and I wiped all that out."

It shouldn't be too surprising that bad-ass Billy Carter got wiped out in a barroom brawl, and gave up his idea of being a tough guy after that. He was physically small, so small he couldn't meet the Marine Corps weight requirement, but they took him anyway. "I was one pound underweight. When I got out of high school I weighed 119 pounds. But when I was in boot camp, I gained thirty-six pounds."

Billy Carter served as an enlisted man in the Marines from 1955 to 1959, including a tour of duty in the Far East. He considered becoming a career man but, he told us, "backed out at the last minute." The Marines, he said, had a policy at the time that prohibited enlisted men from taking their dependents overseas. Billy and Sybil Carter had wasted no time in having children; three were born in the first six years of their marriage. With the prospect of another tour of duty overseas coming up, and Sybil Carter opposed to another separation, he left the Corps.

Billy Carter returned to Plains for what he thought would be just a temporary stop while he tried, at twenty-two and with a wife, young children, and a high school diploma, to earn a living. The Carter warehouse and the commodities business were doing well under the direction of Jimmy Carter. But Billy Carter took a number of jobs away from the family business—construction work, traveling salesman. He tried to go to college. In 1961, when his wife was pregnant with their fourth child, Billy Carter registered as a student at Emory University in Atlanta. He struggled two years; not deportment but English proved his downfall. Handicapped by his sketchy Plains high school education, as well as a seven-year absence from the classroom, twenty-five-year-old Billy Carter couldn't make it as a college student. However, he enjoyed one course in particular. He met a young Emory political scientist who was a student of the populist leader Tom Watson. Billy Carter remembered that his mother had kept a batch of correspondence between his grandfather, Jim Jack Gordy, and Watson. Billy Carter dug out the letters, read them avidly, thought for a time about writing something on Watson and populism, and ended up by donating the letters to Emory—and leaving school. These were not happy times for Billy Carter. His mother once remarked, "I loved Billy more [than Jimmy] because he needed it more."

In 1963, Billy Carter returned to Plains and the family business—much to his own surprise. "I'd have bet anything when I left in '61 that I'd never come back," he says. The year 1963 marked the beginning of his own "new life." Whatever his feelings about Plains and his family, Billy Carter went to work at Carter's Warehouse for his brother. As Jimmy Carter turned more and more toward politics and the outside world in the mid-1960s, Billy Carter turned more and more toward home concerns and the Carter agribusiness. He began running the warehouse operations in everything but name in 1970, the time when Jimmy Carter ran again, successfully, for governor.

Before and during the 1976 presidential campaign, Carter's Warehouse received two bank loans from the National Bank of Georgia. NBG at the time was headed by Carter's "closest friend in the world," Bert Lance. The loans, totaling about $7 million, were for peanut-processing equipment and for lines of credit. When a federal grand jury began investigating the financial affairs of Lance, Billy Carter was summoned to testify. While Lance was the primary target of the investigation, Justice Department lawyers were also interested in the financial practices of Carter's Warehouse. Among practices that first attracted attention were reports (1) that the Warehouse had been delinquent in its payments on the loans to the tune of $600,000; (2) that warehouse records may have been falsified, and (3) that Jimmy Carter and Carter's Warehouse claimed $1.1 million investment tax credits for improvements and construction when filing federal taxes, but that up to $250,000 of the money remained unused in Carter's bank account.

All this activity raised a logical question: Why all the expansion in the family business just at the time that Jimmy Carter, the majority owner of the warehouse, was running for President? Speculation centered on the possibility that some of this money may have found its way into the Carter presidential campaign, especially in the spring of 1976, when federal campaign funds were being held up. President Carter, at an April 11, 1979, news conference, denied that there had been any mingling of funds. And in any case, Jimmy Carter had more than a fig leaf of protection. Others

had administered the loans and run the campaign finances. Whatever happened to Jimmy Carter, of course, Billy Carter would be
in a position not unfamiliar to him over the past ten years—covering for his older brother.

In recent years, Billy Carter has let his hair grow out to normal length. He wears horn-rim glasses for near-sightedness (like
his father), and he has had all of his front teeth capped. His famous
Carter smile, as least, is false. He has developed an allergy to
peanuts, and breaks out in hives on close contact with them. When
Billy Carter was running the Carter business, his weight would
vary greatly, as low as 160 pounds in October, when the farmers
were bringing their crops in to Carter's Warehouse, and as high as
200 pounds in the slow season. He prefers his weight at around
180, but realistically owns two black "funeral suits," one with a
thirty-three-inch waist, the other thirty-eight inches.

Between 1970 and 1976, the Carter agribusiness grew steadily
under Billy Carter's management. After the election, Sybil Carter
ran the warehouse while Billy Carter traveled. In 1977, Donnel
Jeffrey "Jeff" Carter, Jimmy Carter's youngest son, came back to
Plains to begin working in the business. Currently, the business is
administered by a blind trust, which has put it up for sale. Since
the gas station was also being run by an employee of the Carters',
Billy found himself in 1977 all but retired from his duties around
Plains, a casualty of his brother's victory. He had nothing much to
do any more, and he started playing the role of the clown prince.
While his public appearances and his new enterprises became so
well-paying that he made perhaps $500,000 in 1977, these activities
also served to keep a restless, troubled mind occupied.

The relations between the brothers remained, outwardly,
brotherly. Billy Carter carried the heavy burden of looking like
something of a loser, the brother of a constantly successful
brother, now President of the United States. Part of Billy Carter's
way of dealing with this has been to make outright fun of himself,
to pose as a stock figure. Another way has been to make somewhat
covert fun of his brother and of the Carter legend. "I'm not the
Carter who promised never to lie," he says to audiences.

A third way, increasingly, has been to act self-destructively
and, indirectly, to try to damage his brother: linking arms with the
Libyans; making pointed remarks about Jewish influence in the

American press; pissing on an airport runway; cutting down Kirbo, Jordan, and Powell, his brother's closest associates. It's clear that inwardly one part of Billy Carter resents his brother, the President. Billy Carter still seethes inwardly at the older brother who ordered him about, and who supplanted him just when he was about to enter his inheritance. From a little brother's perspective, Jimmy Carter has taken from Billy Carter some of his manhood.

By early 1979, the heavy burdens of being Jimmy Carter's brother and dealing with the pressures of the Warehouse investigation had become too much for Billy Carter. He went through a public breakdown and was hospitalized at a U.S. Navy alcoholism clinic, the same San Diego hospital where another victim of alcoholism, Mrs. Betty Ford, had begun her own drying out and psychotherapy. At last, Billy Carter had a chance to confront, with the help of professional therapists, the deep familial feelings of being a Carter from Plains.

VIII

IN HER INNER HEALING WORKSHOPS, Ruth Carter Stapleton quotes from Corinthians. The beginning of inner healing, she says, comes with the individual. We must begin by saying, "I am the problem. . . . Ruth, you're nothing but a clay pot." In pottery making, the high pressures of the kiln often cause objects to shatter or crack. The same intensities produce pots of strength and utility. The Carter family exerted intense pressures on the Carter children; cracking occurred, but equally, strengths. The real Carters emerge as complex adults, not clay pots—or media inventions and pasteboard figures in a national soap opera.

Out of an exceptional, though by no means unique, passage through childhood and adolescence, their personalities emerge. Jimmy Carter's own story completes the circle of brothers and sisters "all too much alike," yet different.

6

"Just an Ordinary Little Boy"

MANY QUALITIES OF CHILDHOOD elude the records and the remembrances of others. Jimmy Carter, in conversations, interviews, and in his autobiography, tells us—sometimes directly, sometimes indirectly—of other qualities, themes that run through his childhood and link to characteristics present in him today. As Jimmy Carter told us, "It's fallacious to believe that the election result for any public office is going to change the nature or character of a person."

From the very beginning, Jimmy Carter saw himself as an outsider. Even today, as the most important insider in the political life of Washington, he still stands by choice outside. Though he was born in Plains, on October 1, 1924, he moved with his family three years later to a farm in Archery, a collection of eight to ten houses near a flag stop, now abandoned along with passenger service, on the Seaboard Railroad line. Jimmy Carter lived in Archery until the age of seventeen, when he went away to college. A dirt road connected Archery to the outside world. To get to Plains, Jimmy Carter had to walk along the railroad tracks. As Carter recalled, "My life was spent in a fairly isolated way, out in the woods and in the streams and swamps and fields . . . my whole environment was completely rural."

Carter saw Plains as a "center of commerce, education, and religion." The population of Plains in 1924 numbered about 550. Yet for Carter it represented a "metropolitan community." Even then he stood apart: "During my childhood I never considered myself a part of the Plains society, but always thought of myself as a visitor." Jimmy Carter takes all his schooling in Plains and goes to Plains for church—the hub of social life in small towns—and yet considers himself outside of Plains society.

The streets of Plains—the outside world—where as a little boy he would go to sell his peanuts, sometimes intimidated him: "I felt lonesome and timid as a small salesman." A price has to be paid, as well as made, being an outsider in Plains, and in later life. Timidity appears as a trait basic to Jimmy Carter's character, a trait to be overcome, compensated for. He begins to work on it early. As he tells it, when he was about seven or eight he had an "unpleasant experience," one of the few he remembered, when a "wise guy" at the local garage played a trick on him by offering to buy his peanuts and then maneuvering him to get the boy to step with his bare feet on a lighted cigarette. Jimmy Carter fought back the tears, trying to toughen up in the company of men. He didn't want to cry, or be made the target of jokes.

Other contradictions besides the enterprising salesman who is timid appear early in his childhood. An outsider to the segregated society of Plains in some ways, he became an insider in other ways. Jimmy Carter tells us another story of his boyish enterprise. Saving money from the sale of boiled peanuts, Jimmy had enough by the time he was nine to purchase five bales of cotton. Storing them in his father's barn, he sold them a few years later at a good profit. With his gains, he then bought five houses from the estate of the local undertaker. From the mid-1930s until 1949, he informs us, he collected "sixteen dollars and fifty cents in rent each month from those five houses. Two rented for five dollars each, two for two dollars each, and one for two-fifty."

Jimmy Carter sounds proud of his business enterprise, of his busy life on the farm. But the formal name for the system he describes is "tenancy farming," or sharecropping. Croppers lived in shacks, not "houses." Southern tenancy, like slavery before the Civil War, was the economic basis for the social and political order of a caste society. The tenants' clapboard shacks were the worst in the land; outhouses were a luxury. The workers, blacks and whites, lived like serfs, held to the land by debt, ignorance, poverty, and dependency on the landlord. If the workers were lucky, the planter-owner might be paternalistic.

It is not likely that the growing Jimmy Carter, with his photographic memory and eye for detail, would be unaware of the tenancy system around him. He became an insider in the system, and profited from it. If he could remember the rents he charged for his shacks—two for two dollars a month—he could surely have remembered as well what they looked like inside and out. He chooses to suppress—the sin of omission. He does not lie to us. Instead he embodies a life of opposites: outsider-insider, openness-suppression, mythic pastoral–economic reality, the ordinary-extraordinary child.

II

ADULTS CAN HAVE two childhoods: what actually happened and what is remembered. For many of us, but especially for figures in public life, there may be a third childhood—the reality they wish to share with the public. All three childhoods must be established, as far as possible, by the historian or the interpreter, and played off against one another as accurately and completely as possible. Remembered reality, the way Jimmy Carter views his own life, becomes a major part of the historian's actual reality. If Jimmy Carter exaggerates or suppresses—edits—parts of his past, these changes become not historical inaccuracies but a part of his mental landscape, "facts" and "truths" in their own right. Before analyzing his words—whether in his autobiography or in interviews, speeches, statements, diaries, and letters—would-be interpreters must know if the words and their editing are his own. Jimmy Carter personally assured us that the composition of *Why Not the Best?* was completely his rather than the work of Jody Powell, Jerry Rafshoon, Hal Gulliver, or any of his other associates who helped on the book. Carter told us, and offered proof, that they were his words, his paragraph order, his overall structure.

Jimmy Carter's words testify to the intense relationship between him and his father, an intensity that persisted as young man Carter went out into the wider world. The flat prose in which

Jimmy Carter conveys his life with Mr. Earl in *Why Not the Best?* should not mislead readers about the strong emotions that still persist. When critics complained, as did Norman C. Miller in the *Wall Street Journal* at the two-year mark in the Carter presidency, of Jimmy Carter's "bland, even boring presence," they revealed that they had missed the high personal pressures contained under the composed exterior Carter has created. To call him "bland" is similiar to labeling nuclear power plants "benign" because their exterior brick facades are so ordinary-looking.

Jimmy Carter starts off his account of his childhood with an extraordinary statement. His father, he tells us, "was thirty years old when I was born, stood about five feet eight inches tall, and weighed 175 pounds." The newborn infant Jimmy Carter could hardly have known these facts firsthand; he had to ask or ascertain them when he got older. But why bother writing down these measurements in his autobiography at all? He doesn't give his mother's size or, for that matter, his own. The answer must surely lie in the lesson his father had taught him from his earliest days on: Jimmy Carter had to measure up to his father, and to his father's standards. He appears always concerned with how small he is and how much he weighs. Gloria, he remembered, was bigger than he was when they were growing up. At seventeen, he worried about being too small for Annapolis and stuffed himself with bananas and lay in bed resting to put on weight. He weighed 121 pounds when he entered Annapolis and 135 pounds when he reported on board his first submarine. The question "Am I big enough?" recurs as a steady theme in Jimmy Carter's life. Facing Gerald Ford in their first televised debate, Carter worried about their respective heights and acknowledged his feelings of awe. At the June 1979 economic summit in Tokyo, he later confided to acquaintances that he was worried about his ability to measure up as "leader of the free world." The other national leaders seemed "more experienced."

Carter's feelings about his father, and his mother, were necessarily mixed, as with any of us. Outwardly, he worshiped his father, who "worked harder than did I or anyone else," who was "an excellent tennis player" he could never beat. Carter says he never considered disobeying his father. These feelings may have been genuine. But with them co-existed other feelings. His father, Jimmy Carter has said, was his only "close friend." As the first-born and the only Carter male child for thirteen years, he had his father's prime attention. When Mr. Earl went fishing, he would take little Jimmy along. When he made the rounds of his farm properties, Jimmy would ride beside him. Jimmy Carter remembers that as a little boy on hot summer days, "I would lie under a tree and sleep until Daddy got through in the field and came back. We were very close. . . . During the times when I was very young, when my mother was out nursing, I would come and get into bed with my father and sleep with him."

The perfectionist Mr. Earl had special standards—he expected "a performance that was exemplary"—for his namesake. He had a special nickname for him, too. Mr. Earl called Jimmy Carter "Hot Shot," or simply "Hot." The name "Hot Shot" carries two possible meanings: one, an admiring recognition of someone displaying drive; the other, a somewhat sarcastic put-down for implied egotism, for someone who thinks he's hot stuff.

Gloria Carter Spann says that her father "called Jimmy 'Hot.' Jimmy always said, 'I can't let him stick me with a name like [that].' " When we talked to him, Jimmy Carter said, "My father called me 'Hot Shot' when I was a little kid. . . . When he called me 'Jimmy,' I knew he was angry with me. . . . When I was a little baby, he'd say, 'Come here, Hot Shot.' I don't know why. I don't know what it meant to him. . . . I never thought about it at the time." In 1943, at Annapolis, however, Jimmy wrote to Gloria, "Please do not call me 'Hot.' " While no stranger should make too much of a family nickname, small children have been known to be sensitive to the meanings of the names they are called by their parents. James Earl Carter, Sr., can't tell us what "Hot" meant to him, and Jimmy Carter says he has forgotten. "Hot Shot," then, will have to stand as a symbol both of a father's incitement to his son to pursue "exemplary performance" and of a father's pointed judgment on that performance.

III

HOW DOES A SMALL BOY come to terms with such a powerful-seeming father? One way, of course, would be to love that father and try to earn his love in return. With Mr. Earl, that could be quite hard. "No matter how well Jimmy did," Gloria Carter Spann remembered, "Daddy always said he could do better." Jimmy Carter's account, in an interview with us, put it another way. His father, he said, "was very tough but fair." Young Jimmy Carter, in any event, kept trying to please his father and to become like his father. Measuring himself against the best he knew, his father, he gave his best, trying to "measure up."

Another way for a son to measure up to a father—and handle ambivalent feelings about the man who appears to love him but always pushes him—would be to learn to toughen up, to act like a "man." American boys traditionally have been trained to be manly. A generation or two ago, "little men" didn't cry; they were quick with their fists; they stood square and upright. (In many homes, this brand of manliness is still treasured.) Sometimes, however, being a man may be hard, especially for an undersized, quiet, well-behaved little boy. A posture of standing apart—avoiding people, withdrawing into books—may offer better defenses against the outside world. Jimmy Carter's mother testifies, "He was shy . . . he wasn't an extrovert." After the episode with the wise guy at the garage, Lillian Carter told us, "He cried, but he didn't want to cry in front of men."

Toughness can take many forms, mental as well as physical. Gerald Rafshoon, Jimmy Carter's close associate since 1970, told us he can understand a great deal about Carter's childhood in this respect, more so than other men. "I can empathize with him," Rafshoon said. "I was an Army brat and a Jew—a hell of a combination. And living in twelve–thirteen places, you're always the new kid, and I was kind of a weak kid—you know, I wasn't very athletic. . . . I always would feel I was going to get beat up, and so I had to develop my mind and talk my way out of things, and I kind of sense in Jimmy this kind of guy. . . . Here he was probably the most affluent kid in town . . . the smartest. Of course, his mother might be the most liberal in town, not that he was a great liberal. He was different from the other kids, so therefore he had to develop a way of being himself, saying what he wanted to say, and yet getting along, to be able to tread water. And I think that trait developed as a child, as a local politician, as a state politician, and as a presidential candidate. . . . You know, when they used to say Jimmy Carter was wishy-washy and never got off the fence, well

. . . goddamn, he said *too* much, he used to say everything. But he had a way of getting along with diverse audiences. And I think he probably built that up, growing up the way he did."

The shy small boy makes up for any insecurities by learning to be resourceful; he faces the world with determination; and he gets along, accommodates to people, with a smile. The original smile may have been the result of a malocclusion; eventually the smile masks the basic shyness as well as the learned toughness. Jimmy Carter beams good will to his father, his friends, his customers, to everyone—until they deceive him, or make fun of him.

Another way of dealing with Mr. Earl—on the evidence of *Why Not the Best?*—was to get angry. Few people today need instruction any more about the "normal" feelings of rivalry, even barely suppressed rage, that exist between father and son (as well as mother and daughter). One night Jimmy Carter's parents had a party for their friends. They made so much noise that, as he remembers it, he went outside to sleep in his tree house. After the guests departed, his father called to him, but the young boy refused to answer. "The next morning," he says, "I received one of the few whippings of my boyhood, all of which I remember so well." The passage hints at a suppressed anger—the little boy's and the grown man's—at his father for what was perceived as an unjust whipping. It was, after all, his parents who had made the noise.

This anger becomes explicit in the very next paragraph: "One of the rare times I ever felt desperately sorry for my father" was when he ordered a tailor-made suit of clothes, the first of his life. The whole family gathered to watch the great event of Mr. Earl putting on his made-to-measure clothes. "Daddy opened the box with a great flourish," Jimmy Carter recounts, and "began to put on his suit. Alas, some terrible mistake had been made! The custom-made clothes were twice as large as my father." Carter adds, "I remember that no one in the family laughed."

This is a strange juxtaposition of narratives. Emotionally, however, the clothes story is very much in the right place. The boy-man is allowing himself to win out over his father, to laugh at him safely. By humiliating his father in memory, he gives vent to his anger at the unjust whipping. Because the two paragraphs seemed worrisomely pat, we specifically asked Carter if *he* wrote and arranged them. He said he did.

Jimmy Carter in this passage cuts his father down to size, and reduces his stature a bit; Mr. Earl wasn't large enough for the suit of clothes. Jimmy Carter finally gets some of his own back for the father who always beat him at sports and worked him so hard in the fields. It is not an unhealthy reaction; in reducing his father a notch or two, while still believing him great and powerful, the boy could see himself as a match for his father, and imagine himself having more or less the same dimensions. Moreover, it is also emotionally healthy to find a bit of clay in any great statue's feet.

Jimmy Carter's father did him another "injustice," with a different outcome. The Carters were getting the boy ready to go to Columbus, Georgia, to visit Lillian Carter's parents, the Gordys. His father, wielding the clippers he used to shear the mules, cut his son's hair for the big trip. "Daddy's hand slipped and a big gap was cut out of the hair on top of my head. After studying the situation for a few minutes, he decided that the only solution was to clip my head completely. . . . I was deeply embarrassed and wanted to stay at home until my hair grew out. Finally, Daddy found a cap that I could wear, and I went to Columbus to visit for about a week and then returned home. Later, my mother asked my grandmother what she thought of me, and Grandma reported that I was a fine boy but acted in a very peculiar way. She told Mother I was the only child she had ever seen who slept and ate while wearing a cap." This time, Jimmy Carter tells the embarrassing joke on himself; he doesn't, in memory, nurse along a constant, emotionally crippling resentment.

IV

THE REMEMBERED EPISODES of the father's clothes and the gapped hair, trivial and "personal" in themselves, suggest something about the formation of Jimmy Carter's attitudes toward authority and discipline. As we have noted, he mainly accepted his father's "authoritarianism," rather than revolt openly against it. Jimmy Carter, as a quiet, well-behaved "good little boy," did not give vent to anger. As his sister Gloria Carter Spann remembers, when he was angry "he went to his room with a book, shut his door, and no one was allowed to disturb him." For the well-behaved boy who became a disciplined, controlled adult, deep anger cannot be expressed; it must take another form. In retrospect, Jimmy Carter places his father in a humiliated posture or he turns his feelings into a joke on himself. More conscious retort is not allowed, to his father, or to his latter-day adversaries. Only that throbbing vein in his temple, gives away the depths of his anger.

When Jimmy Carter openly disobeyed his father, punishment followed. Jimmy Carter, as we have noted, calls special attention to this when he summons up memories of the six whippings handed out to him by his father. Some people might dismiss this incisive memory by saying, "Well, all kids are whipped. So what?" Jody Powell, one of Carter's closest associates and his press secretary, did just this in talking with us. Others might say the memory of six whippings—not five, or seven—is another trick of recollection, much like his recitation of exact numbers throughout his book. The fact is that Jimmy Carter did not *have* to write about the whippings in a campaign-year book intended to help him win the Presidency; he wouldn't have bothered unless they were really of importance to him. These remain extraordinary events in the memory of Jimmy Carter; library research and census records could help him with his other figures, but no record of his whippings existed for him to crib from forty years later, except the record of deeply felt memory.

The whippings followed Jimmy Carter's transgressions against authority. They stirred rage and resentment, but he accepted the punishment. Loving his father as he did, Jimmy Carter learned to control his anger. "I used to get angry," he told us. "Yes, of course, as would any child." Then his next association: "Daddy felt that when I wasn't in school, I ought to be working, and that was part of it. And he was much stricter on me than many other fathers were on their children." His father "worked hard himself," Jimmy Carter went on, and because he asked as much, or more, of himself as he did of his son, the demands seemed justified. "I never disobeyed my father in that when he said, 'Jimmy, you do something,' I failed to do it. But on many occasions I did things that I knew my father didn't like, and I was punished very severely because of it." His father's authority, exercised in the family, appeared legitimate. Jimmy Carter felt no revolutionary zeal or rebellious desire to overturn such authority.

V

BESIDES THE PARTY WHIPPING, Jimmy Carter gives the specifics of two others. His "most vivid," "most memorable" whipping came after he took out an extra penny from the Sunday school collection instead of putting one in. "That was the last money I ever stole," Jimmy tells us. The other recalled whipping came when he hit Gloria with his B.B. gun. When the child Jimmy Carter gives way to open anger—a muffled echo of violent episodes in the Carter family past—punishment quickly follows.

Jimmy Carter's feelings about his father required more acceptable ways of expression, as well as more "acceptable" targets. His sister Gloria and childish jokes like the disappearing act aboard the Alabama-bound train provided more suitable outlets for anger. The familiar technical term for this is "displacement." Lillian Carter told us, "He was always laughing and kidding; he teased his sisters to death."

There remains one other acceptable channel for the displacement of the angry feelings a son may feel about a father who sternly disciplined him and constantly pushed him. He can make common cause with the other victims of injustice. In Jimmy Carter's life, the oppressed people who were closest lived just up the road and worked the land for Mr. Earl. Nowhere, quite naturally, does Jimmy Carter flatly state that he "identified" with blacks or sharecroppers because it was a way of dealing with his father or of "getting back" at him for perceived injustices. Supposedly, Jimmy Carter learned his racial liberalism and compassion from his mother, the now-established legend. Yet Jimmy Carter himself, as we saw, has insisted that James Agee was telling his story—even though the James Earl Carter, Sr., of Archery was undeniably one of the two or three most substantial landowners and merchants in his community. Carter has often talked about his special "relationship" with the poor. "I do have unique experience," he said during the 1976 campaign, "and one of the strongest and best of these is my relationship with poor people. That's where I came from. That's where I live. Those are my people—not only whites, but particularly blacks." This feeling runs too deep to be dismissed as political oratory. The black and the poor exist as Carter's "people" in his emotional past. There he can be both Mr. Earl's princely first son and a victimized little boy.

Jimmy Carter recounts a childhood episode suggesting a way that competing and contradictory identities can exist within the same person. In 1938, the heavyweight fighters Joe Louis and Max Schmeling met for their second match. Since Mr. Earl had the only radio for miles around, his black sharecroppers gathered outside his Archery house to listen to the broadcast of the fight.

The emotions stirred by this fight may be hard to grasp for those too young to remember. The twenty-three-year-old Louis, an American Negro, came from an impoverished Alabama farm family that had migrated to Detroit. The German Schmeling, thirty-three, had beaten Louis in their first meeting in 1936. The rematch was played out against the background of Nazi German expansionism and Hitler's Master Race dogmas. The American Negro track man Jesse Owens had won four gold medals at the Berlin Olympics in 1936, and Hitler had refused to acknowledge Owens at the awards ceremonies. Though Schmeling told American reporters that he was not a member of the Nazi Party, the theme of the Nordic champion versus the "childlike" Negro proved too powerful to resist in the sports pages. Louis met with President Roosevelt, who told him the country's hopes were in his corner. When Carter notes that there were "heavy racial overtones encompassing the fight," he is understating for a change.

Since Mr. Earl's tenants had respectfully asked to listen, Mr. Earl propped the radio in an open window so that the Carter family could hear inside while the blacks, forty or fifty in all, sat and stood outside in the yard under a large mulberry tree. Everyone observed the "accepted priorities of a racially segregated society," Jimmy Carter noted in his terse way. Louis demolished Schmeling in less than two minutes of the first round. "My father was deeply disappointed in the outcome," Jimmy Carter writes. Then: "There was no sound from anyone in the yard, except a polite 'Thank you, Mr. Earl' offered to my father." But once the blacks had filed out of the yard and across the railroad track to one of their own houses, about a hundred yards away, "pandemonium broke loose inside the house, as our black neighbors shouted and yelled in celebration of the Louis victory." The story reads, in memory, not just as if Joe Louis and the blacks had won but little Jimmy Carter as well.

Perhaps interpretive biographers should not make too much of this small triumph of a small boy over a powerful father and master. But Jimmy Carter often uses parables in his speeches, a carry-over in all likelihood from his years as a Sunday school teacher at Plains Baptist Church. And this sounds like one of the parables.

There is another anecdote told to illustrate a moral point; it, too, deals with childhood feelings of aggression and love. Jimmy Carter describes how, "like all farm boys," he had a slingshot and how he picked up little white round rocks for it from the railroad bed. "One day I was leaving the track with my pockets and hands full of rocks and my mother came out on the front porch and called me. She had in her hands a plate full of cookies which she had just baked for me. She asked, 'Honey, would you like some cookies?' Really, nothing much happened, but I remember it vividly. I stood there about fifteen or twenty seconds in honest doubt about whether I should drop those worthless rocks and take the cookies which Mother offered me with a heart full of love."

Carter writes that his reason for telling the story is to illustrate how hard it was for Southerners to give up the "rocks" of segregation and to accept the blessing of a "new and free relationship." On the surface, he has told a political parable. It may be a personal parable as well, since the young child with the slingshot could not have been thinking as a politician when he experienced what became a vivid memory. The parable sounds like a small Southern boy in the process of choosing between his father and his mother, and of giving up masculine aggression and white male supremacy —the rocks hurled from a slingshot—in favor of the softer, more compassionate acts of taking and giving, the nurturance embodied in the cookies. Probably Jimmy Carter doesn't know exactly what his story means, on its deepest level, in his own mind. The sensible outsider's reading, then, treats the story in symbolic terms, expressing the pulls of masculine and feminine on the young boy and, beyond, on the society in which he was growing up. Critics who demand a "tougher" President Carter fail to recognize his balancing of these contrary impulses, in himself and in his Administration.

88

We do know that Jimmy Carter's feelings toward his father, and thus toward authority and power and, by extension, toward politics—for power is what politics is about, even the politics of love—remained ambivalent. But then so did his feelings toward his mother and, by extension, toward tenderness and compassion. Jimmy Carter took on many of his mother's values, as well as his father's.

How much of each came together in Jimmy Carter, and in what measure, is difficult to know. One of Jimmy Carter's friends in Plains, P. J. Wise, declared that "Jimmy's got some of both of them in him . . . a good business head like his father; and I would say he's a little bit stubborn like Miss Lillian." Another contemporary, Virginia Williams, dissented: "I never thought he was like his dad at all." Everyone deferred to Mrs. Ida Mae Timmerman, a wisp of a woman who had known Earl and Lillian Carter as well as their children. "Well, I'm sure he got a lot of qualities from his mother and his father," she said, "but I guess he is a lot like Earl. But Jimmy is just *more* than any of them."

7

Leaving Home

.

JIMMY CARTER'S DECISION to go to Annapolis, he tells us,
dates back to his fourth or fifth year, a time when most children
plan no more than an afternoon's play. Later, as a grammar school
child, he read books about the Navy and Annapolis: "I wrote to
ask for the entrance requirements, not realizing my age, and I
almost memorized the little catalogue when it came. Then I
planned my studies and choice of library books accordingly."
Jimmy Carter sees himself as a planner, even as a little boy; his
self-image credits him with long-range plans which contain within
them the steps to the final goal, as well as the goal itself, and all
with no room for self-doubt: "There was never any question about
it [Annapolis], as I recall, in my life from the time I was a tiny
child," Jimmy Carter told us. "The folks used to, you know . . .
make conversation about when you grow up. Some kids said, 'I'm
going to be a fireman,' or some, 'I want to be a policeman,' or
some say, 'I want to be a railroad engineer.' I always said, 'I want
to go to Annapolis.' And I honestly believe at that early formative
stage of my life I didn't have a clear concept even of what Annapolis was; I never had seen the ocean."

Nothing seems more natural than that Jimmy Carter should
have gone to Annapolis and made the Navy his career. The military
academies are filled with Southern boys—following a strong tradition, seeking free education, and achieving mobility. But Jimmy
Carter's choice, looked at more closely, does not seem quite so

natural. His family had no strong military tradition; no Confederate heroes dominated the scrapbooks. Annapolis offered engineering training—technology for the broader world—but then so did Georgia Tech. While the Carters were not old rich in the early 1940s, they were certainly well off. If Alton Carter could send his son Hugh to the University of Georgia, Mr. Earl could have done the same for his son Jimmy. As for social standing and political office —sometimes one and the same in small towns—the state university at Athens offered the best way to rise in Georgia.

Yet Jimmy Carter went to Annapolis and chose a career in the Navy, a life as different from his life in Plains as he could find. The Navy meant a new world of water; Jimmy Carter never did see the ocean until he entered the Naval Academy. Instead of the familiar boundaries of the land, the Navy represented open horizons, an unbounded place for ambitions, far from the confining grids of farm and small town—not social mobility in the usual sense, but movement in a fluid situation. In the Navy, a determined young man could test himself and see how well he measured up against rivals of a different sort from those in the Carter home, in the Archery fields, in the streets of Plains, and in school.

Lillian Carter's youngest brother, Thomas Watson Gordy, an enlisted man in the regular U.S. Navy, inspired the young boy's choice. Uncle Tom became Jimmy Carter's childhood hero; he was distant, and he did not whip little boys. He handed out punishment to other men. Uncle Tom was the fleet lightweight boxing champion. Jimmy Carter remembers the photograph of him "standing proudly with boxing gloves, slightly in front of a group of other men whom he had beaten."

Many young boys look up to another man, a substitute father figure, in addition to their real father. Uncles often play a father-hero-adventurer's role, like Uncle Ben in Arthur Miller's *Death of a Salesman*. Uncle Tom Gordy served as the model who offered escape to Jimmy Carter. Since young Carter wanted his father's love, and could never rebel openly against Mr. Earl, he quite naturally later in life associated his father with his decision to go to Annapolis. "My Daddy's service in the Army during World War I as a first lieutenant caused him to hold in high esteem the military training at service academies," Carter would later write. Talking to us, he fleshed out his spare formal account: "The reason I went to Annapolis, I believe, was because of my mother's youngest brother, Tom, who died in 1975; he was kind of a hero of mine . . . he became a radioman third class and a radioman second class . . . and the fact that he was in the Navy and the fact that my Daddy wanted me to go to a military academy, I think it was the thing that decided me to go to Annapolis instead of West Point."

The two contrary voices—the demanding father's and the freewheeling Uncle Tom's—meshed in seeming harmony; he could heed them both, though they spoke different messages. Jimmy Carter managed to serve his uncle, who sent him gifts, and his father, who worked him hard, combining impulses that would exert opposite pulls. For most of his young life, from age four through his twenty-ninth year, he kept the competing forces in rough balance, though the conflict never ended completely.

From the perspective of Archery in the late 1930s, much more practical issues were on the Carters' minds. Appointments to the military academies came from Senators and Congressmen. Mr. Earl had begun cultivating his Congressman, Stephen Pace, in hopes of obtaining the long-desired appointment to Annapolis, and also because Pace specialized in legislation concerning peanuts.

Lillian Carter remembers the Annapolis appointment as something of entitlement. "After he was twelve and thirteen, we knew he was going to Annapolis. . . . Because it was easy to get an appointment."

In Jimmy Carter's memories, the outcome was no sure thing. He worried about the Navy's physical requirements. Malocclusion, the fact that his teeth did not perfectly meet, interfered with his enjoyment of food. Retention of urine, the Navy's circumlocution for bed-wetting, scared the mystified Plains high schooler. As he unabashedly tells it, he wondered if that meant "the last clinging drop" of urine on his penis after urinating might leak, and cause his disqualification. Flat feet, the fear of fallen arches, drove him to a home remedy—rolling his soles on Coca-Cola bottles for hours each week to raise the arches. Worried most of all that he would be too small and too underweight to make the grade, he not only stuffed himself with bananas but gave up a part-time job so he could rest more—on the boyish theory that if he used very little energy what he ate would all go to weight. Later he would remember all this as his "ridiculous and secret fears" that he would not meet the requirements.

They were not so ridiculous. He *was* thin and small—five feet three inches and 121 pounds at high school graduation in 1941. Nor were his fears very secret: Jimmy "was always wondering if he'd ever grow," Gloria Carter Spann reminds us. Some grown men might shrink from telling such stories about the bodily worries of their childhood. Talk of physical concerns seems for Jimmy Carter another part of his testimony to the truth within, another form of his kind of off-putting openness.

He also worried about the academic requirements. His schoolmate P. J. Wise remembers him as something of a grind because of Annapolis, studying all the time, while everybody else was out playing and having a good time. After the years of trying to measure up to Mr. Earl's standards, he now had to meet the Navy's.

If they are lucky, schoolboys and girls encounter an extraordinary teacher and person when they are young. For many children in Plains, the coach, Young Thompson Sheffield, served that role; for Jimmy Carter it was the sainted Miss Julia Coleman, the English teacher (later superintendent of schools). She loved books, just as Lillian Carter did, but had no other interest in life except her young charges, unlike Lillian Carter. Julia Coleman was stout and she limped, the victim of polio or a birth injury. As Virginia Williams, a former student, recalls, she "stood on one foot and propped the other small leg." She wore her hair pulled back, and "had a big nose." Jimmy Carter remembered all that, and more. "Miss Julia remains alive in my memory. She was short and somewhat crippled, yet she was quite graceful as she moved along. Her face was expressive, particularly when she was reading one of the poems she loved."

The daughter of a minister, Miss Julia never married. Her whole life went out to her schoolchildren. If a student needed something, remembers Virginia Williams, "she'd give them the money to buy a tablet, or anything." Unable to drive herself, she bought cars and let schoolboys wear them out for her. She gave reading lists over the summer. She put on the plays, musical productions, debates, spelling bees, and word contests. She handed a copy of Leo Tolstoy's *War and Peace* to Jimmy Carter when he was twelve, telling him he was ready for it. From the title, Jimmy Carter hoped it was about cowboys and Indians; still he managed to get through the 1400 pages.

Miss Julia's tutelage of Jimmy Carter reinforced some of the lessons of his parents, without the pain. She helped point the way *from* home, just as that other substitute figure, Uncle Tom, had beckoned to new horizons. Miss Julia's teachings suggested the existence of other prizes in life to Jimmy Carter than those offered in the business world of his father. Searching for the best in him, she also set ambitions before him. As one schoolmate recalls, "I bet she had as much to do with Jimmy . . . she used to tell us, 'Some of you could be President.' " In hindsight, everyone contributes to a winner—and defeat is an orphan. Still, Jimmy Carter has his own accolade for Miss Julia Coleman; he allots her almost as much space in *Why Not the Best?* as he does his mother. And he quoted her at the very beginning of his presidential Inaugural Address.

Teenage boys had another persistent concern, beyond buck teeth and science grades, in the last years of Jimmy Carter's high school days. In June 1940, radios, now electrically powered, brought the sound of German soldiers marching into the Channel ports of France. In December 1941, the Japanese attacked Pearl Harbor and Guam, where Uncle Tom Gordy was stationed. In January 1942, the Carters received official word that Uncle Tom Gordy was missing and presumed dead. Jimmy Carter was seventeen; a boy of seventeen could pick his branch of service and march away to training camp right after his eighteenth birthday. But Jimmy Carter, no more bellicose than his paternal ancestors, and just as respectful of a dollar, chose to wait for his Annapolis appointment; the glory of action and the red badge of combat would come after he got his commission, and his education at government expense.

He missed the fighting entirely, as it happened. Two years passed before Congressman Pace could arrange his appointment. Though Jimmy Carter does not mention it in his autobiography, he spent the first year of the war at Georgia Southwestern College in Americus. Southwestern was the local junior college; Plains high school graduates went there, if they went to college at all. As Plains people tell the story, Jimmy Carter had won a scholarship to Southwestern, beating out Plains's number two student, Eloise ("Tenny") Ratliff. Dark-haired, pretty Eloise came from a large family, and her parents could not afford the hundred

94

dollars to send her away to college, even the state school in Americus. Jimmy Carter, so the story goes, gave his scholarship to her.

II

SOUTHWESTERN SERVED ONLY as a stopping place for Jimmy Carter on his way out of Plains. The Annapolis appointment came through, to begin in June 1943. In the summer of 1942, eighteen-year-old Jimmy Carter enrolled at Georgia Tech in Atlanta as a Naval ROTC student to take more preparatory courses recommended by the Navy.

At Georgia Tech Carter caught that peculiar giddy, intense Saturday afternoon fever so common in young American males, and nowhere more so than in the South. He became a loyal football fan of the Tech Yellowjackets that fall, staying in Atlanta on weekends for the big games rather than traveling back to Plains. Even after going to Annapolis, he maintained his strong loyalties as a "Tech man."

Later the politician Jimmy Carter would call upon his association with Georgia Tech as he traveled around, both in Georgia and in the United States, meeting, in his words, "hundreds of Tech alumni in top leadership positions in government and business," and replaying old football games in that fraternal way men of affairs often use to break to social ice in their wheelings and dealings with each other.

The year Carter spent at Georgia Tech was the first full year of America at war. War produced prosperity at home. America's gross national product had been $91 billion in 1939; by 1945 it reached $215 billion, despite the fact that 15 million young men and women in the armed services were not contributing any goods or services to the GNP. Farmers particularly enjoyed the new technology and the war boom; new fertilizers, high-yield seeds, insecticides, and machinery helped increase crop bounties by 25 per cent. The farmers' old fear of surpluses—and lowered prices—dissolved as America became, in the admiring phrase of the period, the bread basket of the world. America, *Time* magazine proudly announced, was becoming "suddenly rich—everywhere, all at once." The new prosperity included Mr. Earl.

His son, meanwhile, had achieved his own success, away from the father. Jimmy Carter reported to Annapolis in June 1943. An ambition, held for fifteen years, had been rewarded. Failure might have called into question his ability to measure up; it might have been intolerable. Success would mean that Jimmy Carter had been right about himself, that his sense of self was justified, and that he could go on to achieve other ambitions. He was almost nineteen years old, stood about five feet six inches, and weighed less than 130 pounds.

Going to Annapolis for Carter also meant traveling beyond Georgia for the first time. He felt homesick. He kept a diary during his plebe first year. It is a log of anger, and a lot of control.

Carter had always tried to get along with others and keep his composure. At Annapolis, he encountered the hazing system— punishment by paddlings and other schoolboyish cruelties. No one could say whether these absurdities ever produced a better officer corps; they constituted "tradition," and they were perpetuated. In the aftermath of the war, a great deal would change at the service academies. Annapolis, for example, would graduate its first black midshipman, tougher curricula would replace Mickey Mouse courses, and healthier, more sophisticated attitudes would sweep away the practice of smacking other boys' buttocks. In 1943, however, when Jimmy Carter entered Annapolis, the hazing tradition had not yet come apart.

Jimmy Carter was much like most of the other young men of Annapolis in the war years—white middle-class Christians, rural and small-town sons of important local personages, salutatorians or valedictorians of their schools, the pride of the Miss Julias. He came from the Deep South and, in his quiet, stiff, skinny kid's way, stood somewhat apart from the others; but the major division at Annapolis was drawn by class year, not section or size. In Carter's account, however, he was picked on for his Southernness. In his remembrances, he emerges, once again, as something of an unyielding hero, not quite forsaking his roots but still reaching out beyond them.

His toothy smile—his sign of outward peace and good will toward others—got him into instant trouble instead of protecting him. On July 7, 1943, the first night in his regiment, he wrote, "Of course all of the plebes were rather apprehensive about what was to come. We later found out that our fears were well-grounded." Right after supper, Carter wrote, "the halls were lined with young-sters who were anxious to try out their new authority. . . . We had to tell our names and home state to every youngster we saw. . . . My main trouble was that I smiled too much. I soon learned to concentrate on a serious subject when passing a group of the yap-ping 3/C. I also learned how to 'wipe it off.' " In fact, he never did wipe the smile off his face to the satisfaction of third classmen. His last diary entry, in May 1944, returns to his proud defiance of the hazing. "I got beat with a serving spoon twice at noon for not wiping a smile off to the class of '45. Tonight they were out to make me stop it, but beat me four times before I did. Twenty-seven licks each time. It's really sore tonight, but was well worth it."

The spoons had long handles and the paddler could get a good purchase. The wooden breadboards had smaller handles but wider paddling surfaces. A Yankee upperclassman named Weidner led a group of hazers intent on making the boy from Sumter County sing "Marching Through Georgia," the battle hymn of General Sher-man's army. Plebe Carter refused. "Weidner is kinda mad at me now. He said—'Learn "Marching Through Georgia" ' three times and I said, 'Sir,' every time. He was pretty mad and yelled it again and told me not to say 'sir' again. He really got mad when I said 'aye, aye' with no 'sir.' Told me to come around, but I haven't been yet." Though the paddling continued for several days, Carter stubbornly refused to sing. Eventually, an Arkansas upperclass-man intervened, and Carter wrote in his diary, "I don't think Weid-ner went for the idea so much, but my rear end was getting in worse shape." He had not sung, any more than the lone hero, as he saw himself, had stopped facing the world with his smile.

His classmates gave a less serene account of these days. Like other plebes, he was denied food and repeatedly required to "shove in," that is, to sit at mess without touching the table. Once, Plebe Carter was knocked across a wardroom with a bread platter. Classmates say he would march angrily to his quarters, eyes ice-blue and face white with fury. "But he would never let it out," remembers his fellow plebe Arthur Middleton, "never kick a chair or throw a book like the rest of us."

97

His life with his father had prepared him well enough for
certain challenges. He accepted stoically, though inwardly seething, the upperclassmen's whippings administered in the name of
rightful authority. Though he may have questioned the justice, as
he did with his father, he accepted the legitimacy. Nineteen-year-
old Jimmy Carter could write sarcastically that the Navy kept its
men in woolen "Blue Service" uniforms "although the temperature is ninety degrees every day. The Navy really uses judgment
about everything. Never just blindly follows regulations—always
quick to make a change for the better." He could remember, thirty
years later, that Annapolis "was sometimes a brutal form of training and testing." Yet he maintained his outward composure, and
inward loyalty. "My impression is that I enjoyed it all, even the
less pleasant parts."

Though he accepted the Annapolis way of training and leading
men, as he had accepted his father's whippings, he did not allow
his acceptance to dull his common-sense ability to see the errors in
the military way of doing things. In part, he felt a pride in passing
the test. Hazing represented one side of the passage to manhood.
Failure to endure the rites meant exit from the tribe. As Carter
writes, "If one ever showed any weakness, he was assaulted from
all sides with punishment and harassment, and forced out of the
academy." It was another lesson of life, taught at Annapolis, outside of the classroom. At its worst, not showing any weakness
could mean not admitting a mistake, because this might be taken
for weakness; at its best, it could mean stubbornly holding to one's
rightful beliefs and acts. Years later, an unbending Jimmy Carter
persisted in supporting his friend Bert Lance, and his energy man,
James Schlesinger, past the point of good political judgment.

Stubbornness aside, his refusal to sing "Marching Through
Georgia" represented something of an ironic situation. Carter had
left Georgia, and the South, to go to Annapolis and be more than a
Southerner. In an essay on domestic commerce that Jimmy Carter
did as a schoolboy in Plains, he reported, "The West raises lots of
wheat that people in the East cannot raise and the people of the
East raise cotton." William Greider, the reporter who uncovered
the essay, observes; "It is a small thing, perhaps, that the little boy
thought of himself living in the East rather than the South." Later,
as a grown man, he would take speech lessons to rid himself of his
regional accent.

At the Academy, however, upperclassmen thrust his South-ernness at him. Jimmy Carter was not one to fight for the Lost Cause, though Yankee classmates may have pushed him so that he would defend, without being defensive, the South. He had, after all, not only grown up with blacks, but also identified with them in deeply hidden ways. Carter already had begun to stand apart from those mixed feelings of guilt and pride that so many white South-erners have had about race and the special burden of the white South.

Thoughts of status, rather than segregation, occupied what-ever social consciousness he displayed as a middie. His friends recall Carter's references to the family "plantation" back in Geor-gia; pointedly Carter admonished sister Gloria in a letter home, "Don't write me on lined notebook paper with a pencil." Jimmy Carter had not come to Annapolis to remain a Southern cracker. He was reaching out to broader horizons beyond Georgia. He re-mained Mr. Earl's son, yet he was no longer only Mr. Earl's son; again he juggled different spheres rather than discarding one in order to grasp the other. His contacts with home became less fre-quent, but were still full of emotion; he was putting distance be-tween himself and Plains.

III

AS IN MANY WARTIME SCHOOLS, the Annapolis courses put Jimmy Carter and his classmates on an accelerated track. He fin-ished four years of work in three, and the class of '47 graduated in June of 1946 instead of 1947. Carter sailed through gunnery, sea-manship, navigation, astronomy, engineering, and naval tactics, plus Spanish. In tribute, *Lucky Bag,* the 1947 yearbook, said, "Studies never bothered Jimmy. In fact, the only times he opened his books were when his classmates desired help on problems." The exaggeration testifies to the impression he made on his class-mates; he finished fifty-ninth in a class of 820.

He liked ballroom dancing and cross-country running (his best sport, given his small, wiry size). He also took instruction in after-dinner speaking, and described it as "one of the most fear-some requirements." Standing up in front of people and talking to them did not come easy for Carter; he may have acted somewhat superior, but he still felt a shyness in groups. He excelled then as now at solitary efforts like ship and plane recognition; he would study silhouettes for hours. He got hands-on experience at the controls of naval aircraft.

In the summer of 1944, as the Allied forces landed in Normandy and pushed toward the Rhine, the class of 1946 got its first sea duty. Jimmy Carter's assignment took him aboard the U.S.S. *New York,* an old battlewagon consigned to patrol duty off the East Coast and in the Caribbean, far from combat. The trip became memorable for two reasons. First, the duty roster put Jimmy Carter in charge of keeping the after "head"—the ship's toilet troughs—in sanitary condition; for someone who got seasick easily, it proved to be a vivid experience. Second, the *New York* had a close encounter with a German submarine, or what the ship thought was an enemy sub. The *New York* took evasive action and broke a propeller; it may have been hit by a torpedo or it may have hit a hidden reef. The *New York* headed back to port, and the Navy awarded everyone, including the midshipmen, a campaign ribbon. In retrospect, the whole voyage sounded like a service comedy on television. Jimmy Carter, however, took it all seriously.

Carter remained something of a solitary figure at Annapolis, as he had been at Southwestern and at Georgia Tech. Annapolis classmates, interviewed in the summer of 1976, could be expected to be doubly kind to Carter in memory; he had served with them as a comrade, and he stood a very good chance of being Commander in Chief of the Navy they had served. One such classmate, Dr. Francis Hertzog, now an ophthalmologist in Los Angeles, compared Carter to General Robert E. Lee. "In some respects," said Hertzog, "I felt like he was an even better person than Lee. Maybe once in a thousand years a person comes along who will have the control of their own mind and can utilize it to the extent he can his." This did not blind ophthalmologist Hertzog to the possibility that a human being lived under the hero's mantle: "Carter was very well liked by his company. But he was a loner. He did not make close intimate friendships. He went out of his way to be perhaps more friendly to more people, but he didn't need other people's close bond of friendship to support his own ego and personality—he had a very strong character."

Carter's undergraduate life seemed typical of that of his class-mates at Annapolis. Perhaps he studied more and appeared stand-offish (snobbish, one classmate complained), but he fitted into the competitive atmosphere. His class of '47 turned out thirty-two admirals, two generals, and two Medal of Honor winners. Two officers became prisoners of war in Vietnam, and heroes to their class-mates.

More immediately, the class of '47 shaped up as neither heroes nor winners. They were shipping out into the doldrums of the peacetime Navy. Naval officers, who had received their free Annapolis educations thanks to the government, had to continue to serve to pay back this generosity. Nearly half his class of '47, however, continued to leave the Navy before putting in the required tour; many got out the way they got in, through senatorial or congressional influence. No fewer than 250, according to recent records, forsook military life and became businessmen.

Jimmy Carter himself agonized about getting out. "The postwar Navy," he recognized, would go nowhere for a while: "It was a time of great disappointment. . . . I became most disillusioned with the Navy, and the military in general, and probably would have resigned had not I and all Annapolis graduates been serving 'at the pleasure of the President.' " The dream of the four-year-old boy had foundered upon reality. The Navy didn't look at all like Uncle Tom's postcard life. The Annapolis dream embraced going to college and getting out of Plains; Jimmy Carter hadn't been prepared, long-range planner that he may have been, for the mothballed Navy of 1946.

His first post-Annapolis assignment came by lot, and he got "almost the last choice," the U.S.S. *Wyoming,* an aging battleship converted into an electronics and gunnery experimental vessel. In 1947, the following year, Carter boarded the U.S.S. *Mississippi,* which replaced the decrepit *Wyoming.* He became the officer in charge of teaching enlisted men high school level courses and also the electronics and photography officer. He tried to make the best of his situation, a tough assignment in itself. His ships earned the name "Chesapeake Raiders" because they operated in the gunnery practice area of the Chesapeake Bay. After two years, disillusioned and unhappy, he reached for a lifeline out of the Navy.

Jimmy Carter tried for a Rhodes scholarship, though he does

not mention this in his autobiography. The estate of the English empire builder Cecil Rhodes at that time awarded scholarships to white male North Americans for study at Oxford University in England. Appointments came by state and region, with former Rhodes winners serving on the screening committees. Carter applied, made it through to the end of the screening, and then the board rejected him.

His failure to measure up in the eyes of the Rhodes committee stands as his first real loss, and he took it hard. We learned about the Rhodes rejection when we were talking with him about his defeat in the 1966 Georgia governor's race. The two failures appear connected in his mind. When we asked him about the effect of the 1966 loss, he responded, "I had only two major setbacks. I tried for a Rhodes scholarship when I got out of the Naval Academy [actually he applied two years later], and I didn't get it. . . . That . . . forced me to acknowledge that I was not superior, as I thought I was; and to be defeated in the governor's race was another major thing that happened." On another occasion, he declared that he should have won the Rhodes: "I got to the final screening board and there was another fellow in there with me. He was a tall gangly fellow, real peculiar-looking guy. We were the last two. He studied Elizabethan poetry, and the interviewing board asked him something about current events, and he said he wasn't interested in anything that happened after Queen Elizabeth died. . . . They asked me every question they could think of. I answered them all. Current events, Philosophy. Music. Nuclear physics. But the other kid got the Rhodes scholarship. I didn't even feel bitter about it. But, as a matter of fact, he went over there from Georgia and he had a nervous breakdown."

His account sounds bitter, in spite of the disclaimer. Its tone calls up the story of Carter's father's custom-made clothes. Retelling both stories, Carter in the end salvages his own superiority, even out of defeat.

Though hardly commendable, Carter's response to rivals follows a familiar and not unhealthy pattern. Defeat hurts, but it is not allowed to destroy his sense of worth. Though it forces him to acknowledge that he is not as superior as he thought, that thought in turn allows him to rise superior to his loss and restores his sense of self-esteem.

But why must he feel superior? Superiority, for Carter, represents winning. It is the voice of his father that tells him he must excel, must win. More than most of us, Jimmy Carter must listen to that voice and measure up to its demands. Carter responds to defeat by going out and finding another, or more demanding, contest. When he felt that his energy speech scheduled for the Fourth of July, 1979, was not in shape for delivery, he postponed it and broadened its theme to address the whole moral posture of the nation. "Losing" in the polls, he asked for the resignations of his entire cabinet and staff; in effect, he declared the end of the first Carter Administration in the summer of 1979, and was trying to put together a second, "winning" Presidency.

In the case of the Rhodes he looked for a new challenge tougher than the one he had failed. He applied for submarine service, and won his transfer.

8

The Embryonic Feeling

SOME MEN MARRY THEIR MOTHERS: "a gal just like the gal that married dear old Dad." Jimmy Carter married someone very much unlike his mother; he married someone who impressed people as quiet, shy, lonely, and yet hardworking, independent, and determined to do something better than to stay in Plains forever—someone, it seems, very much like himself. Rosalynn Carter, Jimmy Carter often said during his 1976 presidential campaign, has been an "equal extension of myself." Once in the White House, they seemed to grow even more alike, despite the demands of the presidential office. When he took up jogging, in his grim, determined way, she did too—proudly measuring off her circuits at Camp David. By the spring of 1979, she was up to four miles per run. (He claimed to do ten miles by then.)

Their outward similarities of character appear to be so noticeable that one interviewer after talking to each of them separately declared that he had just met "two Jimmy Carters." There may be something more than exasperation in that observation. Jimmy Carter, without the support and hard work of Rosalynn Smith, quite possibly would have achieved no more—and no less—than the standing of a wealthy southwestern Georgia agribusinessman. Today he might be a state legislator, a more urbane Mr. Earl, with season tickets to Georgia Tech football games.

The union of Jimmy Carter and Rosalynn Smith, like most marriages, has been special, personal, unique; but again, like most marriages, it has played out certain general social patterns. Students of the American family speak of the "two-person career"—a marriage in which the husband and the wife both strive to advance one partner's lifework, typically the husband's. Jimmy Carter has had such a marriage. Dr. Peter Bourne, the psychiatrist who first became a friend of the Carters in the early 1970s, says simply, "All the Carters submerge their needs to his." With the recent drive for greater economic and psychic equality between the sexes, marriages arranged to benefit the dominant male, helped by his dutiful wife and children, may no longer be as common as they have been in the past. Jimmy Carter married at a time when men, particularly men from rural and small-town America, could profit from a "male supremicist" marriage before the idea began to be discredited.

Jimmy Carter also married on what seems like impulse. He took Rosalynn Smith to a movie and came home later that night and announced to his mother that he had met the girl he intended to marry. For someone who had carefully planned his Annapolis career since the age of four, his decision may sound out of character. But by marrying a hometown girl, and his sister Ruth's best friend, he stayed in character, taking a part of Plains, and family, with him as he reached out to another, larger world.

II

THE FAMILY of Rosalynn Smith lived in Plains proper. While her father, Edgar Smith, owned some farmland, he earned his living mainly as the town garage mechanic and school bus driver. Smith was a staunch Methodist who would not allow alcohol in his house. He wasn't one of life's winners, despite his abstemious habits. His land eventually became part of the Carter family holdings; unlike Mr. Earl, Edgar Smith had experienced the full draining force of the 1930s Depression. Then he fell victim to leukemia in 1940, at the age of 44. He took to bed to die, his life brightened mainly by his pretty curly-haired daughter, Rosalynn. His deathbed instructions were that his children should all go on with their education: "I want you to have a better position in life." To get them started, he left a little money specifically earmarked for all of them to begin college.

Rosalynn Smith remembers her life after Edgar Smith's death. "We were very, very poor and we worked hard. It was just a very bad time," she says. Her words echo Jimmy Carter's memories of his childhood; and just as other Carters dispute his accounts, so, too, do other Smiths challenge her version. Her brother Murray Smith, now a high school teacher, once noted that "a lot has been written about how destitute we were. I guess by New York standards we were, by the standards of south Georgia we were not. We had what we needed." Lillian Carter added: "People ask me, 'How poor was she [Rosalynn]?' I said, 'I didn't even think she was poor.' She had the most beautiful clothes in town." With the Smiths, as with the Carters, the memories appear to conflict because different qualities of life are being remembered. For Rosalynn Smith at thirteen, the loss of her beloved father devastated her childhood in her memories. For the younger Jimmy Carter, a loss of another kind—his seeming inability to gain his father's love —created similar memories of a harsh childhood.

As the oldest, Rosalynn Smith had to take care of her brother Murray and her other brother and sister while her mother, Allie, was working part-time as a post office clerk. Rosalynn Smith also worked in a beauty parlor and helped her mother sew. Just entering adolescence, she suddenly had to act more mature and learn to put other people's needs first. She had been just another "normal" small-town girl who loved to dance to records and to the radio; she had played basketball, read books, and got good grades. She had always been extra neat, conscientiously striving for perfection in order to please her father. After his death, she never felt she was doing enough to help her widowed mother; Edgar Smith's death took much of the security and spontaneity out of her life.

At seventeen, Rosalynn Smith went to Georgia Southwestern to study interior decorating and secretarial skills for two years. She would catch glimpses of her best friend Ruth Carter's brother Jimmy at his house, around town, and at parties. The young midshipman paid no attention to her until the summer of 1945, when he returned from his second year at Annapolis. At that point, they saw each other in a new way, and he decided to marry her.

Ruth Carter was the sister Jimmy Carter was closest to; Rosalynn Smith was not only her best friend but was like her in many ways—school smart, pretty, a perfectionist, a "daddy's girl." Even as children, Rosalynn Smith and Jimmy Carter had separately developed similar personalities. She had no close friends except for her family and Ruth Carter, and in the end Jimmy and Rosalynn Carter became each other's best friend. Jimmy Carter has referred to his father as his "closest friend." He now refers to his wife in the same way.

When young men "fall in love at first sight," we know that usually a "second sight" may be involved. In his heart that summer night, actually in his unconscious, Jimmy Carter knew that he had found the right woman for him. He was not quite twenty-one years old; she was eighteen.

Midshipman Carter's surprise announcement stunned his mother. She remembers her response: "Jimmy, she's just a little girl! She's Ruth's friend." All the while, Lillian Carter was thinking, she says, "My Jimmy is so much more sophisticated than she is. He's been dating girls who are graduating from college, girls from New Jersey. . . . This little girl Rosalynn is naïve." Lillian Carter came later to cloak her feelings about "little" Rosalynn in softer tones: "She was real young, and we would have liked her to finish her education, but she didn't want to." On July 7, 1946, Rosalynn Smith and Ensign Jimmy Carter were married at Plains Methodist Church.

III

THE NEWLYWEDS promptly set off for Norfolk, Virginia, and Carter's first assignment aboard the U.S.S. *Wyoming*. As a Navy wife, Rosalynn Carter learned to live with her husband away at sea. Their apartment may have been small, his ensign's pay of $300 a month not much grander; but they were far from the confining world of Plains and of Carters and Smiths. She had to cope alone at home, yet she seemed to thrive on the responsibilities and to grow. Jimmy Carter remembers their early married years in terms, now familiar, of apartness and union; their life then was "one of constant separations interspersed with ecstatic reunions and the

melding of ourselves over the years into a closer relationship."
Rosalynn Carter says, "I loved those years. We were so close. We
studied books. We listened to the Rachmaninoff concertos and
memorized Shakespeare."

The Carters were also seeing the postcard places of Uncle
Tom Gordy, and they were having children—three boys born at
three different naval bases: John William (named after Rosalynn's
grandfather), born in Portsmouth, Virginia, in July 1947; James
Earl in Hawaii in 1950; and Donnel Jeffrey in New London, Connecticut, in 1952. Rosalynn Carter's official White House biography carefully speaks of how the Carters "faced the uncertainties
of military life," as the peacetime Navy had shrunk from three
million to under one million men. But Rosalynn Carter remembers
the Navy years as a good period, one of relative freedom and even
glamour, certainly by Plains standards.

At first Jimmy Carter dominated the family, as his father Earl
had, and made the decisions—about money, work, and play—that
have been the traditional patriarch's privilege. He admits, "I was
very domineering and demanding." She says, "I never thought of
asserting myself or trying to do anything different. I was just happy
having babies, going all over the world and feeling very independent to be away from home for the first time."

Gradually, roles shifted. With Carter gone four days a week
at sea, his young wife had to learn to fend for herself. She also had
to learn to assert herself and to raise her voice in their family
decision-making. Sometimes the two would argue; her style would
be to raise her voice, his to control himself and to grow quieter and
quieter. But his silence did not mean he would win the argument
by ignoring her. Usually, they remembered, arguments would end
in compromise. Jimmy Carter, characteristically, governed his
emotions and accommodated others.

Rosalynn Carter, during the Navy years, had become a person in her own right. The two had become friends, and when Carter
began trying to figure out what to do about his life in the becalmed
peacetime Navy, he talked the possibilities over with his wife. To
say they grew to be friends in a companionable marriage, rather
than in the old male-first patriarchy, is not to say that Rosalynn
Carter achieved marital equality by contemporary definitions of
the word. If it was a partnership, then she occupied the position of

junior member. The Navy years became a pattern for their later partnerships. When Jimmy Carter decided to return to Plains and take over his father's businesses, Rosalynn Carter learned accounting and kept the books for the peanut warehouse. When Jimmy Carter decided to go into politics, Rosalynn Carter learned to give speeches at Lions Clubs, shake hands in beauty parlors, and stand in for him at the smaller meetings so that he could attend to the larger matters. Sometimes the toll in personal energy could be heavy.

Rosalynn Carter had always been a shy person. The solitary work of bookkeeping suited her, but making public appearances could fill her with terror. Once when she was on her way to give a speech on mental health during her husband's tenure as governor of Georgia, she had to ask her driver to stop the car so she could get out and be sick. Sometimes, too, the prospect of another day of public activity could reduce her to tears, and she would sit on the edge of her bed in the morning crying at the thought of the afternoon's schedule. To this day, she remains rather tight-lipped about these public demands on what she regards as her limited talents. "All my life," she acknowledges, "has been a challenge."

Jimmy Carter, like many ambitious husbands, had a different image of his wife and helpmate. "Everyone has always underestimated Rosalynn," he has said. He knew shyness and had hated public speaking himself. Rosalynn Carter, the naïve little girl from Plains, wasn't being asked to do anything that Jimmy Carter, the shy, timid boy from Archery, wasn't doing himself.

Unlike the wives of many rising American men in traditional marriages, she kept pace with her husband, socially and intellectually as well as on the jogging paths. She cultivated her public image—as he did his. As the governor's wife, she received instruction from the German consul's wife in Atlanta on the ways of "gracious" entertainment. A pert, natural-looking woman, Rosalynn Carter nevertheless bought a shelf of wigs to wear at public functions. In her forties she underwent a so-called eye tuck, in which a plastic surgeon in an hour-long operation tightens the skin around the eyes by removing snippets of esthetically offensive sagging or bagging lids.

The task of remaking the inner self, as most of us can testify, may take considerably longer than a cosmetic eye lift. Jimmy

Carter had come from a family where the sons and daughters were told to believe they could achieve anything they set their minds to. Rosalynn Smith did not have the security that comes from being told as a child that everything is possible. Jimmy Carter gave her that security. Together the young Navy couple had studied music, poetry, and Spanish; later he helped her with her public appearances, so she could help him. According to Greg Schneiders, the young aide who became close to Jimmy Carter during the campaign, "Because Jimmy Carter has personally traveled that road from introversion and shyness, he could understand how difficult it was for Rosalynn." Carter, according to Schneiders, would be a sympathetic but firm instructor. "He would not say, 'Why don't you just forget it.' That's not his way. He would say, 'I understand and sympathize with how difficult it is for you to do this.' But the idea of not doing it was never considered." Jimmy Carter had become a sympathetic Mr. Earl to his closest friend and wife.

Looking back on those days, Rosalynn Carter acknowledged that she often wondered if she could indeed do the things her husband expected of her. But she said she always tried. "Jimmy believes I can do anything, he really does. He has given me confidence." As the governor's wife, she had her assignments and she did them well: speeches on behalf of Jimmy Carter's mental health and drug abuse programs, receptions for visitors to the mansion, a round of parties, spread over eight weeks, for 250 guests to "introduce Jimmy." He would praise her performance; the next time was a bit easier and the recognition was headier. As she learned, her confidence in herself grew and the insecurities about her social standing and status diminished. Dr. Peter Bourne described the process almost clinically: "It is an incremental series of measured successes that she's dealt with at her own speed. . . . She was willing to take on whatever was at the fringe of her confidence, and build gradually for bigger and bigger accomplishments."

Jimmy Carter has been considered something of a sexual prude. His young staff—Hamilton Jordan, Jody Powell, and the others—were known to carouse a bit; Greg Schneiders lived with a young campaign worker (they later married); Jack Watson was divorced; and the marriage of Jerry and Betty Rafshoon was shaky (they later divorced). Supposedly, Jimmy Carter disapproved of these comings and goings because of his strict Southern Baptist upbringing, as well as for fear of possible voter reaction. But, according to Peter Bourne (also a divorced man, though remarried), Jimmy Carter fervently believed in marriage not for reasons of morality or politics but because, in Carter's words, "my marriage has been so good for me."

Rosalynn Carter brought her husband a close supportive relationship. Her loyalty and help over thirty years earned her an unchallengeable place in his life. The physical affection the Carters show is so open that almost everyone who spends any time with them comments upon it. He constantly reaches out for his wife, takes her hand, and draws her to his side. They kiss and hug in public, their knees often touch when they sit in church. In meetings and at official dinners, they sit together; his official White House schedule lists a regular weekly luncheon meeting with Rosalynn Carter. While most public men publicly display affection toward their wives, the Carters' love affair seems singular.

IV

JIMMY CARTER NEEDED a good supportive marriage in the dreary days of his naval service as a Chesapeake Raider. Two years out of Annapolis, however, his career began to look up. In June 1948, right after the Rhodes setback, he applied for, and won, a berth at submarine school in New London, Connecticut (the decision was jointly taken with Rosalynn). Submariners make up an elite in the Navy, much like carrier pilots; they wear special insignia and get special pay. It is a proud service, and Jimmy Carter judged his five-year period as a submariner "one of the most interesting and enjoyable of my life." Still, his subsequent accounts of these years illustrate again his characteristic tendency to exaggerate. Jimmy Carter never was a "nuclear submarine commander." He left the Navy sixteen months before the first American nuclear submarine ever put out to sea. He served as a junior officer on four conventionally powered subs, and then spent less than a year in the nuclear propulsion prototype program, most of that in training in Schenectady, New York, far from blue water. He has much to be proud of about his service, but the record should be clear on what that service really was.

In December 1948, Carter was assigned to Hawaii and the

U.S.S. *Pomfret*, his first submarine. On his maiden cruise, out of Los Angeles, the *Pomfret* encountered a major Pacific storm. For five straight days, Carter tells us, he was seasick. Warren Colegrove, a fellow officer on the *Pomfret*, remembers his being "pretty dreadfully sick . . . but he would never permit it to interfere with his standing the watch." The heavy weather almost cost him his life when an enormous wave lifted him off the submarine while he stood duty watch on the bridge. Carter says pure chance brought him down on the deck about thirty feet aft of where he had stood; if the current had been running broadside, he would have come down in the dark sea. He perhaps can be pardoned for feeling watched over by Providence. "I don't have any fear at all of death," he has said.

Different shipmates of Carter's have different memories of those years. Warren Colegrove remembers a young officer whose interests in politics seemed to be surfacing. "He would talk about the '48 election. . . . And he was also interested in social areas, very, very concerned about the plight of the black man in his home state. . . . There was a nagging concern about this." But Frank Andrews, the skipper of the K-1, the sub Jimmy Carter served on later, says that he can't remember one political conversation in his two years as Carter's senior officer.

One reason for the difference in these accounts might be that, as Andrews himself suggested to Colegrove, "I was a captain and you were one of his buddy officers." Charles Woods, who also was on the K-1, recalls a junior officer who liked to needle everyone. Andrews remembers the "big smile and big laughing." His fellow officers called him "Jim," not "Jimmy."

Of the dozen Navy men interviewed for our project, every one agreed Jim Carter had worked hard. "He was Regular Navy," Andrews says. "He was just a hardworking officer trying to get ahead, like the rest of us were in those days." To a man, they remember him as intense, always reading technical manuals, always apart, different from the rest. They liked and respected him —his smile and his professionalism helped—but he made no real friends. "He never really got close to anybody," says Colegrove. He remembers Carter as "always apart," working on a sonar problem while the other officers played poker after dinner, or stretched out in his bunk with his nose in a book, ignoring everyone (as his mother had removed herself from the family years before).

Carter has a different memory of his submarine years. In interviews, he has talked about how close he felt to the other men. "What I liked about being in the submarine is that it was embryonic," he once recalled. "There was a feeling of personal privacy because of the closeness. People respected the privacy of others more. But there was also a sharing of responsibility. It was for me a time of unreserved masculine behavior. There was on the submarine, once we pushed off for several months, a kind of liberation from the restraints of civilized life. There was a degeneration of behavior, a closeness just among men which I liked."

Duty in a submarine under water for extended periods of time had made many others before Carter think of womb life and what it may have been like. Since we were concerned with the theme of closeness-apartness, we asked him to talk more about his memories of submarine service. His remembrances of the pleasures of being "embryonic," he explained, were connected to the threat of claustrophobia (which drove one seaman mad). "I said I never did feel any adverse effect from claustrophobia because there was an embryonic feeling that you were protected in your isolation," Carter offered. What did that have to do with "unreserved masculine behavior" and "liberation from the restraints of civilized life"? Carter responded, "When we would shove off from Pearl Harbor for a three- or four-month cruise at sea, going to Wake Island or Guam or Hong Kong or up the Chinese coast . . . you didn't have the responsibility of the daily payment of bills, and the concern about reports, and the concern about family. You were a warrior, and there was a masculinity about it—a freedom from constraint—that was, I think, a part of the consciousness of almost everyone who has been in a war. I don't know if it's an admirable thing for me to say, but that's the way it is to feel. . . . It was a throwing off the restraint indigenous to showing courage and the feeling of contribution to your nation, and there was—in one word —I think, this freedom."

Carter offers a tangle of recollections and associations, candid and provocative, the kind of testimony that might be made at a religious revival meeting or in a therapist's session. Jimmy Carter is not the first young man to feel in the company of men certain emotions that seemed to be lacking in other relationships. A man can be heterosexual, married, a father, and still find a pleasurable closeness in all-male endeavors, like the world of the submariner.

It could be a closeness with qualities and meanings somewhat different from those experienced by his shipmates, who did not feel he was close to them in the ways they took for granted: playing poker, swapping stories, pub-crawling on liberty. In so many of Carter's relationships, closeness appears involved with physically standing apart—separation—yet emotionally being one, merging. The word "embryo" usually has maternal associations, but for the particular character of Jimmy Carter, the need to be close is entwined with the memory of his father, who had been his first companion, his "close friend," yet never really close, or a friend.

Submarine service made "demands" on us, Carter remembered; duty was "tough," "dangerous"; "high standards" had to be met—just as in the house of his father. In the family of the Navy, as in the family of Mr. Earl, Jimmy Carter developed his own relationship to authority and to discipline. "Life on a ship," he says, "is a heavy discipline; to move in the submarines is a heavier discipline." While observing discipline, Carter nevertheless would criticize a superior if he thought him wrong, something not usually done in the Regular Navy. As Colegrove recalled, "There's a certain amount of deference given to the commanding officer, right or wrong." But right or wrong, logical way or Navy way, Carter carried out orders, just as he had obeyed his father.

When the time came for Carter to give the orders, his command style showed the influence of this contradictory attitude, at once questioning and obedient. Aboard submarines, and in other dangerous elite services, a certain informality of command exists. Leadership often depends not so much on the orders given but on the projection of leadership qualities. Where a high level of cooperative work is required, in compact quarters or on small-team missions, the leader must first be able to reassure his people, win their confidence, and then to communicate with them in an unharried manner. Ramrod postures and martinet orders don't fit aboard a sub. Jimmy Carter's fellow officers remember how he developed a submariner's style of leadership. Colegrove says, "One of the most outstanding characteristics of a submariner is that he's a low-key, easy-to-get-along-with individual. And it's probably predicated on the fact that you're all smashed together on a very small boat and you have to get along."

When the K-1 was commissioned, the officers and crew prepared as a humorous souvenir a listing of every man's sayings, the identifying tag lines of the months they had spent together. Carter's line was "Watch it, these are my engineers." He would be recorded as looking out for the men under his command. In the submarine service Jim Carter felt close to other men, in his way; he got along with them, in his way. His feelings of closeness and his manner of relating to others who worked with him became linked to a distinct style; it would not be such a great leap from working in the close quarters of a sub to working with a tight little band of associates in a political campaign. His associates had a way of becoming family. His message was, Trust me, for I trust you. His leadership, he believed, would never *mis*lead those who worked with him, his followers, people with whom he felt close. With others, in Georgia politics, in the Washington establishment —the *un*close—he would have trouble as a leader.

The K-1 assignment ended Carter's active sea duty. In 1952, he eagerly applied for work on one of the Navy's prototype atomic submarines, the *Sea Wolf* (the other was the *Nautilus*). This assignment followed an interview with Admiral Hyman Rickover.

V

RICKOVER'S PERSONAL INTERVIEWS for nuclear assignments have become the stuff of Navy wardroom legend. Supposedly he put interviewees in straight-backed chairs with one inch sawed from the two front legs, and the chair placed so Rickover could direct sunlight, by moving a Venetian blind, into the eyes of the already unsteady victim. Supposedly he told one candidate, "You have thirty seconds to make me mad." The candidate knocked all the papers from Rickover's desk. No reaction. Then he went over to the tabletop models of the nuclear ships Rickover had helped develop, and smashed them all. The candidate was selected.

Carter's own interview lasted for two hours. Rickover allowed him to talk on any subjects he wished—current events, seamanship, music, literature, electronics—and then began to ask questions. "In each instance," Carter says, "he soon proved that I knew relatively little about the subject I had chosen. He always looked right into my eyes and he never smiled." Finally Rickover asked Carter how he stood in his class at the Academy; Carter proudly answered fifty-ninth in a class of 820. Instead of congratulating him, as Carter expected, Rickover asked, "Did you do your best?" Carter gulped and had to confess, "No sir, I didn't *always* do my best." At which point Rickover gave him a long look and said, "Why not?" The interview ended.

Twenty-two years later, a book title would be born, in tribute to Hyman Rickover. In it, Carter says that the Admiral "had a profound effect on my life—perhaps more than anyone except my own parents." Later, during the 1976 campaign, Carter raised that estimate: Admiral Rickover had quite simply "changed my life." Rickover's example showed Carter the "small effort" he was actually making, "compared to what I could do."

In some ways, Hyman George Rickover appears to be an unlikely example and mentor for Jimmy Carter. Rickover was born in 1900, making him about the same age as Jimmy Carter's father. He grew up on the tough, crowded streets of the Near West Side in Chicago, where Italian and Irish and Jewish immigrants elbowed and jostled each other for blue-collar jobs and living space. His father owned a tailor shop. Hyman Rickover was small, thin, wiry, with a prominent nose, large Adam's apple, receding chin. A generation of junior Navy officers came to know him as compulsive, driven, fiercely competitive, a perfectionist, quick to cut a subordinate with his laser eyes, glacially slow to give praise—descriptions strikingly similar to those later used for his junior engineer Jimmy Carter.

Rickover won an appointment to Annapolis at the end of World War One. He was a true outsider; the sons of immigrant Jews were almost as rare around Bancroft Hall then as black faces in the first years after World War Two. Rickover, as anyone who has dealt with him knows, can be a figure of great personal force, emanating that mysterious quality called "presence." His bearing would explain in part why the twenty-eight-year-old Jimmy Carter felt so profoundly affected by his eleven months of service under Rickover's command.

But that may be only part of the answer. For Jimmy Carter especially, Rickover's approval meant passing another test. Carter had, a few years before, failed the Rhodes interview. Now, though still a junior officer with no real battle stars in his military folder, he had secured the Rickover stamp of approval, and with it entrance to a hot new program. Rickover tried very hard to make candidates lose their composure; Carter did not. Rickover tried to fail people; Carter passed. With Rickover he had measured up successfully. Moreover, Rickover demanded that Carter do better, just as Mr. Earl had demanded. Carter himself saw Rickover's standards of performance as the "impersonal demands of a perfectionist." Mr. Earl's standards had been the *personal* demands of a perfectionist.

Mentors, or second fathers, have become familiar figures in life and biography, thanks to the work of Erik Erikson and others. The mentor figure may not feel the emotional involvement that the younger man feels. In the eleven months that Carter worked in the nuclear program, Rickover saw him perhaps every two or three months. To Rickover, a friend recalls, "Carter was just another engineer," one of four young officers working on a propulsion project, the sodium-fuel *Sea Wolf,* that proved to be a dead end. Rickover gives the impression to friends that he didn't even remember Jimmy Carter. For Carter, however, Rickover became an emotion-laden figure, as mentors do. Feelings about the first father often transfer to second fathers.

Among these displaced feelings were some negative ones. "Deep within," Carter says of Rickover, "I had an adverse reaction to him." The anger existed initially: "You know, I felt like he was pushing me too hard, because I had been a pretty good officer when I got there." But then, Carter says, he accepted the legitimacy of Rickover's demands, because the Admiral demanded more of himself than he did of anyone else: "He expected the maximum from us, but he always contributed more . . . and we finally realized that no matter how hard we worked . . . he always did more himself." The words echo the same terms that Carter had used in describing his father. In the person of Rickover, Carter had the model of an older man he could emulate without too many "adverse reactions deep within."

Carter observed and copied the Rickover style. When Carter served in the Georgia state senate, he carried through a promise to read every line of every bill up for vote; later, in the White House, he tried—often to the dismay of both his friends and his critics—

to maintain the same kind of control over paper work, attempting the impossible (his critics said) task of reading 350-page administrative documents. It may not be a practical "presidential style," but it sounded very much like the way Rickover ran his office. Rickover, for example, gets involved in controlling every phase of his nuclear operations by "reading the pinks." Every typist, under pain of instant dismissal, is required to insert a pink sheet, with suitable carbon, in the typewriter whenever *anything* is typed. The pink sheets go to Rickover every day, and he reads them every day. Rickover's operation, of course, involves at most 300 people; the Presidency presídes over a bureaucracy of three million.

VI

WHEN HIS FATHER DIED in 1953, Jimmy Carter turned his back on his naval career. A decade of his life, rooted in the ambition of a four-year-old boy, ended. His request to resign predictably angered Rickover, who regarded it as "a breach of loyalty." In a sense it was; Carter was shifting his loyalties from Navy to Plains, from mentor to father. Carter had to invoke the assistance of Georgia Senator Richard Russell, head of the Senate Military Appropriations Committee, to get out of the Navy.

Freud observed—and our own eyes confirm—that young adults face two challenges: learning how to work and how to love —*Arbeiten* and *Lieben*. In the Navy, Carter had survived the hazing, the hardships, and the discipline of military life, trying to become tougher, more competent, and more self-disciplined in the process. The Navy represented Carter's first real work experience; it set his style of self-discipline, building on the discipline he had learned from his father. It also helped to shape the way he made decisions; it established his pattern of behavior toward his co-workers; and it set its mark on his sense of competence. The Navy had been a time of preparing, becoming, a transit through young adulthood in the family of peers. His own family had been growing, too, and his competence as a loving husband and father had also been challenged.

Yet neither test, of work or of love, had been decisively met.

He had hoped that his transit would lead him to the Navy's top job —Chief of Naval Operations. Realistically, the odds were against Carter's beating out competitors with campaign stars and distinguished battle records. The years between his eighteenth and twenty-ninth birthdays had been—ironically enough, for someone so determined to measure up and succeed—a kind of moratorium.

9

"A Man Like My Father"

JIMMY CARTER RETURNED to Plains with his wife and three sons in November 1953. Rosalynn Carter had fought the decision to move back. "She almost quit me," Carter would later remember. Perhaps Jimmy Carter might never make CNO, but Rosalynn Carter had come to like the life of a Navy wife. Some elemental force would have to exert a great pull on Jimmy Carter to cause him to resign from the Navy, and risk divorce, in order to return home. By most accountings, that force has been labeled economic. But like so much else about Jimmy Carter, the explanation is more complicated and rooted in his deepest emotions.

When James Earl Carter, Sr., began dying of cancer, shipmates remember his son Jimmy Carter discussing the family's large financial stakes in Sumter County. Carter started talking about the family's "plantation" in Georgia, Frank Andrews says. "He used that word . . . and about all the people who worked on it. I remember it clearly because it was just about the only time he wasn't talking about the ship or the Navy." Another officer recalled how Carter agonized about his decision: "I remember talking to him about it at—really at great length. And he'd come from this little town of Plains, Georgia, and it was almost like a medieval idea, that one man, his father, was responsible for the souls in the town of Plains, Georgia . . . without his father, those 1500 people were not going to have any means to live."

The Carter holdings could not be thought of as a "plantation" with manicured lawns stretching out from an antebellum manor house. Still, Mr. Earl owned over thirty parcels of land around the county. The land was worked by about 200 tenants, and if spouses and children were included, the figure might reach 1500. Although Mr. Earl had been cutting back a bit in his business activities, with an eye on travel and retirement, he still had his seed and fertilizer businesses in town. He still was a private banker of sorts. In the spring he would give cash loans or extend credit to the farmers who purchased his seed peanuts and seed cotton; in the fall he would collect, after they sold their crops. Mr. Earl, as it happened, died between spring credit and fall collection. By Lillian Carter's reckoning, the Carters' agribusiness had $100,000 in accounts receivable on the books that summer of 1953 (others claim it was more like $40,000 credit outstanding and $50,000 cash in the bank).

Lillian Carter had never concerned herself with the details of her husband's agribusiness and his land dealings. In her view, the business had to be "saved." "He had to come back," she told us. "Everything we had was on the line. . . . Jimmy saw the situation and he went back up to Schenectady where he was living and called me one morning about two o'clock, and he said, 'I have no alternative; I'm coming home.' " In reality, alternatives existed. Carter could have requested leave to settle his father's estate, collected the debts, and sold off the business. He didn't. Instead, he recalls, he felt "a pull on me that was irresistible to go back and re-cement my ties to my birthplace."

Carter hadn't really cared, at least for a decade, about the land parcels that Mr. Earl had pyramided on his way to becoming a powerful man in Sumter County. The "irresistible pull" bringing Jimmy Carter back to Plains came not from the family estate but from his father. In death, Earl Carter reclaimed his first-born son. Jimmy Carter had become a "changed" person in the Navy. In 1953, he experienced yet another such change—a rebirth of a special sort that rejoined him to his father after a long, pained separation.

In an interview, Jimmy Carter recalled that he hadn't seen his father "since I was about seventeen years old." In fact, he saw his father—and his mother—during his Navy years on an average of once every two years. In denying these meetings, Jimmy Carter substituted feelings for fact. To us, Carter explained that the reunions occurred so infrequently because of Navy regulations: "As you know from the policies of the armed forces, there just wasn't much time off." Actually, there was time off. Military officers in the years after World War Two routinely had thirty days leave per year. Carter chose not to spend his leaves in Plains. Jimmy Carter had left his father and the world of Plains far behind him. The growing distance between the two men was expressed in the racial argument the father and son had when the twenty-seven-year-old officer was home on leave. Jimmy Carter told his father about a party given by the British officials in Nassau, where a black sailor in the crew was refused an invitation. Not one of the white submariners would go. Mr. Earl couldn't understand. "There was simply no way that I could explain the reasons to my father. After that, he and I agreed to avoid racial subjects on my rare and brief visits home."

At Mr. Earl's deathbed, their disagreements were put behind them. Jimmy Carter says he spent hours by his father's bedside, talking about old times together and catching up on the eleven years when they had grown apart. As the man he remembered as his strong, powerful, large father wasted away before him, the son's feeling of love reasserted itself. His "re-cementing" was to the ties to his father.

Jimmy Carter would later say he came to know the man his father really was, or at least to see another side to him. He describes a deathbed scene that did have a grand medieval-lord quality about it. In that last month of Mr. Earl's life, Carter declared, "I'd say a thousand people from around that little community out in the country, from way back on the creek, came to our front door to bring Daddy a quail they had cooked, or a fresh loaf of bread, or some fresh-picked flowers. And they wouldn't want to talk to him or bother him—they knew he was very sick—they'd say 'I hope you give this to Mr. Earl, tell him I thank him for what he did for me.' " Many of these visitors, Carter tells us, were black. But black or white, he says, Mr. Earl supported them in hard times, gave them clothes, paid secretly for their children's education. Watching all this, Carter remembered, "I just thought that my daddy's life was much more significant than mine would be if I were Chief of Naval Operations. I thought about it, it was the worst decision I ever had to make."

Just as Carter may pump up his chances for Chief of Naval Operations, so too he may inflate the vision of Mr. Earl's last days. The actual number of visitors doesn't matter. What matters is what the numbers tell us about Carter's feelings. The death of a father often causes a child to re-examine his own life. Mr. Earl, a figure of limited vision and little worldly experience, Mr. Earl, the seg-regationist and paternalist, became a big man again. Lieutenant Jimmy Carter compared his life to his father's and decided his father's had been better. "He was an integral part of the commu-nity," Jimmy Carter concluded, "and had a wide range of varied but interrelated interests and responsibilities. He was his own boss." Carter wrote in his autobiography that his decision to resign from the Navy and go home to Plains meant that he would live a life "with a potentially fuller opportunity for varied public ser-vice." The trite words can be read to mean that Jimmy Carter, having learned to love his father again, also wished to learn to love others, as it seemed to him his father had done.

Ruth Carter Stapleton had remembered how, on the day of their father's death, her older brother had cried and declared his intention "to be a man like my father." A few years later, Carter's close friend John Pope recalls the day they went on a quail-hunting trip together and Carter came dressed in his father's World War One cavalry leggings and lace-up boots. Jimmy Carter has a repu-tation for frugality, and a good pair of boots is a good pair of boots, whatever the deeper symbolism. Still, in returning to Plains, Carter did take up the path of his father's footsteps, measuring himself and his own strides against Mr. Earl's.

II

JIMMY AND ROSALYNN CARTER and their three young sons moved into a new public housing project in Plains. Jimmy Carter had carefully put aside a few thousand dollars by buying savings bonds during his naval service; he also would be heir to the Carter

business. Technically, however, the ex-lieutenant could say he had
no assured income and was therefore entitled to public housing.
His apartment was in a white-only project; its major attraction was
the rent, thirty dollars a month. Jimmy Carter had learned the
value of a dollar from his father, and in the streets of Plains. His
penny-pinching was reinforced by the Puritan ethic of unostenta-
tious and abstemious living, as much a part of Southern as of New
England culture.

During their first year back in Plains, drought parched the
fields of southern Georgia. Carter sold over 2000 tons of fertilizer,
but with the bad harvest, the people his father had lent money to
could not pay back their debts. His net profit, Jimmy Carter
claimed, turned out to be "less than $200." Carter at first served
as his "one and only employee," an unintended version of his
desire to be his own boss like his father. He loaded the fertilizer
bags himself, often working sixteen hours a day. Rosalynn Carter
took a correspondence course in accounting. Jimmy Carter set out
to relearn farming and to apply to his new business his Navy engineer's attention to detail and his deep and total dedication to success. He crammed through books, sought out the county agent,
talked to Uncle Buddy, observed the experienced farmers, and
went to short courses at the agricultural experimental station in
Tifton, Georgia. "I learned rapidly," he recalls. He threw himself
into the task of making money as he had into his studies at Annapolis and his engineering responsibilities in the submarine service.
He only knew one way to work: flat out.

The agribusiness benefited from his intelligence and energetic
efforts. It also benefited from market forces. The peanut and fertilizer business stood on the edge of major change just as Earl Carter
was dying. Carter's classmate P. J. Wise remembered: "You had
to get with it, or either get out of the business—that's what it
boiled down to." In the 1930s and 1940s, Wise recalled, a farmer
who got a yield of one ton of peanuts for three acres considered he
had "good peanuts." By the 1960s and 1970s, if the same farmer
did not get roughly two or three tons per acre he would be a loser.
Better fertilizer and new planting and cultivating techniques helped
make the difference; increased mechanization, the use of dryers,
the introduction of grading of different types and varieties of peanuts, all transformed the business for planters and suppliers like

Carter. By the 1970s, peanuts had become Georgia's leading cash crop.

Jimmy Carter built the first dryer and the first shelling plant in Plains, and his friend Wise, expert at electrical work, wired them up. Engineer Carter took advantage of the new technical developments, plowing back after a while $100,000 a year into improvements; he invented some devices himself.

In the nature of the subject, the details of business enterprise tend to glaze over the eyeballs. Carter's efforts sound pedestrian: enlarging and modernizing his warehouse; dealing with wholesalers, tenants, farmers, and the Southwest Georgia Seed Association. It was a life lived day by day without any great events. In the end, though, he had a business grossing $2.5 million annually, and he controlled 3170 acres of farm and timberland. Buying and selling land, like his father before him, he traded off good land for better land. By 1976, his personal fortune had been pegged at $814,000; his net income from 1970 through 1976 would reach $137,000 in a good year, $46,000 in a less successful year. In June 1979, he disclosed that his net worth was just over $1,000,000.

Earl Carter had been a hardworking, successful businessman-planter. Jimmy Carter measured up to his father in this respect. His success confirmed his own feelings of self-confidence; it also proved to be an essential foundation of his political career, providing the money that fuels campaigns for office. Carter, perhaps, had not come back to Plains just to make money. But for over fifteen years his daily life pulsed around the major American occupation of buying and selling, with a bottom line at fiscal year's end to measure how he had done. By the objective standards of the profit and loss sheets, he had done extremely well indeed.

III

MARY ANN THOMAS, one of the freer spirits of Sumter County, once told us that there were two ways a propertied white middle-class southwestern Georgia male could spend his time when he reached the age of forty: "He can chase women and drink at the country club or he can go into politics." Thomas exaggerates to make her point that the challenges of small-town life narrow considerably for successful men in middle age. Some men do party a bit, others find civic duties to perform. Some men do both. Jimmy Carter, no twenty-four-hour-a-day Puritan, knew how to have a good time—but invariably, by all testimony, in the company of Rosalynn Carter.

The Carters saw a great deal of two other couples in the 1950s, John and Marjorie Pope and Billy and Irene Horne. The "Three Musketeers," as Billy Horne calls them, used to go dancing at the Americus Country Club, the American Legion Post, or over to Albany, which boasted a nightclub. They also danced with the Sumter Squares. On weekends, the Musketeers would think nothing of driving 500 miles to the Georgia shore or to the beach on the Gulf Coast. The men liked stock car races, major meetings such as the Daytona 500 and the Darlington 500 but also any dusty oval where the Fords and Chevys raced. Friends remember weekends of all-night partying, of rounds of drinks, and of one memorable trip when the Musketeers lost all their money at the resort gambling tables and could not afford to pay for their hotel rooms; they slept on the beach.

Like his father, the demanding but fun-loving Mr. Earl, Jimmy Carter had a partying side. It went into eclipse more and more as his interest grew in politics, and as religion became of greater importance in his life. But it has never been entirely suppressed. He accepts that pleasure-seeking side in those around him, sometimes with a touch of envy. His brother, he says, lived the life that he might have enjoyed, for a time at least. Those who expected President Jimmy Carter to impose his own supposedly prim standards on his staff—and on the nation—overlooked Carter's own past. It is not just that he gets some vicarious satisfaction out of the styles of his brother or some of his younger aides. His own pleasure side exists—up to a point. His lust, as he told *Playboy* magazine, has remained in his heart.

IV

JIMMY CARTER'S BAPTIST RELIGION instructed him that sexual intercourse outside marriage is a sin; the Bible, "which I believe in," says so. Bible reading, churchgoing, and daily prayer have always been a part of Jimmy Carter's life. On an "eventful day," he once said, he might very well say a silent prayer as many as twenty-five times. His mother thought that the religious fervor of the Carter family had been overplayed in the campaign: "We made a Christian home, read the Bible, and had prayers; but Jimmy was no different from other children." But others remember that young Jimmy Carter put himself into his churchgoing with the intensity of his other activities. He was baptized at eleven, formally becoming a member of Plains Baptist Church. Twelve-year-old Jimmy Carter would borrow his mother's old black Plymouth on Sunday mornings and drive around the countryside picking up boys his own age who did not have a way to get to church. "He was so tiny he could hardly see over the steering wheel," recalls Mrs. Anne Dodson, a childhood friend. Small-town social life usually centers around church and school, and Plains was no exception. The Plains Baptist Church and the Sumter County school board became entry points for Jimmy Carter's new public life.

In the mid-1950s, up-and-coming businessman Jimmy Carter did what his father did before him and became a Sunday school teacher. Not just everybody could teach in the Bible classes of the church. According to Clarence Dodson, husband of Anne and a Sunday school teacher himself, "They had to be active members of the church, members of the Bible class, and they had to have training at special Bible courses, and know the Bible extremely well. . . . Jimmy," he added, "is a Bible scholar and a very fine preacher." Other neighbors recall that Carter taught a Bible class for young girls while he was an Annapolis midshipman. Carter also served as a deacon of Plains Baptist and a leader of the Royal Ambassadors, a troop of boys organized like the Boy Scouts for camping trips and also for religious retreats. Carter learned a special style of leadership in these Baptist church functions. Baptists believe in running their churches along decentralized and charismatic lines: power belongs to the people, but leadership has to guide and inspire them. To the Navy style of relaxed, small-team authority, Carter added the Baptist mode of democratic persuasion as his way of leading. The man in the White House combines submarines and Sunday school in an "unpresidential Presidency." The style has cost him dearly.

Carter became one of the doers around Plains; every town has that small group of people who serve on committees for the hospital building drive and the community fund. Carter got the town to build a swimming pool, welcome relief for children from the oppressive heat of the Georgia summer. (Only whites could use its segregated facilities.) He worked for the library board and later the Sumter County school board for six years.

This time of service proved to be a time of testing. In 1954, the U.S. Supreme Court had declared school segregation unconstitutional; after eight decades of separate and unequal facilities, school desegregation had been mandated. One after another, like so many candlepins, Jim Crow laws came tumbling down. But the Jim Crow practices took longer to change; the Court had delayed implementing its desegregation order for a year, and then gave segregated school systems "a reasonable time" to comply. The challenge was direct: Were the messages of Sunday school to be preached and honored only on that day? Jimmy Carter's answer, characteristically, accommodated the demands of religion and politics, of whites and blacks.

Jimmy Carter did not join the school board until two years after the Warren Court decision. But he came in time for the fight. Unlike World War Two and Korea, the civil rights combat would not pass him by or leave him in its backwaters. In the two decades from 1956 to 1976, the drive of millions of black Americans to achieve full civil rights, and the determination of millions of white Americans to oppose them, dominated the moral life of the South and the nation. No Southern white male adult—certainly not one of the rising doers of the community—could long ignore or escape the issue, even if he had wanted to. Jimmy Carter's critics claim he trimmed and dragged his feet, along with thousands of other "community leaders" during those years. His admirers counter that he acted with moderation, and occasionally with courage, in situations that Northerners and other outsiders cannot fully grasp. From our perspective, both descriptions are correct.

The lot of blacks in the Deep South in the immediate years before *Brown vs. Board of Education* had improved since Reconstruction in some ways, and in others not at all. Lynchings had dropped from several score a year to no more than four or five a year, though dozens of other blacks might be killed by law officers in line of "duty." The White Knights of the Ku Klux Klan kept a low profile, but Jim Crow still ruled in schools, churches, hospitals, buses, and waiting rooms. The prevailing argument in defense of the sorry state of the blacks' segregated schools was "If we educate the Negro, then who will work the farms?" In those years before the Warren decision, 12,000 blacks lived in Sumter County, half the population. Home for them was run-down "niggertown" in Americus, the dusty south side of the tracks in Plains, and the pitiable shacks rented from the white farmers.

Jimmy Carter himself has looked back with some amazement at how he managed in those days to maintain a white man's tunnel vision of Southern reality. "It seems hard to believe now," he says, "but I was actually a member of the county school board for several months before it dawned on me that white children rode buses to their schools and black students still walked to theirs. I don't believe any black parent or teacher ever pointed out this difference." Just as he had suppressed his memory of his family's role in the tenancy system, so too he had managed to overlook the realities of school segregation. Nevertheless, the injustice of the situation rankled him once he did notice it. By no stretch of the word did he favor integration then; he wanted, he said, only to make some school facilities more "equal" so they could remain "separate." Blacks should have buses to ride to their own segregated schools.

His views seemed to be close to those of his neighbors. When a group of white citizens came to protest the planned location of a black school as being too close to a white school, Carter proposed a measure relocating the black school. He did not object to the fact that white teachers got sick pay, while their black counterparts did not; and he voted for a proposal to use the surplus funds from the sick leave fund to give white teachers a raise, but not black teachers. While on the board, however, he also pushed for a plan to consolidate the county schools with the Americus school system. To get approval of the plan, he made speeches throughout the county, his first real taste of politicking. His opponents, led by his cousin Hugh Carter, accused him of being an integrationist, even though the plan called for separate black and white schools. The plan lost, and Jimmy Carter emerged from his school board experience in character, with a mixed reputation; some considered him a liberal, others a conservative. His friend Warren Fortson preferred the term "humanist."

Nothing he did over the next ten years in Plains would change that image of ambivalence. Jimmy Carter himself is the source of two "racial anecdotes" intended to reveal his moderation during the late 1950s and early 1960s. One day, he recounts, two recruiters for the White Citizens' Council approached him; one was the chief of police of Plains, the other the local railroad depot agent, who happened to be a Baptist preacher. They asked him to join the local chapter being organized. He refused. Jimmy Carter never liked to be told, then or now, what to do, especially by those whose authority he didn't respect. In a couple of days they were back, with some of his friends and customers. They warned him that he was risking his reputation and the loss of business; they were even willing to pay his five-dollar dues for him. Again, perhaps from pride as much as anything else, he refused, saying he would rather pack and leave Plains than join. They boycotted him but only for a time and unsuccessfully.

The second test of Carter's racial views occurred at the Plains Baptist Church in 1966. Now State Senator Jimmy Carter and preparing to run for higher office, he had a position in the community to uphold. The pastor and eleven of the church deacons had voted to recommend to the congregation that blacks be excluded from entering the church on Sunday. In the past, blacks had attended special services—weddings, funerals, and sometimes baptisms—by invitation. But black groups, responding to the calls of young ministers like Martin Luther King, Jr., and his deputy Andrew Young, had started holding pray-ins at white churches throughout the South. The Plains resolution spoke of barring Negroes and all other "civil rights agitators." Carter, the twelfth deacon, had missed the first vote. He and his wife and children had gone to Atlanta for the weekend. His friend John Pope, a casket manufacturer, advised him to stay away, saying, "It wouldn't be healthy for your public image to get involved right now." Carter told Pope that there was "no way" he would miss the vote at his church. That Sunday morning, 200 people crowded into the white-painted church and heard Jimmy Carter urge the meeting to reverse the deacons' decision. It was God's house, he said, not theirs. Lillian Carter noticed the vein on her son's forehead throbbing, a measure of his feelings.

In the vote that followed, the only six in favor of keeping the services open were Lillian, Rosalynn, two Carter sons, Jimmy

Carter, and one other member of the congregation. About fifty voted on the other side; others did not vote at all. Later, some of the non-voters told Jimmy Carter they agreed with him but did not want to speak up openly.

The resolution stood until 1976, when presidential candidate Carter cast another vote, this time with the majority, to repeal the resolution. That vote, however, rubbed feelings raw in town; the deacons fired the minister, the Reverend Bruce Edwards, who had voted with Carter. One faction, more pro-Edwards than anti-segregationist, resigned from the church and formed a new church, the Marantha Baptist Congregation.

His detractors have argued that Jimmy Carter in 1966 had an eye on broader political horizons, where moderation on race would be useful. Carter had, in fact, begun to think about a life beyond Plains once again, this one in politics. He turned over in his mind the two racial experiences—the White Citizens' Council and the church vote—and drew a lesson from them. "In each instance," he remembered, "there was a small group of extremely fervent advocates of maintaining the strictest racial segregation. My own belief, in retrospect, is that a majority of the members of the community chose, perhaps reluctantly, to abide by the law in a quiet and unobtrusive manner."

He also seemed to have learned from this—not in retrospect, but at the time—a fundamentally moral approach to politics: that people are basically good, although misled by their leaders, a handful of men with special interests. The good people also needed leaders, or a leader, to rally them and to recall them to their best side. But such a leader must know and take into account the feelings, right or wrong, of the "irate" citizens. At the bottom of their complaints, even their racism, was some need of justice. The demagogue exploited these needs; the true and good leader, free of special interest, fulfilled these needs; he helped people. James Earl Carter, Sr., had walked part of the way down this particular path, in his own paternal manner, shouldering the white man's burden. His son Jimmy saw himself going farther.

V

CARTER HAD a third important "racial experience" in this period, one that he omits from his autobiography; Jimmy Carter does not emerge as a hero/leader from it. The experience illustrates the persistence and complexity of race in the South. It also illustrates both Carter's conveniently selective memory and the limits of his powers of accommodation.

In 1942, the year Jimmy Carter went off to college, a Christian commune called "Koinonia" had been founded on 440 acres of treeless, eroded farmland in Sumter County some seven miles from Plains. The founder, Clarence Jordan, a cousin of Hamilton Jordan's, wanted to live a life patterned after the examples of the early followers of Jesus. He believed in Christian sharing: "Koinonia" is the Greek word for "fellowship," used in the second chapter of Acts in the New Testament to describe the disciples' living together with all things in common. Jordan and his wife, Florence, also believed in Christian non-violence—and had the radical idea of practicing, seriously and without compromise, what they preached. During World War Two, they counseled conscientious objectors. Later, when mechanization drove black tenant croppers from nearby cotton farms, the Jordans invited a few blacks to join the fellowship. But Jordan was no outside Northern agitator; he could claim to be Southern-born (in Talbot County about fifty miles from Plains), a University of Georgia graduate, a Greek scholar with a Ph.D., and a Baptist minister, trained at the Southern Baptist Seminary in Louisville, Kentucky.

But with all his credentials, Clarence Jordan never threw them, or his weight, around. He favored persuasion rather than confrontation. While he would not go out of his way to start a fight, he would not go out of his way to avoid one either. He knew how to farm, how to organize, and how to raise funds for his struggling enterprise. Eventually Koinonia came to own 1400 acres in Sumter County, with a handsome arbor of trees, all planted by the communards. In the 1950s, the Jordans raised cotton and peanuts; they built a pecan-shelling plant and eventually a bakery and a candy kitchen. They set up road stands to sell their produce and baked goods.

Clarence Jordan seemed like a saintly madman, perhaps more mad than saintly. He remained a presence in Sumter County until he died in 1967. His cousin Hamilton Jordan described him as handsome, honest, "the greatest man I've ever known." Because Jordan told us that while sitting in his White House office a few doors away from his boss, President Jimmy Carter, we asked him if he wanted to amend his statement in any way. Hamilton Jordan said no.

In general, the people of Sumter County left the Koinonians alone until the mid-1950s, when the great changes were set in motion by the federal courts. Reading about all the evils of race-mixing every day in their newspapers, Sumter County whites remembered that integration already existed in their own back yard. And if they had forgotten, Clarence Jordan gave them an excuse to remember.

Early in 1956, two black students wanted to enroll in the segregated Georgia State College of Business in Atlanta. Jordan agreed to help them with their applications, which required endorsements by two university alumni. The executive secretary of the state board of regents, however, ruled Jordan ineligible as a signatory because he had graduated from a different school in the university system. Jordan went home without signing the applications. The front page of the Americus *Times-Recorder* informed Sumter County inhabitants the next morning that Clarence Jordan had signed the applications of two Negro students.

Dallas Lee, author of an affectionate biography of the Jordans, *The Cotton Patch Evidence,* described what happened next: "The threatening phone calls started that night. The egg market in town closed like a trap, signaling what was to become a massive, thorough boycott. Petty vandalism—fences cut, garbage dumped on the land, corn taken from the fields—became routine overnight. Homemade signs along the Albany Highway advertising Koinonia's roadside market were torn down repeatedly until the vandals finally hauled them off. Sugar in the gas tank ruined the engine of a Koinonia vehicle. Bullets from a heavy-caliber pistol were fired into the roadside market."

On July 26, 1956, shortly after ten P.M., an explosive crashed into the roadside market, damaging the front of the building, ripping off a section of roof, and wrecking refrigeration equipment and other fixtures. Shortly after the bombing, the Koinonians took out a newspaper ad expressing regret that the actions of one or two persons should bring shame to the whole county. The Americus *Times-Recorder* deplored the use of force and coercion, "the very things that our Southland is being subjected to by the United States Supreme Court."

On July 31, Koinonia ran a second ad, an open letter in the *Times-Recorder*. The letter stated that Koinonia had not made a public statement about its beliefs before, "largely due to the fact that we wanted no one to think that we were trying to force our ideas on them. We wanted simply to live our own lives under God." The letter cited a number of scriptural passages; it mentioned the commune's crops; its cattle, hog, and poultry endeavors; it said Koinonia Farm borrowed from the local bank, had mortgaged land and good credit, and currently supported about sixty people. The letter also stated that Koinonia was incorporated as a non-profit religious organization and that it had no connection with any outside group. "Please do us the favor," the letter closed, "of not believing a rumor until you have checked the facts. We welcome visitors, and will be glad to answer any questions about our life."

If anything, the boycott intensified in August. Koinonia could not get its cotton crop dusted or ginned. It could not obtain fertilizer; its insurance was canceled. The farm's poultry produce could not be sold. Farmers who had cooperated with Koinonia in egg-grading and marketing would not buy the hens or the poultry equipment; some 4000 laying hens had to be given away or butchered. A mechanic who serviced Koinonia vehicles suddenly refused to be available. Koinonians found it difficult to obtain hardware supplies. They lost their checking account and were refused loans.

On January 1, 1957, night riders welcomed the New Year by spraying Koinonia's sign at the farm entrance with bullets. A few nights later, raiders chopped down nearly 300 of the apple, peach, and pecan trees that had been planted on four acres, and destroyed the farm's beehives. On January 29, 1957, automatic weapons raked one of Koinonia's buildings. On Easter Sunday, a convoy of cars drove by and deposited a crudely written note: "Get Out, You Mongrels."

Finally, the Sumter County law, in its majesty, took note of Koinonia and its persecutors. A grand jury convened, subpoenaed records, investigated, and in seven days, on April 5, 1957, returned a "no-bill." Not only was no one indicted, but the grand jury concluded that Koinonia had committed the violence on itself in order to raise funds from "outsiders."

One merchant moved to break the boycott. Herbert Birdsey of Macon, Georgia, who owned the Birdsey Flour and Feed Store chain, wrote Koinonia Farm to declare his Americus store open to the community. Early Sunday, May 19, a bomb ripped the front of Birdsey's feed store. "No one, with the possible exception of those guilty of the crime, could believe that such a thing could happen in Americus, a city of peace-loving, churchgoing, cultured people," said an Americus *Times-Recorder* editorial. The editorial added that violence was "foreign" to the Southern way of life. The bombing must have been the work of extremists, red-necks, or "outside" agitators.

Almost twenty years later, some other outsiders looked into the Koinonia events wondering what role, if any, the Carters of Sumter County took in all of this. Lillian Carter remembered her husband had told Clarence Jordan that he and "that bunch" would not be welcome at Plains Baptist Church, where Mr. Earl served as a deacon. Mr. Earl, she said, "was particularly against mixing the races, and he'd heard that there were colored and whites living together and all. He just didn't want any of that in his church."

When Robert Scheer, in his *Playboy* interview, asked Jimmy Carter about Koinonia, Carter told him, "I went there several times in the Fifties and Sixties. They couldn't get anyone else to shell seed for them, and I did. I went down there a couple of times to talk to Clarence Jordan . . . I knew Clarence Jordan when we were going through the years of integration."

Scheer then asked Florence Jordan about Carter; she said, "I have to say I'm sorry, but I don't even know the man. I've never met him, and we've been living down the road for 34 years. People came here from all over the world, but he hasn't come seven miles."

Distressed at the prospect of catching Jimmy Carter in a lie, Scheer returned to Carter, and in Scheer's words, "pinned him down on what stand he *had* taken when he heard about the shootings and bombings at Koinonia." Carter replied in what Scheer

calls a sarcastic tone, "I didn't shoot at them or throw bombs."
Scheer pressed on: "But did you speak out against it?" Carter
replied, "There was a general deploring of violence, and the grand
jury investigated it and I think everybody was embarrassed by it.
It was done—if it was done—by a fringe element. This was a time,
I'd say, of very radical elements on both sides."

When we asked the various parties about Koinonia, Hamilton
Jordan affirmed that his cousin and Carter knew each other. The
widow, Florence Jordan, strongly dissented. "I don't know him,"
she said of Carter. "I just don't know a thing about him. I'd be
afraid to say anything about him. He has never come over here; he
has never helped; neither has his mother." Then she added, "I
don't think the Carters ever withstood a great deal of pressure."

Warren Fortson, the former Americus lawyer, knew both the
Jordans and the Carters. As he told us, anyone visiting Koinonia
wouldn't win a lot of friends, but they wouldn't be judged a communist or a nut, either. Fortson suggests that Carter might have
met Clarence Jordan, talked, and promised help. Carter, perhaps,
didn't lie. Fortson believed it would be more a matter of a vague
recollection, and taking the wish and the promise for the deed.

Scheer's own expert witness is Jack Singletary, an unusual
Georgian from a "patrician family." Singletary went to Annapolis
and to Koinonia, becoming a member of the commune for a couple
of years, until he moved to his own farm nearby, without, he says,
giving up his progressive ideas. According to Singletary, he ran
into Jimmy Carter on the street in 1953 or 1954, and the Carters
invited him to their apartment. Carter told Singletary that he
shared his views about "the race question," and he told Singletary
the story of the black sailor on his submarine who didn't get invited
to a party in Nassau. "He was proud. He wanted me to know
this," Singletary said.

The "progressive" Singletary had got caught in the same boycott net that pinned down Koinonia. He adds a personal note of
tragedy to the narrative. His oldest child had acute leukemia, and
he was using the telephone at a local store to keep in touch with
New York, where the boy was hospitalized. According to Singletary, the sheriff and a Georgia Bureau of Investigation agent went
to the storekeeper and told her to keep Singletary out of the store.
"Our little boy finally died of leukemia," Singletary says. "It was

when the boycott was on and we had our friends from Koinonia come over for the funeral. Rosalynn came the next morning and brought a ham. We invited her to stay and she did; we had a very informal Quaker-type service and put the body into a little box that Koinonia had made. We took it down to a little playground there where he had played and buried him without any remarks." Rosalynn Carter, Singletary was told later, immediately drove back to Plains, confronted the Baptist preacher, and angrily bawled him out for not presiding at the burial. "He said he reckoned he'd be run out of town if he did it, but she made him come . . . we finally had a graveside service," Singletary says. He concludes that "that's a little insight into the kind of person she is, and I'm sure that Jimmy was with her."

Koinonia provides, as a roughly drawn map does, a general idea of how far Carter dared venture in the 1950s into the terrain of race and politics. More than seven statute miles separated the "pure" Christians of Koinonia from their neighbors—the peace-loving, churchgoing, community-fund doers. The proper conservative, blinkered traditions of small-town life did not make it easy for even the Best People to accept the unconventional or the odd. Koinonia, Warren Fortson declares, had "real kooks"—vegetarians, hikers, seminary students, freelance writers, conscientious objectors. Not everyone had come from an old-line Georgia family or won an Academy appointment. Jimmy Carter would not naturally take to oddballs. They seemed like "radical elements," to be avoided as much as the low-class racists and night riders. Perhaps he only knew them as "kooks" by hearsay, but that would be enough.

The Carters could relate to Jack Singletary, but not to the others. Clarence Jordan fits somewhere in the middle. Carter may have met Clarence Jordan and offered to help, unknown to Mrs. Jordan. Possibly, Carter's need to think well of himself, a need in all of us, might have caused him to exaggerate his encounters with Clarence Jordan into a mental reality less disturbing to his own conscience. As in one of Friedrich Nietzsche's aphorisms (*Beyond Good and Evil*, Book IV): " 'I did this,' says my Memory. 'I cannot have done this,' says my Pride and remains inexorable. In the end—Memory yields!" In truth, Jimmy Carter did not forthrightly take a stand in Dixie back then. Those who wish he did, or criticize him for his silence, overlook his acceptance of Southern conventions; more importantly, they ignore his accommodating, trimming character, shaped by his boyhood. People still make the same mistake today in their demands for a "stronger" Carter Presidency.

By the mid-1950s, a distinct Jimmy Carter style had begun to appear in his public words and deeds. He acts to integrate contradictions and to avoid confrontations, if possible. He seeks to understand both sides of issues, especially the race "issue," to call for the best in each side and to settle for accommodations, a living together yet partially apart. Koinonia, in the 1950s, tells us exactly how apart.

In *Why Not the Best?* written with an eye on the Presidency, he managed both to chasten himself for his tardiness in recognizing the injustices of segregation and to put in a good word for the "Seg Academies"—the private school arrangements used throughout the South to avoid real integration of black and white schoolchildren. The private schools, he wrote, "absorbed the children of unyielding white parents and had value in a difficult time, serving in a way as community safety valves." Similarly, when he returns to Plains these days as President, he makes a point of attending both the Plains Baptist Church and the breakaway Marantha Baptist Congregation (both, by the way, still all white). His position, or positions, may be politically expedient; but his expediency accords with his character.

Carter the young boy tried to integrate the complex, clashing loves, angers, and identities of his childhood; Carter the mature man tries to balance the complex, clashing forces of his society. The character of the boy and the character of the man do not openly war with each other; they stay in step. With such a balancing character, an ambitious, intelligent, restless man could go far. The strains of race, class, caste, and identity cut deeply into the grain of American life, in the biggest cities no less than in the Plainses and Albanys of the country. These relations are complex, and often contradictory. Jimmy Carter contained these same complexities within his character. They provide a partial explanation for his campaign successes in Georgia and national politics.

10

Winners, Losers

THE PASSION TO BE A WINNER has been a constant in Jimmy Carter's life. The word "loser" is among the strongest terms of criticism he knows. The life of a politician, then, might seem a strange choice for someone who doesn't like to lose—since losing is, in theory, always a 50 percent possibility—just as the life of a politician would hardly sound appealing to a man who judged himself shy, reserved, and not a backslapper. In politics, more than in most activities, rejection can be swift. By Jimmy Carter's own testimony, the rebuffs encountered during his first days of campaigning for elective office tested his sense of esteem. He has often recalled how lonely and unappreciated he felt starting out in politics. "Most of the time, in those early stages, when you say, 'I want to be Congressman (or Governor or President),' and then you walk away, you know there are a lot of jokes and a kind of smirking and you feel very humble. To walk in front of a service station and talk to five people and say, 'Would you vote for me for Congress,' and quite often you feel that you are not quite worthy in their eyes. You think more of yourself, but you're kind of sure that they don't think you are qualified to go to Washington."

Still, he could have tried some other public life, a religious ministry, for example, perhaps something like his sister's evangelical mission. He has said he considered such a life back in the early 1960s; indeed, the idea has never been completely abandoned. President Carter has even talked about doing Christian missionary work after his White House days end. But politics offers a bigger public arena than a religious ministry. Politics is not only a field of winning and losing. It is also an area where great waves of love flow back and forth. The office seeker can proclaim his affections for the "people," and the people can give him adulation and attention in return. This is the up side of the experience of being rejected or ignored at gas stations or plant gates. The smirks stop, the people listen, and their eyes reflect not scorn but approval. Their votes—approval, love—reaffirm the lifelong process of proving yourself, and improving yourself.

Politics can also be an arena for the release of strong internal feelings against established authority. When that authority can be seen as using its power unjustly or illegitimately, a fight can be waged with a grim, unceasing, justified aggressiveness. A life in politics made sense on many levels for the son of James Earl Carter, Sr.

II

WITHIN TEN YEARS of Jimmy Carter's return from the Navy, he had replicated his father's successes: Sunday school teacher, church deacon, community leader. Mr. Earl had been a state representative from Sumter County; Jimmy Carter in 1962 decided to run for the state senate. He cast himself, in his recollections, as the lone and public-spirited David against the Goliaths of entrenched political power in southwestern Georgia.

The reality of that first political campaign does not always match the romanticism of his remembrances. A Carter of Sumter County hardly fitted the role of powerless little David. Mr. Earl had cultivated Congressman Pace. Naval officer Carter made a point of meeting Georgia politicians on his trips to Washington, D.C. After the death of James Earl Carter, Sr., the Democratic Party leadership of Sumter County offered Lillian Carter a chance to complete the remaining year in her husband's term; it was "man's work" to her, and she never considered the idea seriously. A close friend of Mr. Earl's got the appointment. Over the next eight years, Jimmy Carter often thought about challenging his father's replacement.

In 1962, a reform in the Georgia election procedures—the first of the great 1960s changes that helped clean up the rotten-borough system of the state and of the Deep South—opened the way for Jimmy Carter's run for state office. The reform became law in October, a short time before the elections, and Carter decided at this last minute to run for the new seat.

Carter threw himself, his family, and friends into what he remembers as an "amateurish whirlwind" campaign. He made no speeches but shook thousands of hands, introducing himself to indifferent strangers at gas stations, barber shops, and feed stores. His opponent, Homer Moore, had been elected in the September primary under the old rules, and many people thought Moore had reason to feel aggrieved about having to run again for a seat he had already won. But Carter pressed on, secure and righteous in his cause. With only Quitman County to report, Carter led by seventy votes. But Joe Hurst, a Democratic Party functionary, ran Quitman County, and Hurst backed Moore. When the final returns came in, Moore had won the election by 139 votes. Carter's observers counted 333 people voting that day in Quitman, but Hurst reported 422 ballots in the box. Incensed and frustrated, Carter met the next day with his friends and family. What had happened had not been all that unusual in Georgia politics, and usually the losers went along with the result. But Carter reacted differently. John Pope recalls: "I saw the real burning desire to win that I had not really seen before. It really meant everything to him."

Carter began to gather affidavits and other evidence of fraud. His friend Warren Fortson agreed to represent him. Carter tried to get a newspaperman from nearby Columbus to look into the Quitman County irregularities. The reporter assigned, Carter says, knew Hurst and said he didn't see any story. The Columbus papers, in fact, called Carter a sore loser. Through his cousin Don Carter, a newspaper editor, Carter got in touch with John Pennington, an investigative reporter for the Atlanta *Journal*. Pennington looked into the charges and wrote a series of stories that made it impossible for state leaders to ignore the episode any longer.

Don Carter also recommended the help of Charles Kirbo, a lawyer who had been a classmate of his at the University of Georgia. Kirbo, a south Georgian some nine years older than Jimmy Carter, worked for King and Spalding, one of the two or three best law firms in Atlanta. At first Kirbo hesitated; then he received a call from his good friend Griffin Bell, also an established lawyer. "Griffin asked me if I wouldn't go down there and help Jimmy," Kirbo explained to us. "I went down there and met him and his wife and his family and his friends who were supporting him, and for five or six weeks thereafter I saw him a good bit, talked to him on the phone, was in his home, and I recognized him as a bright, friendly man. . . . He was not aggressive, but you could tell he had a general force about him and was determined to turn that election around." The friendship of the two men continued from that 1962 election fraud case—for which Kirbo billed Carter $2500—through the years of the Carter Presidency.

Because of Charles Kirbo's age and role—the silver-haired fox among the thirty-year-olds on Carter's formal staff—some people naturally assumed that Kirbo has played a mentor's role in Carter's life, similar to that of Hyman Rickover. This analysis, however, overlooks the differences in the Jimmy Carter of 1952 and 1962. The consolidation of his character had taken place in the years after his father's death. No one person again would ever have an extraordinary influence on him, "changing his life." The important interplay in the mature Jimmy Carter is between his character and outside events—his own crises and historical developments.

In the fall of 1962, Carter wanted to overthrow a crooked election, and enough like-minded people agreed to help him. In a write-in election, Carter won, 3013 to 2182, carrying Sumter County by nearly four to one, and winning Quitman County too.

Carter's first serious political activity had been rewarded with success; the 1962 race had confirmed his public style. Ambition, hard work, true grit, persistence, and a near-religious commitment will win out. Personal campaigning works, whether he makes one-on-one contact with people or uses his family and friends as extensions of himself. Well-connected acquaintances also help—Don Carter, Kirbo, Bell, Fortson, Pennington. While all politics involves such mutual systems of support, Carter's very first network transcended political labels and traditional affiliations; John Pope, the Goldwater conservative, and Warren Fortson, the "radical," both support him. He joins opposites, convincing disparate people of his commitment to honesty, decency, and morality.

He may leave others cold. In this first encounter, he seemed,

142

in some eyes, a scary combination of Machiavelli and Norman Vincent Peale, of gut fighting and Godliness. He self-dramatizes even the genuinely dramatic—much as Lillian Carter gilded the "lily" in her life. Carter's idealized portrait of "the citizen-politician" glosses over the normal ambiguities of politics, its mixture of virtue and vice. As the journalist William Greider points out, "Even in Quitman County, Georgia, politics is more complicated than good guys versus bad guys. Where Jimmy Carter describes honest citizenry struggling against political tyranny, others see a somewhat less dramatic situation—two long-established political factions—the ins and the outs—both eager for the spoils and both scrapping with dirty ferocity." Greider might have added that the fight was a segregated one, between white-only factions.

But the myth of good against evil, little guy against big guy, emotionally sustains Jimmy Carter, even if it has little basis in political reality. It creates a self-confidence that allows him to walk with righteousness and to run with certainty. When he believes in his cause, he can feel himself a David of virtue versus the Goliath of entrenched authorities. In his televised speech of April 5, 1979, announcing plans to combat the rising costs of energy, he pictured the chief villain as the "foreign oil cartel" and its allies in the domestic oil industry. The oil interests, giants like Mobil and Exxon, would try to defeat his public-spirited plans in the Congress. He urged viewers to join him in the fight against companies that put profit ahead of country. In point of fact, while oil-company profits are indeed high, and going higher, a lot of that profit goes to stockholders in the American middle class. Exxon, for example, has 690,000 stockholders—most of them the same citizens Carter asked to join him in the fight against the oil giants.

Back in 1962, Jimmy Carter saw himself leading the fight against the "establishment," whether hacks like a Joe Hurst or the smoother operators of the party. Carter cast himself as the amateur, beating the professional villains at their own game. In such moments, Jimmy Carter will fight on relentlessly, even after the ballots have been counted. As the good little guy, he can fuse his aggressive impulses against unjust authority with his feelings of love for the "people." Carter makes love and aggression serve each other. "I have spoken a lot of times this year about love," he declared during the 1976 campaign, "but love must be aggressively translated into simple justice." Machiavelli's Prince and Dr. Peale march hand in hand. In the summer of 1979, when Carter's rating sank lower and lower, commentators speculated that he might step aside out of despair. They underestimated his deep-seated unwillingness to accept defeat whatever the ballot count.

III

AFTER THE PROTRACTED, exhilarating fight to win the state senate seat, Jimmy Carter's four years in the senate—his only legislative experience—seem almost anticlimactic. As with his term on the Sumter County school board, liberals thought him conservative, and conservatives thought him liberal. While civil rights marches and sit-ins roiled the South, State Senator Carter kept a low profile. Surveying his non-record, *Newsweek* magazine concluded, "Mostly, he avoided the subject." He did, in one of his first speeches, urge the abolition of Georgia's "Thirty Questions," the infamous literacy test used to exclude blacks from the polls. At the same time he voted with the segregationists for amendments to the state constitution.

Almost everyone agrees that Senator Carter was hardworking. He had pledged—foolishly, he later admitted—to read in Rickover fashion every bill before he voted on it. To get through the 800 to 1000 bills before the senate each year, he took a speed reading course and kept his promise. He claims to find "almost unbelievable" his discovery that these bills all carried special-interest provisions, carefully tucked away. State Senator Carter bristled at "entrenched authority"; he particularly resented the "special deal" pay bills for state government department heads, and pushed for a uniform method of establishing salaries. "I lost that battle while in the legislature," he says, "but did win it later while governor." A similar pattern unfolded with Carter as President over the dams bill; beaten in the first round with Congress, he persisted in seeking to eliminate some of the dams and eventually won. Carter, though an accommodator, sticks to long-term goals.

Reg Murphy, the former editor of the Atlanta *Constitution* and a critic of Jimmy Carter, first met Carter during the 1963 legislative session. "I remember him as clear as yesterday," Murphy says. "I used to dread to see Jimmy Carter come walking down the hall, because he was going to tell me about some comma or fault in the newspaper—some little nitpicking thing, instead of dealing with what I considered to be the important thing, whether we were getting mainly the tempo of issues right. We just never got along."

Murphy remembers Carter as a loner. "He was not one of those committee people who could work in the senate—that's probably a life pattern." Murphy also says that many of the other fifty-five senators were not comfortable with Carter. "He didn't have many friends in the state senate then. In fact, when he ran in 1966 almost none of his old senate colleagues were working in his campaign or interested in it; they were probably opposed to it." Murphy remembers that Carter couldn't give a good speech: "He'd get up to speak and the doors would open and they'd begin to trickle away."

Murphy makes no effort to paper over his low opinion of Carter. The editor earned the dubious honor of writing a disparaging column about Jimmy Carter's presidential aspirations, with the headline "Jimmy's Running for What?" But Murphy's recollections ring true. Carter did not banter with his fellow senators or make the small talk that greases committee work and other legislative relations. Carter didn't make scintillating speeches. He did do his homework and he mastered details; he became fascinated with the details of government, learning how it was put together, just as he had avidly studied nuclear engineering. He served as one of two legislators on a commission to study the needs of Georgia's educational system (remaining silent on segregationist proposals to close the state schools). He could be counted a fiscal conservative who questioned expenditures.

Critics and supporters alike can probably agree on one proposition: Carter's talents, whatever they might be, did not lie in the legislative process, though he was good in his way. He needed a broader constituency with whom he might have a more direct and intimate connection while preserving his loner qualities. Yet, perversely, he wanted to run for Congress—the national legislature —in 1966. He had begun to prepare for the race two years earlier, when Howard "Bo" Callaway had become the first Republican to be elected to Congress from Georgia in a hundred years. The passage of civil rights legislation in 1964 had shattered the traditional commitment of white Southerners to the Democratic Party. Georgia, along with other Deep South states, voted for Barry Goldwater, and Callaway came in on the Southern Republican tide in Carter's own district.

Callaway, a wealthy textile scion, graduated from West Point just a little before Carter finished at Annapolis. Callaway had won battle stars as a tank commander in Europe. As a member of the state board of regents, he initially blocked Carter's efforts to secure the four-year college campus for Americus. By 1966, Callaway had risen to the leadership of the Young Republicans of Georgia; Carter coveted a similar role with the Young Democrats. Jimmy Carter did not like Bo Callaway. "When we were around each other," Carter candidly remarks, "both of us were somewhat tense."

Carter's enmity ran deep. Callaway personified the Establishment, the entrenched powers who governed in their own interest, callous to those beneath them. The youthful Jimmy Carter had been willing to accept legitimate authority even when it punished him; it was for his own good. Carter had no respect for merely selfish authority whose only moral claim to power was that it was established. The Callaways, Philip Alston, an old Carter friend, explained to us, "come out of a different stratum of society than Carter. Callaways are money people; they are to the manner born, so to speak—landed gentry. . . . Jimmy felt that the Callaways were not as enlightened in their stewardship of this world's goods, of which they had an immense amount. . . . Jimmy considered himself a better article, a better human being." Carter, Alston concluded, "wanted to whip the Callaways."

Carter admits to a "natural competitiveness" with Callaway, measuring himself against his self-assured, attractive upper-class rival. The Carters of Plains counted themselves well-to-do by Sumter County standards. In Atlanta, the wider world, the Carters did not count. When Callaway became the Republican candidate for governor in 1966—and when the leading Democratic candidate, Ernest Vandiver, withdrew from the race for health reasons—Jimmy Carter, as much for personal reasons as political considerations, decided to give up his campaign for Congress and run for governor.

As with his race in 1962 for the state senate, he made a last-minute entrance, against the odds. Kirbo advised him not to do it: "I told him it was a big gamble, that I was afraid he didn't appreciate how much money it would take, and he said he had some money, and was willing to spend it. I think he said he had $70,000 or $80,000 to spend on it." But Callaway began the race as the favorite, and Carter wanted to take him on.

Carter, as usual, worked intensely. He and Rosalynn shook thousands of hands; they took down the names and addresses of the people they met, and each was sent a hand-written note. The hard work and personal campaigning, however, could not make up for the overall amateurishness of the campaign. Carter had a "low recognition factor"—he was "Jimmy Who?" He couldn't be conveniently classified as liberal or conservative. "I believe that I'm a more complicated person than that," he maintained. Bruce Galphin, an Atlanta reporter covering a Carter appearance at the Atlanta Press Club, observed, "It is hard to meet Senator Jimmy Carter and hear him talk about state government without liking him and admiring his integrity. . . . Here was a breed of politician new to Georgia's big contest: subdued, frank even about his deficiencies." Carter's frankness brought a refreshing quality to the 1966 campaign. "His honesty is almost painful. He admitted the unique problems of big cities were new to him. . . . He said Vietnam wasn't an issue in the Georgia's governor's race—an honest position—but then went on to talk about it, to admit it was complex and finally to confess, 'I don't have any solution.' "

Charles Kirbo would later comment about candidate Carter's style: "I've seen him keep talking until people misunderstand him. But I don't think he does it deliberately." Carter's need to explain himself, to reveal his thoughts and feelings, had surfaced early in his political career.

The fastest route to recognition for a political unknown normally involves advertising, either paid commercials or "free exposure" through staged appearances. Carter didn't know how to manage either. He had been running commercial spots with a country and western sound on radio. A young adman named Jerry Rafshoon, who had come to Atlanta three years before, heard the Carter ads and felt appalled. The radio tune went "Jimmy Carter is his name, Jimmy Carter is his name . . ." And, Rafshoon says,

147

"I thought to myself, Jesus Christ, this would be a challenge, because for one thing, it's a terrible tune; secondly, he has no name or recognition, and they're just repeating his name. What is he? Is he a country and western singer? . . . So on a lark, I called Hal Gulliver and said, 'Your friend Jimmy Carter needs help.' ''

Gulliver, a newspaperman, later became political editor of the Atlanta *Constitution,* Reg Murphy's old job. Gulliver liked Carter as much as Murphy disliked him, and he arranged for Carter and Rafshoon to get together. Rafshoon liked Carter even before their first meeting. "I remember watching him with all the others on television and thinking I was going to vote for him. He obviously wasn't really articulate, but his earnestness and sincerity and the fact that he could say 'Negro' without slurring it—that was before he said 'black' . . . really contrasted with Lester Maddox the madman and Ellis Arnall the fading liberal."

Carter also picked up some other new friends. William Gunter, a lawyer, had met Carter during the winter of 1964, when both served on a commission to rewrite the rules of the Georgia Democratic Party. The two men and their wives became good friends, and in May of 1966, when Vandiver withdrew from the governor's race, Gunter urged Carter to run. A graduate of both the University of Georgia and the Georgia Law School, he knew how to tap into the state political network. Gunter introduced Carter to Robert Lipshutz, an Atlanta lawyer active in Jewish community affairs; Conley Ingraham, another lawyer, who got David Gambrell of King and Spalding to pledge support; and Philip Alston, a lawyer and fund raiser.

Gunter himself did not know Alston, but he wanted to meet him because Alston knew Mills B. Lane, the head of the Citizens and Southern Bank and the acknowledged "chairman of the board" of the Establishment that ran Georgia—or thought it did. Alston had decided for himself that Ellis Arnall would not be able to win the election, and he liked the idea of a new face. Carter and Alston made some small talk—both men had been in the Navy— and got on to more substantive matters, "the main one was race relations." Carter convinced Alston he would move to get rid of the old traditions.

Though Carter had won over Alston in their private meeting, Carter could not win over many of Alston's friends. The Alstons gave a dinner party with the right people invited to meet Jimmy and Rosalynn Carter; as Alston tells it, "It was a fine, diverse group of people. But he and his wife are modest. Timid may be a good word; shy may be a better word. They simply didn't come across that evening."

Carter met another Georgian who helped his campaign and later became a close friend and associate, a large affable banker from Calhoun, Georgia, named Thomas Bertram Lance. As Lance remembers, "I applauded Carter as a businessman and told him I'd help him."

Carter never did get Mills B. Lane's vote in 1966. But he held on to the friendship and support of Lance, Rafshoon, Gunter, Gambrell, Ingraham, and Alston. They could not make up for his late start, poor organization, and low recognition. Carter finished third in the Democratic Party primary. In the runoff between Maddox and Arnall, Maddox won with the help of Republican crossovers (who figured Maddox an easier candidate to beat). Carter refused to support Maddox, a stand that made him look like a hard loser to his critics once again.

In the general election in November, Callaway came in first, with Maddox and Arnall (a write-in candidate) splitting the Democratic vote. Callaway did not have a majority, and under an anachronistic law the election went to the state legislature, where Maddox was chosen governor. "This entire experience was extremely disappointing to me," Carter later said. "I was deeply in debt, had lost twenty-two pounds [down to 130], and wound up with Lester Maddox as governor of Georgia." His mother, less guardedly, remembers that "he cried like a baby." Defeat and its aftermath set in motion a major change in Jimmy's interior life, a change that he says affected all his subsequent behavior. His father had taught him how to win, not how to lose. Jimmy Carter needed to master a new discipline: to lose in the world, if necessary, without losing a sense of self and of self-worth.

Shortly after the 1966 election, Carter seriously injured one of his fingers while working on a cotton gin. The result is a mallet finger, permanently bent. At a farmers' meeting, Carter held up his finger and said that he had "paid his dues." He meant that he had labored like an ordinary farmer. His sister Ruth has talked about "accident proneness" as a way of connecting the physical with psychological states. Without going that far, it is possible to see that, symbolically, Jimmy Carter had "paid" for the loss of the election with the loss of the full use of his finger.

11

Born Again

A WEEK BEFORE the 1966 election, Jimmy Carter and Charles Kirbo and the small band of friends helping in the campaign for governor could feel a surge toward victory. "We were rising," Kirbo says. "He was coming on strong, and he got confident as hell." Kirbo thought he ought to caution Carter. Carter told Kirbo not to worry. "I'm not going to get too confident," he said. "I can take a licking."

Carter lost, and a few weeks after the defeat, Kirbo remembers, he went down to Plains for a meeting with Carter to "regroup" and figure out what to do next. "I said, 'How you been doing?' He said, 'Oh, pretty bad.' I said, 'Aren't you the same fellow who told me that you could take a licking?' He said, 'I knew it was going to be bad, but I didn't know it was going to be that bad.' "

Just how bad Jimmy Carter felt after his defeat has been a subject of debate. Dr. Peter Bourne, one of Carter's early supporters, and a psychiatrist and specialist in mental health, told us, "He did have an acute reactive depression to losing in 1966. It was the typical classic description of depression."

Jimmy Carter appeared equally forthright when we asked him about the aftermath of the 1966 defeat. "When you run for an office, and you've failed," he replied, "there's a requisite reassessment of your life's future. Are you going to lower your standards, or lower your aspirations and accept the degree of mediocrity in service, or—that you didn't anticipate—or are you going to just dig in . . . and go on to strive again? And to that extent, obviously, it was a psychological problem, but I've weathered it—obviously."

II

CARTER MORE THAN weathered his public failure, without lowering his aspirations. Obviously, too, because he is Jimmy Carter, he lets his feelings show through more than most people do. As Charles Kirbo explains: "Nobody likes to get beat. Some people can swallow it and keep it in their bosom, but Jimmy is a man that expresses his feelings. If he feels bad about something, he comes out with it. Some people can hold it to their bosom; some of them just break down."

Jimmy Carter reacted to defeat, we believe, on two levels. Outwardly, he cried, moped a bit, felt let down and unappreciated—and then began the business of running for office again. At a deeper level, however, intense and conflicting emotions festered beneath his surface adjustment. He felt troubled by "hatreds" and "frustrations." Carter dealt with this turmoil in a way that—as much as any single event in his adult life—gave the decisive shape to his public person. It determined, finally, his life as a man.

The period of outer adjustment ended in a matter of a few weeks. Work and renewed dedication to achievement provided the therapy. His campaign wound up costing more than the $70,000 to $80,000 he thought he would have to spend. Some $15,000 in unexpected bills turned up. Kirbo, understanding how tight Carter could be with his own money, knew how much that hurt. But invitations to speak began to come in. People around Georgia now knew him; he had a network of political friends. In four years, Georgians would elect a governor again; Carter would have another chance to measure up.

III

THE PERIOD OF Carter's inner adjustment to his circumstances in 1966 culminated in his famous religious conversion experience. But, despite many references to his "new life" as a born-again Christian, the experience has remained rather veiled. No description of the episode—or episodes—exists in *Why Not the Best?*—an odd omission for such a careful person. Carter himself, during our interview, placed the experience "in 1966, the period of a couple years, 1967 . . ." Whatever the mystery, Carter clearly did not follow Paul's route on the road to Damascus; no light and voice from the heavens knocked him to the ground.

He had paid off his debts, he had put back on his slight frame most of the weight lost in the last frenetic weeks of the race. At the age of forty-two he had a successful business and a healthy family. As he analyzed it, it still wasn't enough. He felt inadequate, an incomplete man.

One Sunday at Plains Baptist Church, he listened to his minister delivering a sermon entitled "If You Were Arrested for Being a Christian, Would There Be Enough Evidence to Convict You?" As Carter later described his mood on this Sunday: "I was going through a state in my life then that was a very difficult one. I had run for governor and lost. Everything I did was not gratifying. When I succeeded in something, it was a horrible experience for me. I'd never done much for other people. I was always thinking about myself." And so his answer to the pastor's question was no. That realization set him to thinking, he remembers. He began to try to change "for the better." He tried to form "a much more intimate relationship with Christ." At this point, his younger sister, Ruth Carter Stapleton, a psychologist of sorts in her own right, offered him some counseling.

On an autumn day in 1966, Ruth Stapleton recalls, she and her brother drove from Plains to Webster County to go for a walk in the pine woods on some property the family owned. According to Mrs. Stapleton, "I talked about my awareness of Christ, and I shared with Jimmy how it was to come to a place of total commitment, the peace and joy and the power it brings.'' He wanted to know what she had that he didn't have. She asked him whether he would give up his life and everything he had for Christ. He answered yes. She asked if this included politics. He could not answer yes. Ruth Stapleton says she replied that if that were so, he would never find peace. In her recollection, he became very emotional and cried. He does not remember this. Not long after their talk, however, she says her brother "went off and did lay missionary work for about a year" around Massachusetts and Pennsylvania.

When Carter talked to us of his experience, he didn't so much contradict this version as pick it up where his sister left off. The "very tangible evidence" of his new life came when he threw himself into the work of a Baptist lay preacher, knocking on strangers' back doors in towns hundreds of miles distant from Plains. He particularly remembers an assignment in the coal country around Lock Haven, Pennsylvania: "I'm not sure about the year . . . May 1967. [It was] what we call a pioneer mission. Before I went, there had been identified 100 families of non-believers. . . . I was assigned the responsibility along with another person, Milo Pennington, from Texas, to go into these homes and explain our own faith and seek their conversion. Milo Pennington was not well educated. He happens to be a peanut farmer—there aren't very many of them in Texas—and he did the work and talking. It seemed to me he was the most inept person I had ever known in expressing himself. He fumbled and didn't know what to say and I thought, 'Oh, I could do much better. . . .' But he had done it before and he was a deeply committed person.''

Pennington apparently succeeded in converting fifteen or twenty families. "The whole week was almost a miracle to me," Carter said. "I felt the sense of the presence of God's influence in my life. I called my wife on the phone one night and she said, 'Jimmy, you don't sound like the same person. You sound almost like you're intoxicated.' . . . And I said, 'Well, in a way I am.' . . . It was a new sense of release and assurance and peace with myself and a genuine interest in other people that I hadn't experienced before. I felt then and ever since that when I meet each individual person, they are important to me. I found myself able to say, 'What can I do to make this other person's life even more enjoyable?'—even people that I met on an elevator or in a chance encounter on the street. In the past, I had a natural inclination to say, 'What can I get from them?' Or to wipe them out of my mind. Now it's just a different feeling altogether. It's hard for me to express it."

Actually, by his open testimony, he succeeds in making his born-again experience accessible and understandable, even for non-believers.

IV

AS A RELIGIOUS EXPERIENCE, the feelings Carter describes are hardly unique. In his own words, Baptists "believe that the first time we're born as children, it's human life given to us; and when we accept Jesus as our Savior it's new life. That's what 'born again' means." The Fundamentalist Christian believes he or she came into the first life in a state of original sin. By accepting Jesus, who died for all our sins, those who are born again are saved from a future of eternal damnation and punishment. Hundreds of thousands of American choose this "new life" every year, communicants in a tradition based on the gospel story of Nicodemus. (A rich and powerful Jew, Nicodemus visits Jesus and the question becomes how can Nicodemus be saved? Jesus answers that he must be born again.)

In Colonial America, the born-again process engaged the intellect. The Bay Colony Puritans had to narrate an experience of regenerating grace in order to become church members. The Puritans gave great and lengthy consideration to their own behavior. They kept journals, and reflected on what it meant to be an adult in the world with all its difficulties and misfortunes. When Roger Williams and others broke from the Puritan tradition, the born-again phenomenon became more a matter of the emotions than the intellect. Ministers wanted to reach the ordinary people, who had to be appealed to through their senses, where John Locke said learning took place. People had to be scared, particularly the "simple" people of the farm and the frontier. So evangelists preached damnation and a literal hell where Satan's sinuous-tailed helpers eternally prodded naked sinners with red-hot forks. Rational Puritan tradition, as well as Lockian theory, disappeared; the pietism and the emotionalism, the fear and trembling, remained. Conversion became, typically, a "low class" experience presided over by Bible-thumping, hellfire-breathing evangelists holding forth at revival meetings.

The engineer's mind—and the middle-class, proper Plains upbringing—of Jimmy Carter excluded vivid pictures of an actual heaven with pearly gates or a hell populated with roasting sinners. He read the Bible, but not as a Fundamentalist. His own conversion followed a period of reflection in the Puritan fashion. James Wooten, a former New York *Times* correspondent (and a former Presbyterian minister), has suggested that Carter's conversion came from a businesslike calculation: his religion had not given him any worthwhile payoffs, so perhaps the way to get more for his spiritual investment would be by making a deeper investment of himself. Carter bought into God as he might buy IBM or Coca-Cola.

Other critics have considered Carter's religious stance nothing more than a cloak to win over the "God vote"—more than half of Americans surveyed by Gallup claimed that their religious beliefs were "very important" to them—and to cover over his naked political ambitions. "His religion is important from ten o'clock till noon on Sunday mornings," declares Reg Murphy.

In fact, during the 1976 presidential primaries, Carter did make shrewd use of his religion, so much so that without the support of Baptists, black and white, he might not have won. But Carter's religious beliefs add up to much more than political expediency. Carter's religious conversion, admittedly difficult for nonbelievers to understand, completes the formation of his adult character; to ignore its pervasive effects would be to skip over the experience that brings together Carter's being.

Carter's conversion, cool and bloodless as it might seem—especially in contrast to the experience of walking the aisle at a revival meeting—grew out of genuinely felt emotions. The born-again experience, in common with other spiritual movements, speaks to deep human needs—to longings to bury the past, to inabilities to handle great pain, to yearnings to start anew. The pains and burdens of the past need not be all that heavy. Oliver

Cromwell, another public figure of another time, underwent a conversion experience, too. Cromwell, the great leader of the seventeenth-century "Puritan Revolution," lacerated himself for his sins: "You know what my manner of life hath been. Oh, I lived in and loved darkness, and hated the light; I was a chief, the chief of sinners." Cromwell's conscious acts of sin seem to have been minor derelictions, such as cardplaying and engaging in practical jokes. On another level, Cromwell had to wrestle with his fears of uncontrollable anger, either out of frustrations or out of resentments of his parents' strict authority. But, Cromwell says, he was saved: "God had mercy on me."

Carter also seems to exaggerate his transgressions—"I was always thinking of myself"—while hiding his anger from himself. Carter, too, received God's mercy. He was freed from his sense of sin. He became able "to accept defeat" and "to get pleasure out of successes." In unchristian fashion, he had wanted to win too much, for himself and out of pride. Worse, he could not renounce his ambitions, as his sister had asked. As a renewed Christian, Carter could relax a bit about himself, his "selfish" desires and angry feelings. He had felt himself a hypocrite. The "miracle" of rebirth reassured him of his essential goodness and worth. When he truly accepted God the Father, through Christ, he also had been accepted by God the Father.

As a psychological experience, Carter's "rebirth" also follows some common patterns. His personal life had plateaued, as often happens with men in their early forties. He had wanted another child—the last Carter son had been born in 1952—but no conception resulted. In common with many people, he did not feel happy in all respects with the adult he had become. The confessional language of his religious experience easily translates into terms familiar to most adults. Carter felt filled with pride: "I was always thinking about myself." The technical word for this is "narcissism." Carter says that he used people. The therapist hears "I can't love." Carter says he had "the need to improve." The textbooks talk of the "crisis of generativity."

The conflict between generativity and self-absorption, exemplified in Erik Erikson's biography of Martin Luther, fits the forty-two-year-old Carter as naturally as his work shirt. Through the phases of young adulthood and the approach of maturity, men and women are absorbed in their own careers and concerns. Then, at mid-life, age thirty-five or forty or forty-five, adults typically begin to ask themselves, What have I generated? What have I helped to create? Has my life been productive or stagnant? Can old age be faced with a sense of integrity—"All in all, I would do this over again"—or with feelings of waste and despair? What legacy or guidance is being left for the next generation?

Jimmy Carter first began turning over some of these questions, he tells us, when his father died in 1953. Then he had resolved to be like his father. In 1966, he had to face up to these doubts when—now thirteen years older—he had become everything his father could have wanted for him: farmer, businessman, Sunday school teacher, state legislator—yet still believed that he had failed.

Why this sense of failure? Carter's own explanation, or at least the one he offered us, suggests that he wasn't *enough* like his father. James Earl Carter, Sr., knew how to relax, to take defeat. Jimmy Carter didn't know how. He was too proud, too self-righteous. And so he failed—himself and his father. Through the born-again process, however, God the Father accepts him, and so does his earthly father. It is a salvation in the classic pattern of psychohistory. Luther and Gandhi, the Eriksonian heroes, had made their quest for salvation political acts. Jimmy Carter was in good company.

Such a new relationship with God produces incalculable dividends. Jimmy Carter can identify with his father, earn redemption, and secure for himself the love that supports self-esteem. He can feel he is a good person, and—a potentially scary linkage—because he is "good," he can believe what he does will be "right." Jimmy Carter's encounter with God, he remembers, gave him a supreme confidence in himself. If God is with me, the believer can say, what matter who or what is against me. Self-esteem and self-righteousness make a powerful combination. In Jimmy Carter's certitude that he personally could bridge the deep and murderous differences between Egypt and Israel, he went to the Middle East in March 1979 to hammer together a peace treaty. (That "peace" meant a new round of arms shipments to the two countries, as well as a commitment of billions of U.S. dollars. Time will tell how "right" his good offices were.)

"Rebirth" also made an optimist of Jimmy Carter. Some eighty years ago, William James wrote of the "mind-cure" movement and of "The Religion of Healthy-Mindedness." Mind-curists developed a living system of mental hygiene, wholly and exclusively composed of optimism: *Pessimism leads to weakness. Optimism leads to power.* "Thoughts are things," one of the more vigorous mind-cure proponents would print in bold type at the bottom of each page of his tracts. "If your thoughts are of health, youth, vigor, and success, before you know it these things will also be your outward portion. No one can fail of the regenerative influence of optimistic thinking, pertinaciously pursued."

It is almost as if the youthful Jimmy Carter had read James. In the seventh grade, twelve years old, he put together a booklet entitled *Jimmy Carter's Health Report.* In the section called "Healthy Mental Habits," he wrote:

There are certain habits of thinking which have a good effect upon health. If you think in the right way you'll develop:

1. The habit of expecting to accomplish what you attempt.
2. The habit of expecting to like other people and to have them like you.
3. The habit of deciding quickly what you want to do, and doing it.
4. The habit of "sticking to it."
5. The habit of welcoming fearlessly all wholesome ideas and experiences.
6. A person who wants to build good mental habits should avoid the idle daydream; should give up worry or anger, hatred and envy; should neither fear nor be ashamed of anything that is honest or purposeful.

The believer in such moralism and good works experiences an apparently painless emancipation. "What shall I do to be saved?" William James has the worried Christian ask. Martin Luther and John Wesley reply, You are saved now, if you would but believe it. Lifting the conversion experience from its religious context, James created pragmatism, a secular version of mind cure, and the most characteristically American of moral philosophies. Believe, and you shall be saved, Christian evangelism exhorts. In its version, pragmatism says, Act as if what you believed in were true, and it will come true. In a later era, the optimistic would repeat, after Coué, "Every day in every way, I'm getting better and better," and, still later, pragmatically pursue the Power of Positive Thinking, with the Reverend Norman Vincent Peale.

The Jimmy Carter who kept optimistically claiming he would win in his race for the governorship and the Presidency stands well within this tradition. Positive thinking helps explain his characteristic exaggerations and his conviction that Providence watches over his successes. It also helps explain some of his characteristic energy. The belief that sinners can be emancipated places a great demand on activity; success seekers must take a positive hand in the journey to grace. The mind-cure movement of the turn of the century marches on today in courses and books that instruct Americans on how to get rid of their "erroneous zones" and be the people they want to be, and how to get control of their time and their lives. Carter has been a star pupil in the self-improvement school. The same Evelyn Wood Speed Reading sessions that, almost two decades ago, helped State Senator Jimmy Carter brush up on his skills now occupy President Jimmy Carter in the White House. His official schedules also make room for jogging and Spanish instruction and music lessons. Carter fits in the American grain of thousands of upwardly mobile men and women in business and sales. His "ordinariness" in this regard undercuts efforts to make him into a villain, or a hero.

Carter's born-again experience changed his politics as well as his life. It pointed the way to what became his distinct, highly personal approach to political leadership. That week in Lock Haven, Pennsylvania, offered an intoxicating epiphany about public life. Jimmy Carter—Annapolis graduate, nuclear-submarine officer, recent candidate for governor, an intelligent, proud, literate, well-spoken man—walks door-to-door with the poorly educated, inept, elderly Pennington, a man in his seventies at the time. Old Pennington does all the talking—and it works. He makes converts among the non-believers: fifteen, sixteen, twenty, the total rolls up. "It's almost a miracle," Carter says. The experience changes him. He even sounds different on the telephone talking to Rosalynn Carter. Carter had been a man of science—a "cultural consolidator," in Erik Erikson's term. He had integrated the dominant technological development of his time—nuclear power—with his own identity development. But Science and Reason and Intellect could take him only so far in life. The voters had rejected him. Old Pennington, on the other hand, could reach people through feeling and belief. If a religious missionary—or a political leader—"gets down" with the people, feels with them, then he can win them over, convert them, lead them. For a politician, that can be a miracle. In 1966, Carter ran for governor as a bright young engineer. By 1970, in his second try, he put himself forward as a man of the people—a peanut farmer and businessman.

V

IN HIS POLITICAL CAMPAIGNS, Carter repeats the themes that the people are good, and that they need leaders as honest and as compassionate and as competent as the people are—a government as good as its people. This catechism comes as much from Southern Baptist tradition as from any experience in the Georgia legislature.

Baptists strongly believe in a divinely ordained form of church government in which all power belongs to the people. But the Baptists' large, loosely structured denomination demands strong leadership to hold it together and give direction to its activities. As a result, leaders emerge with no clearly defined roles—or any clearly defined limitations on their power. A large church bureaucracy develops, but with no rational or structural ordering of power, since the Baptists are unwilling to confer authority upon their leaders and are equally unwilling to recognize that these leaders have attained power apart from authority.

Consequently, Baptist leadership has a style of its own. The authority of the leader is highly pragmatic, observes Richard Shaull of the Princeton Theological Seminary. "It depends on his ability to achieve assigned goals quickly and efficiently." It is also "personalistic," built upon charismatic qualities that attract a following and win spontaneous support. According to Shaull, this Southern Baptist approach to leadership creates a certain innocence about power. The theory, he says, fails to recognize the dangers inherent in power, or to understand the ways in which power corrupts: "To the extent that Baptists are immersed in their tradition, they cannot admit that this is a problem—much less deal with it theologically." In the end the mystique about the leader's identification with the people tends to eliminate the problem. He is nothing more than the representative of the people, whom he serves and from whom he draws his strength. The important thing is that the leader be worthy of the people's trust, and constantly reassure them of this point.

Carter's religious experience, by common agreement, equips him with many admirable personal qualities. His religion can be a source of strength, making him a dynamic leader. But, Schaull argues, the evangelical style of leadership, while high on motivation, is often very naïve in its understanding of what is demanded when traditional solutions no longer prove effective. In such situations, the usual evangelical answer is: if only our national leaders are strong and trustworthy men, with high moral integrity and faith in God, our anxieties will be overcome and the present system will function once again. Symbolic language is used in a magical way —with no clear connection to any specific problem, and at a time when magic cannot resolve political or economic issues.

Equally important, the Baptist evangelical "theology of institutions" tends to be conservative and idealized. The evangelicals believe that certain institutional structures are divinely ordained; no matter how they develop or expand, or how times change, the principles on which they are built will remain valid. When an institution does not work well, the explanation may be that the right people are not in charge or that it is not organized efficiently—not that there is something fundamentally wrong with the structure itself. In the summer of 1979, for example, President Carter evangelically railed against selfish oil companies, but shrank from any serious discussion of nationalizing them.

VI

CARTER'S THEOLOGICAL EDUCATION did not end with his Southern Baptist evangelical experience. If it had, his religious— and political—beliefs would be considerably less complicated, and less waffling. He had other instruction in the writings of the Protestant theologian Reinhold Niebuhr. Because Dr. Niebuhr—abstract, intellectual, a demanding teacher—seems so far from Plains Baptist Church, some critics do not really believe Carter when he says he has read Niebuhr. They scoff at Carter's use of what they see as catch phrases from the great man's work. Reviewing Carter's collected speeches in the New York *Times*, Arthur Schlesinger, Jr., notes: "Mr. Carter mentions sin once or twice, but seems oblivious to the striking incompatibility between his theological professions and his political exhortations. He claims to have read Reinhold Niebuhr, but Niebuhr would have dismissed this belief in the inherent virtue of people en masse as the most arrant sentimentalism."

Schlesinger's attitude echoes a question asked Carter by Bill D. Moyers during the 1976 campaign. A lawyer in a large firm in New York, a friend of Moyers, had said to him, "What bothers me about Jimmy Carter, the human being, is that he strikes me as a decent but provincial and narrow-minded man from the South." Moyers put this comment as a challenge to Carter. Carter's reply did little to dispel the hick image; he went over the colleges he had attended, his travels to foreign countries, his conversations with leaders in foreign affairs, and his extensive readings about American politics, turning the question into one about his ability to lead a pluralistic society. He gave a political speech, and an unconvincing one at that. But how can "provincialism" be judged? Carter says in his autobiography that he has read Tolstoy's *War and Peace*. He gives no aesthetic reaction, only a political one: that the character of the "people" determines history. He quotes Niebuhr and Dylan Thomas, again without much "intellectual" discussion. Carter reads for his own personal purposes; he wants to know what these thinkers mean for his own life and the way he should lead it. He does not read in an impersonal, scholarly fashion, seeking deeper meanings or literary and cultural trends. He reads, in short, for self-improvement, to learn to "govern" himself and others.

In this way, he read Niebuhr, and not just "claimed to." With his friend Bill Gunter he discussed Niebuhr and the work of other Protestant theologians—Tillich, Barth, Bonhoeffer, Kierkegaard. Paul Tillich had a special appeal for Carter, who always appears caught in process and concerned with *becoming* rather than being.

Tillich, for example, suggests religion is a "search" for man's relation to God, which can never be satisfied. The key instruction, however, came from Niebuhr, whose *Moral Man and Immoral Society* offers the best integrated statement of his basic views, and the one most echoed in Jimmy Carter's beliefs and behavior. Niebuhr analyzes the relation of religion to politics, and fuses the two into an inseparable attitude. If Jimmy Carter's politics can't be understood apart from his religion, then his religion can't be understood without relating Niebuhr's words to Carter's born-again experience. Niebuhr showed Carter how to take that sin-dispelling experience into the sin-filled world of politics.

Niebuhr's weighty prose and dense arguments do not make for light reading or easy paraphrase. *Moral Man and Immoral Society* came out in 1932, the time of the Depression and the rise of Hitler's Third Reich. Niebuhr's conception of man's fallen state echoes the views of Sigmund Freud, and Freud's stoically pessimistic views of human nature. Niebuhr attempts to reunite religion and politics, to align individual with social ethics. It is easier for the individual to be ethical, to follow Jesus in his own life, than to be and do so in a society that by its very nature must be immoral in a Christian sense. But the Christian cannot withdraw from society and become an ascetic. The stern duty of a Christian is to bring justice, in so far as possible, to a sinful world. True, the Christian may not get very far. Niebuhr debunks the believers in naïve progress and perfectionism. He attacks both the Enlightenment thinkers of the Age of Reason and the religious idealists who think the introduction of pure love into society will solve all its problems. Neither rationality nor love will lead us to utopia. Against the established middle-class "illusions" of liberalism, whether rational or religious, Niebuhr insists on man's fallen nature. Though man can strive for perfection, he can never achieve it. We must aim, not at a perfect society, but at something "realistic" like limited justice. "Human society," says Niebuhr, "will never escape the problem of the equitable distribution of the physical and cultural goods which provide for the preservation and fulfillment of human life." When President Jimmy Carter dismissed the coal miners' grievances about black-lung legislation—No one makes them go into the mines—or when President Jimmy Carter opposed Medicaid payments for poor women's abortions—Many things in life are not fair—he sounded the "realistic" morality of Niebuhr, more than any doctrine of fiscal conservatism.

Niebuhr's realism is complicated; there are no simple answers. "Political controversies are always conflicts between sinners and not between righteous men and sinners." From this emphasis on realism and complexity comes an acceptance of the world as an imperfect place where some injustice will always exist. Wherever there is social power there will be social inequality.

Niebuhr constantly cited the black man's lot as an example of injustice in society. He kept asking how blacks will achieve greater justice, when it is so clearly in the interest of the ruling whites to keep them submerged. Niebuhr's answer goes to the core of his Christian ethics. The acknowledgment that society will always be characterized by injustice does not mean we ought passively to accept existing inequities. Joining conservative and liberal views, Niebuhr insists on a continuous fight to remove injustice, waged realistically. Niebuhr's analysis of how societies operate, and most people operate, leads him prophetically to advocate "non-violent coercion." Invoking the example of Gandhi, Niebuhr writes, "The emancipation of the Negro race in America probably waits upon the adequate development of [a similar] kind of social and political strategy. It is hopeless for the Negro to expect complete emancipation from the menial social and economic position into which the white man has forced him, merely by trusting in the moral sense of the white race. It is equally hopeless to attempt emancipation through violent revolution."

The realism of non-violence commends it, as does its ethical advantages. "It protects the agents against the resentments which violent conflict always creates in both parties to a conflict. . . . In every social conflict each party is so obsessed with the wrongs which the other party commits against it, that it is unable to see its own wrongdoing. A non-violent temper reduces these animosities to a minimum." Such a message would appeal not only to a Martin Luther King but to a Jimmy Carter as well, for the threat of violence smoldered in Carter's own ancestry and temperament. Niebuhr envisioned a black leader who could "fuse the aggressiveness of the new and young Negro with the patience and forbearance of the old Negro, to rob the former of its vindictiveness and the latter of its lethargy." The problem of fusing aggression and forbearance, of integrating old parental impulses, of bringing together the Old South and the New South, faced Carter, too.

Religion and politics join not in a perfect but in a possible union. The religious imagination makes its greatest contribution to politics by developing non-violent resistance. When foes find elements of common human frailty in each other and can appreciate the transcendent worth of all human life, this creates attitudes which transcend social conflict and mitigate its cruelties. The repentance which recognizes that the evil in the foe is also in the self, and the impulses of love which claim kinship with all men in spite of social conflict, make up "the peculiar gift of religion to the human spirit." Niebuhr offered better guidance to Carter than did his sister Ruth Stapleton, who asked him to forsake politics for religion. She had it backwards; the Christian's duty, Niebuhr insists, must be served *in* this world of coercion, violence, and injustice.

Niebuhr's realism, in the end, becomes an ideal, and an energizing force. The world, Niebuhr concludes, "can be more perfect than it is. If the mind and the spirit of man does not attempt the impossible, if it does not seek to conquer or to eliminate nature but tries to make the forces of nature the servants of the human spirit and the instruments of the moral ideal, a progressively higher justice and more stable peace can be achieved." Though it has gone unremarked Carter's admission that he had "lust in his heart" —that he did not try "to eliminate nature"—was a political and religious statement as much as a sexual confession.

Niebuhr provided Carter an intellectual analysis necessary for a pursuit of political power as a religious vocation. He put in theological terms many of the impulses of Carter's character, formed in his early years in his family, including the need to fuse opposites, to reconcile contradictions, and to accept the reality of complexity. Niebuhr spoke especially to the problems of racial injustice not only as an intellectual guide but as a palpable presence in the South. In 1932, Niebuhr visited the desperately poor coal miners of Pineville, Kentucky. His Committee on Economic and Racial Justice hired Christian radicals to organize tenant farmers and investigate lynchings. In 1934, Niebuhr's followers founded the Fellowship of Southern Churchmen. Niebuhr's role in the South in the 1930s seems largely forgotten; but his theological writings drew upon this experience, and in turn illuminated it.

166

Arthur Schlesinger stumbled. In Niebuhr, Jimmy Carter found a mind more rarefied than his own, but one that was searching along some of the same paths he had begun belatedly to explore.

VII

CARTER, as it happened, had a chance to answer Schlesinger's criticism two weeks later in an interview with the New York *Times* Sunday book editor Harvey Shapiro. Carter's attempt to reconcile sin and goodness wandered; it would not be satisfactory on a college test. He seemed to be saying that the good in a people could be seen in the country's basic values and institutions. People want "a government as good as they are or would like to be . . . so we have some things, our religious beliefs and the ideal of what our government ought to be, that are stabilizing forces. . . . There comes a time in a crisis when the superb qualities of human beings in a collective fashion are evoked in a religious concept or in a government structure that transcends the mundane commitments of people. But it stands there then as a reminder of what people can do." Then, thinking back to Schlesinger's criticism, Carter concludes, "So I don't see the conflict."

To an intellectual there may be a logical conflict, but Carter brings together the contradictory beliefs in goodness and sinfulness. The weld comes from accreted values and institutions—the deposit of time—which Carter's conservative evangelical side enshrines. Goodness lives in these religious and governmental entities as well as in human souls. Realism tells us men will practice injustice; but Christian love tells us they can be uplifted, and recalled to their better selves, idealized in the collective nation and its symbols. Niebuhr would approve; so would Southern Baptist doctrine.

The threads of Niebuhr, evangelism, and the "born-again" experience may clash with one another; yet for Carter they make up part of the same cloth of religious belief. In each, he found a justification for going on in politics. As manifestations of God, who holds in his hands the governance of the world, Niebuhr, religion, and the conversion experience confirmed, intellectually and emotionally, Carter's decision to try to become a good "governor" on this sinful earth.

VIII

AS AUTHORS OFTEN DO, Jimmy Carter offers some quotations in the preface to *Why Not the Best?* The page reads:

> The sad duty of politics is to establish justice
> in a sinful world.
> —REINHOLD NIEBUHR

> Hey, hey, Woody Guthrie, I wrote you a song
> 'Bout a funny ol' world that's a-comin' along.
> Seems sick an' it's hungry, it's tired and it's torn,
> It looks like it's a-dyin' an' it's hardly been born.
> —BOB DYLAN

> Great is the hand that holds dominion over
> Man by a scribbled name.

> The five kings count the dead but do not soften
> The crusted wound nor stroke the brow;
> A hand rules pity as a hand rules heaven;
> Hands have no tears to flow.
> —DYLAN THOMAS

Carter's critics inevitably dismissed the selections as so much window dressing, a typical politician's bid for ticket balancing— Niebuhr for the religious, Bob Dylan for the young, Dylan Thomas for intellectuals (and pantheists). As with his knowledge of Niebuhr, Carter has been challenged about his familiarity with the music of Dylan and the poetry of Thomas. The doubters need not fret. Carter knows the work of Thomas, a moralist in his own way. Fundamental themes connect the theologian and the poet—and link with Carter's own deep emotions. (The Bob Dylan connection, as we shall see, represents a different challenge.)

Carter remembers that he first came across Dylan Thomas'

work in the mid-1950s, when he had just taken over his late father's
agribusiness. Jimmy Carter had a workshop in the back of the
Carter Warehouse with hundred-pound sacks of fertilizer piled on
the floor. Sitting on the sacks, waiting for customers' trucks to pull
up, he passed the time reading. One day he thumbed through an
anthology of modern poets: "I never had heard of Dylan Thomas.
One of the poems was 'A Refusal to Mourn the Death, by Fire, of
a Child in London.' I didn't understand the poem when I read it,
but the last line said, 'After the first death there is no other.' And
I thought about it for a while and I went back and read the poem
again. I couldn't understand it still, so then I went back to my little
desk in the front and I diagrammed all the sentences and I finally
understood what Dylan Thomas was saying."

The saintly Miss Julia had taught Plains pupils how to read a
poem; a diagram would be the naval engineer's added way of understanding complexity. Carter could sense the words challenged
something more than his zeal for self-improvement. Carter didn't
understand consciously the poem at first reading—he needed dia-
grams for that—but he "knew" at once the profound meaning of
the message "After the first death there is no other." It is a message of acceptance and reconciliation. It tells us that we must all
die, and the way of mourning is to stop mourning:

> Nor blaspheme down the stations of the breath
> With any further
> Elegy of innocence and youth.

Basically Thomas' poem is "about" fathers and "Fathering
and all humbling darkness." For Carter, the poem is about the
death of Mr. Earl. He still mourns the death of his father, and tries
to come to grips with the emotions caused by the passing of Mr.
Earl, who meant so much to him in life, and now in death.

When Thomas' own father lay dying in 1952, Thomas wrote
the poem "Do Not Go Gentle into That Good Night," with its
savage cry of refusal to accept death:

> Do not go gentle into that good night,
> Old age should burn and rave at close of day;
> Rage, rage against the dying of the light. . . .

And you, my father, there on the sad height,
Curse, bless, me now with your fierce tears, I pray.
Do not go gentle into that good night.
Rage, rage against the dying of the light.

That time in the mid-1950s when Carter discovered Thomas, required a mourning's end, not continuing rage. He needed to complete the process started when he sat by his father's bedside and
talked about old times together and the eleven years when they
had rarely seen each other. Mr. Earl's death first brought Jimmy
Carter to Thomas' poems, but Carter found Thomas had much
more to offer. He began to study all of Thomas' work, sharing it
with his own sons. The boys, barely grammar schoolers, would
read Thomas with their father and analyze the poems. Later Carter
found other disciples of Thomas in the Georgia legislature. In 1974,
a special legislative session convened to write a new state constitution. According to Carter, he and ten or twelve members of the
senate listened to recordings of Dylan Thomas reciting his poetry,
after the morning work sessions.

Dylan Thomas mastered paradox, in his life and his poetry. A
cherubic-looking curly-haired Welshman, he drank himself to
death in the company of bohemian Americans. He read the *Times*
of London and the *Daily Worker,* wrote profoundly Christian
poems, and professed revolutionary Marxist politics (not unlike
Niebuhr). He could party all night in seedy bars and then recite
poetry in an unforgettably beautiful, deep voice the next morning
at college seminars. His poetry thrived on the reconciliation of
opposites, often life and death. "I make one image," he once
wrote, "though 'make' is not the word; I let, perhaps, an image be
'made' emotionally in me and then apply to it what intellectual and
critical forces I possess—let it breed another, let that image contradict the first, make, of the third image bred out of the other two
together, a fourth contradictory image, and let them all, within my
imposed formal limits, conflict. Each image holds within it the seed
of its own destruction, and my dialectical method, as I understand
it, is a constant building up and breaking down of the images that
come out of the central seed, which is itself destructive and con-
structive at the same time. . . . Out of the inevitable conflict of
images— . . . the womb of war—I try to make that momentary

peace which is a poem." No wonder Jimmy Carter says he feels a resonance with Dylan Thomas; like a Thomas poem, Carter brings together contradictions and conflicts in his paradoxical character.

Carter the politician receives the inspiration of Thomas' poetic vision. The quotation from "The Hand That Signed the Paper" brings the political and the poetic together in one insight. The lines that Carter quotes come after some earlier lines:

> The hand that signed the paper felled a city;
> Five sovereign fingers taxed the breath,
> Doubled the globe of dead and halved a country;
> These five kings did a king to death.

The "five kings" are the fingers of the hand that writes its "scribbled name," and "holds dominion over man." This hand has "no tears to flow." Powerful people can sometimes be insensitive, Carter said, explicating the poem. "The line that I think summarizes my concept of the poem is 'Hands have no tears to flow.' . . . Sometimes the separation between power and people is unrecognized by the strong leaders. And the insensitivity that's inherent in power, that ought to be a warning to us."

As Carter himself says, "It's hard to know what Thomas meant." It is hard, but not impossible. Thomas means that the exercise of dominion—governorship—requires as well a certain insensitivity. Niebuhr understood this, and so does Carter, in his apparently unfeeling comments on abortion, black lung disease, and other "poor people's issues." In early 1975, about a month before the collapse in Vietnam, columnist Mary McGrory asked Carter what Dylan Thomas would have to say about the people who were continuing to die there. At the time, Carter still supported continued aid to the Saigon regime. To McGrory's visible shock, Carter quoted the line: "After the first death there is no other."

Jimmy Carter felt a sensibility in Thomas that corresponded to his own, just as he felt moved by Niebuhr. Philosopher, poet, politician—each fixed on death and rebirth, dominion in the world, and the contradictory nature of existence; "And Death Shall Have No Dominion," affirms one of Thomas' best-known poems. Carter freed himself from the fear of death, in his own life—where he seems fearless—and in the shadow of his father's death. He could enjoy a new life, a rebirth freed of Death's Dominion. He could enter his own Dominion in the political world. The "obscure" Thomas becomes a living presence for Carter, with memorized lines ready for all political occasions. Thomas himself might have liked the contradictory, "forced" fusion of politics and poetry that Carter made of his own work.

If only Carter had stopped there, with Thomas, in his dedication, without bringing in Bob Dylan. On the surface, a link exists between Dylan Thomas and Bob Dylan. Born Robert Zimmerman in Duluth, Minnesota, the musician-singer-composer changed his name to honor the poet he most admired. Superficially, too, the quotation from Bob Dylan's song used by Carter sounds a note of spiritual rebirth. For Carter to claim that Dylan taught him as much about justice and politics as Niebuhr or Thomas, however, raises questions not about Carter's familiarity with a specific work but about his tendency toward the fatuous. The excess of the claim irritates; no one can really believe that Carter believes that Bob Dylan occupies the same intellectual rung as Niebuhr. It is part of Carter's style of exaggeration; he can make the most preposterous statements in the most serious tones. He is, in fact, ticket balancing —"identifying"—with the new generation. Carter's own tastes in his midshipman years and in the Navy ran to classical music. He started to listen to Bob Dylan's music primarily because of his sons; he says he "got to like it and I used to spend three or four hours a day listening to Paul Simon, Bob Dylan, and the Allman Brothers. At home I'd study government reorganization or budgeting techniques while I listened to rock."

Carter met Bob Dylan when the musician toured Atlanta in 1974. Carter invited him to a post-concert reception at the governor's mansion. To everyone's surprise, Dylan accepted. The party, it seems, broke up about two A.M. without the appearance of one of the scheduled guests of honor, Gregg Allman. When Allman arrived at four in the morning, apparently stoned, Carter, who had long since gone to bed, came to the door in jeans, an old sweat shirt, and bare feet. The two men talked until nearly dawn. Allman later declared that the governor of Georgia was "really far-out." On another occasion, Carter visited a Savannah radio station, and the host asked him to dedicate the next Bob Dylan record. Carter agreed; the deejay, disconcertingly, chose to play "Lay, Lady, Lay."

IX

Yet the Dylan connection has an authenticity about it, too. Bob Dylan—and Gregg Allman—represent another, seldom recognized side of Carter's nature, as well as what seemed to be a politically advantageous tie. Carter tries to bring out the best in people and to govern as a leader of the broadest possible flock. A religious-political leader rejects no one in his ministry; for all, to a greater or lesser degree, are equally sinners and equally good. In the White House, Carter remained outwardly tolerant of the personal habits of his young staff; he looked the other way a great deal, until an errant drug prescription, written by his psychiatrist friend Dr. Bourne, caused even more embarrassment than usual and forced Bourne's resignation.

With Niebuhr, Jimmy Carter knew that people cannot be made perfect, but they can be made to live up to the best within them. Carter knew this from his own life as a boy and man. The vehicle for social ennoblement can be government; for personal enhancement it is religion. Government must be as good as the people—basically decent, honest, and compassionate. It must also be realistic—tough-minded and efficient.

Carter also believes that a nation "has a many-faceted character," just like an individual, and just like a man who wishes to lead them. Many-faceted himself, Carter has said he wishes to mirror the contradictory, complicated nature of the people. He could do this both by his intuition (the extension of his own complex nature to that of the people) and by his polls (a scientist's way of ascertaining the temperature of the body politic). With both methods, Carter has tried to stay constantly in touch with the "psychological needs of the country," as his public opinion pollster, Pat Caddell, puts it. The people must be listened to; the leader does not impose his own ideas on them. The people, and their character, determine the course of history, as Jimmy Carter read in Tolstoy.

Carter's leader, like the minister of Southern Baptist theory, draws all his strength from the people. Carter's leader has an extraordinary need to merge with the people, to feel at one with them. Just as his religious beliefs allow him to achieve unity with God, his political convictions lead him to that same unity with the people. He invites them into his family. He merges with them, not only in his rhetoric encompassing everyone into his family, but in his body language. As any number of associates and reporters assigned to him have noted, Jimmy Carter constantly pats, squeezes, kisses, hugs; he touches not like the old-time backslapper but *intimately*. Contact seems necessary to him. In part, he follows a Southern custom; in part, he engages in a sexual communication. But Carter's physical expressiveness has other meanings for him. Nancy Butler, the wife of one of his associates, says touching expresses "a genuine feeling of closeness." Touching embodies his political beliefs about the nature of the people and their leader. It also coincides with his low-key non-oratorical way of communicating with people. When people stay close, body language and symbolic gestures may be more appropriate than words. Closeness and an intimate, unbroken relation with the people also mean support; he owes the people everything, and nothing to the special interests. Carter's only "boss" would be the people, whose needs he knew through the antennae of his own feelings (and Caddell's polls). When he felt besieged about his domestic policies in July 1979, he called guests to Camp David for face-to-face meetings, and also got back "in touch" by helicopter visits to private homes in Pennsylvania and West Virginia. He has to stay close.

Carter trusts the people because, finally, he trusts himself. He and the people merge into one. This revelation came to him during the process of his born-again experiences, when he went door to door. Since he healed divisions in his own psyche, he feels able to be a healer-leader to his countrymen. Certain that he is fulfilling God's commands, Carter has no doubts that he is also fulfilling the will of the American people. The strength he feels comes not from his superior intellect, or from his sophisticated grasp of the issues —however intelligent or studious he may be—but from what he *feels,* and from what he *is.* When Garry Wills interviewed Carter just before his election, Wills asked him if he was afraid of winning. Carter instantly replied, "No." Wills comments, "Yet he reads the New Testament as a devout Christian, and the book seems to be full of warning against worldly power and place, against pride of office and the desire to rule others.''

''I don't feel that at all, I don't know why,'' Carter told Wills. ''I know ministers, teachers, blacks, Jews. I have consulted the best minds on every subject. I am as well prepared as anyone has been, including Roosevelt back in the '30s. I draw my strength from my personal relationship with the American people.''

Someone convinced he stands on the side of God and the People can be a potent force in the Presidency, but only if his goodness is harnessed to experience and ability.

12

White Man's Candidate

JIMMY CARTER'S CONVERSION experience may have helped him, as he said, to come to terms with himself, and with defeat. But in the 1970 governor's race, Jimmy Carter did not intend to lose again. Niebuhr, Tolstoy and Dylan Thomas had given him an intellectual framework for his political style. As Carter saw it, however, victory in 1970 required the support of other forces— former Governor Marvin Griffin, an archsegregationist; Roy Harris, publisher of a racist hate sheet; and the "Wallace vote." Niebuhr had written about politics bringing justice to a sinful world, but as someone once scrawled on a Carter campaign sign, "You Can't Establish Justice in a Sinful World Unless You Win Elections."

In 1970, Jimmy Carter and his supporters played hardball politics—one of the favorite phrases of those Nixon years—in order to win the governor's race. His campaign used tactics perhaps no dirtier and no more demagogic than those used by any number of other ambitious politicians in 1970. Still, it was rough enough, in part because the Carter forces, though inexperienced, played so hard to win. *Time* magazine, an early Carter booster, later called the 1970 governor's race "the most questionable aspect" of Carter's career in Georgia politics. Analysts since have debated whether or not Carter conducted a racist campaign. If by that his critics mean, did he shout, "Nigger, nigger, nigger," to win white votes? then the answer must be No, he did not. But he did play

176

race politics. Other accounts have claimed that he ran a populist campaign. The true meaning of that misused word centers on the redistribution of economic power. In 1970, Carter borrowed populist rhetoric about unfeeling big government and selfish big shots above the law, but he had no populist program to change the rules by which banks and corporations operate. The words echoed the Baptists' approach to government: If leaders lead in the interests of the people, then institutions need not be changed.

In fact, the word that best characterizes the Carter campaign is not "populist" but "expedient." But like so much else connected with Jimmy Carter, a single descriptive label can be misleading. In the Presidency, it has been equally misleading to dismiss him as "decent but inept."

II

CARTER HAD FOUR YEARS to plan his campaign and to work the state this time, unlike 1966. He became state chairman for the March of Dimes, a district governor and chairman of the six regional district governors in Georgia of Lions International. He appeared on the chicken and peas circuit, the typical political route of clubs, civic associations, and professional associations. In all, he says, he had made about 1800 speeches over four years, all of which he wrote himself. As Charles Kirbo explained: "He spent a great deal of time that you and I are not willing to do."

Along with old-fashioned time and effort, Carter had a very contemporary political strategy of "positioning." In mid-1968, Carter had concluded that Carl Sanders, the popular former governor, would be his only real rival (Lester Maddox, the current governor, couldn't run again immediately). Carter wrote a memo to his staff, revealing his own conflicting feelings: "Some images to be projected regarding Carl Sanders . . . More liberal, has close connections with Ivan Allen [then mayor of Atlanta] and Atlanta establishment. . . . Atlanta-oriented to the exclusion of other metro and rural areas . . . pretty boy . . . ignored prison reform opportunities . . . nouveau riche . . . refused to assist local school boards in school financing . . . excluded George Wallace from state. . . . You can see some of these are contradictory, but right now we just need to collect all these rough ideas we can. Later we can start driving a wedge between him and me.''

The wedge would be *race*, though not *racism*. Carter courted the Wallace vote. Where Sanders had barred Wallace from a scheduled speaking engagement in a Georgia state building, Carter indicated that, as governor, he would invite Wallace to speak. Carter also talked about closer ties with Wallace through interstate compacts to equalize college student fees, and cooperation in crime prevention and pollution control. Early in the campaign, he announced he expected "to have particularly strong support from the people who voted for George Wallace for President and the ones who voted for Lester Maddox." He played Wallace's own game of code words at a time when "liberal" and "conservative" had meaning mainly in terms of attitudes toward black Americans. Carter declared, "I don't consider myself a liberal." White people had rights, too, he made it clear.

Carter did not rely on his intuition about Wallace, Sanders, or the voters. He hired William Hamilton, a Washington-based public opinion sampler, on the recommendation of Kirbo. At the beginning of the campaign, Hamilton found that Sanders would have received 53 percent of the vote, with Carter getting 21 percent. Carter still had a recognition problem: 25 percent of the electorate hadn't heard of him, and only slightly more than one half the Democrats queried had any opinion of him. Carter also read in the polls "an awful basic feeling among the people that 'I just don't have any voice any more. The government's pushing me around.' "

The Carter forces portrayed Sanders as a pawn of the Atlanta Establishment, who used his servile position to make money for himself. In attacking Sanders, Carter appealed to the "little people"—poor white rural Georgians. Carter did not invent the phrase "Cuff Links Carl"—one of the Republican candidates did—but he used it to advantage. Hamilton's polls had shown that about one fourth of the undecided voters felt that Sanders had become too close to the Atlanta bigwigs, and too citified. Carter took aim at this group, positioning himself as the conservative and average (white) man's candidate. A Jerry Rafshoon television commercial depicted an exclusive Atlanta club, with a fat cat—a "big money boy"—writing out a check for Sanders. Carter demanded that

Sanders make a public financial statement, which Sanders foolishly refused to do until just before the election. In September 1969, only 1 percent of the electorate had felt Sanders used the governor's office for personal gain; by primary time in 1970, a majority felt Sanders had benefited too much.

Carter's attack strategy accused Sanders of being "linked" with the 1968 Democratic presidential candidate, Hubert Humphrey. Carter ripped open a Sanders campaign button to show that the inside backing was made of an old Humphrey button, and he talked of "deals" with Humphrey. Afterward, a reporter approached Carter and said he, the reporter, thought the button gimmick was "a sneaky way" for Carter to tag Sanders with Humphrey—an unpopular figure in Georgia. Carter grinned his boyish grin and replied, "I think so, too."

Three major Democratic candidates faced each other in the primary: Carter the "conservative," Sanders the "moderate," and C. B. King, a black attorney from Albany, Georgia. From Carter's point of view, King would drain black votes from Sanders; and Carter needed to take white votes from Sanders. According to Ray Abernathy, an Atlanta public relations man who worked in the 1970 Carter campaign, the Carter forces had an operation jokingly referred to as the "stink tank." The stink tank produced a series of last-minute radio ads for King that ran on stations all over Georgia during the last few days of the campaign.

A second stink-tank operation used a newspaper photograph showing Sanders, who had been a partner in the Atlanta Hawks professional basketball franchise, being doused with champagne by some of the team's black players after an important victory. Abernathy says that some Carter campaign operatives incorporated the newspaper photo in a leaflet and distributed it to white barbershops and Baptist ministers around the state. (These stories were circulated widely during the 1976 campaign. Jody Powell's office issued a standard—and unconvincing—denial of Abernathy's story.)

The Sanders campaign didn't do too much to raise the level of the race. Sanders called Carter a "slaver" (a reference to the slaves his ancestors had owned), a slum landlord (the shanties around Plains that young Carter had rented out), and an atheist (State Senator Carter had voted against a constitutional amendment which would have required that God be worshiped in Georgia schools).

Sanders, in fact, had the black vote from start to finish of the primary campaign. But that didn't stop Carter from going into black neighborhoods and campaigning—against the advice of his staff, and contrary to his own strategy of being the "white man's candidate." He did it because of his own self-image of a "good man" who was not a racist. He may have taken aim on the Wallace voter in Maddox country, but then, as he saw it, "these are my folks . . . I convinced the average working man and woman that I was their friend, that if I was elected, I would understand their problems." As for black working people, Carter said, "I would challenge anybody to detect one single statement that I ever made to appeal to these fears and prejudices. I campaigned openly in the black sections of the cities. I guess I was the only candidate who ever has."

As he saw it, he waged a "conservative" campaign. "One of the standard speeches I made—I know it by heart—is that Georgia people are conservative, but their conservatism does not mean racism . . . that we hide our heads in the sand and refuse to recognize that changes are inevitable in a fast-changing technological society . . . that we are callous or unconcerned about our fellow man. . . . Georgians are conservative. So am I." When the Gwinnett County *Daily News* offered sketches of the candidates, it described Carter as one who "advocates conservative government, law-and-order, describes himself as a 'redneck' without the racial connotation."

On primary day, Carter led the three major contenders by polling 388,280 votes, though not by a sufficient margin to prevent a runoff. Sanders finished second with 301,659 and King third with 70,424. In the runoff, Carter whipped Sanders by nearly 150,000 votes.

Carter had run a traditional "anti-incumbent" campaign, for all the so-called dirty tricks (they are part of "tradition," too). A familiar slogan had sounded across the land in the late 1960s and early 1970s: "It's time for a change." Voters tended to blame incumbents for the troubles of those difficult times, and they became the lightning rods for discontent. An unknown, Carter could create his own image, drawing on a blank tablet, arranging himself to conform to what the polls told him the voters wanted. Content

—issues—mattered less, in any case, than his own anima. He practiced personal politics. As early as 1970, the lowly peanut became his identifying symbol. Supporters wore gold peanut pins; peanut bowls stood on lunch tables where Carter spoke; women campaign workers wore peanut necklaces. Carter told his supporters that the "peanut represents what I stand for . . . working in the fields . . . going to church." His personal style won him the grudging admiration of Reg Murphy, his oldest political critic: "Carter's as good a campaigner as anybody you've seen in the last twenty-five or thirty years in American politics. One-on-one, he's probably as convincing as anybody I've ever seen."

Carter's victory in the Democratic primary assured victory in the November election. Against a pleasant Republican opponent, Hal Suit, Carter won with 60 percent of the vote. His running mate for lieutenant governor, the "clown" Lester Maddox, who rode tricycles backward for the benefit of photographers, got 73 percent of the vote, a sharp reminder of the realities of Georgia politics in 1970.

III

THE CAMPAIGN of 1970 served as a rehearsal for Carter's run in 1976. He started early and campaigned personally, with his family, at the grassroots; he used television effectively. Polls took their place next to his intuition about the "people" and guided his moves. He masterfully offered symbolic actions and broad themes, not so much "populist" as nostalgic and mythic. He would shade principle—racial harmony in 1970, possibly illegal financial arrangements in 1976—in order to win. He had learned fast and come far in his new career as a politician. The 1970 campaign displayed the character of Jimmy Carter with all its contradictory virtues and failings.

Politicians must be politic and smooth, but Jimmy Carter's politics invariably bore the stamp of his contradictory personality with its sharp edges. Early in the campaign, for example, Carter had denounced the "seg academies" established to subvert federal desegregation orders, declaring he was opposed to "putting a single dime of taxpayers' money in private schools." Later, however, he visited a private school and supported private education. He told a rally in Fittin, "Don't let anybody, including the Atlanta newspapers, mislead you into criticizing private education." Kirbo explains that some "good people" who had founded private schools for non-racist reasons had come to Carter and had complained about his first stand. Carter's staff had advised him originally to stay out of the private school issue; yet he had insisted first on making his earlier statement, and then on trying to hold to it while elaborating a second position, complex and/or hedging, depending upon the listener's feelings.

If he had not been so often "open" and disingenuous, sometimes to the point of naïveté, he wouldn't have had to cover over his tracks so much. But if he had not learned to elaborate and cover over, he would have been just another George Romney, making naïve, stumbling remarks. Carter did learn this lesson of politics, just as he had learned to recognize hundreds of plane and ship silhouettes in the Navy.

His "position" on race reflects his character. Technically, he spoke correctly. "Conservative does not mean racism," as he kept saying. But he often allowed people to think otherwise. His early life and his identification with the victims of injustice helped make him quite the opposite of a racist. Confident in this self-knowledge and self-righteousness, Jimmy Carter could run a Wallacite, red-necking campaign. As he saw it, he was being "tough" and realistic. As a small boy selling peanuts, when he had been tricked by a wise guy, he learned to toughen himself; he didn't intend to be taken again. George Wallace, in his first campaign for governor of Alabama, had run as a racial moderate; Wallace got whipped, and he swore he would not be "outniggered" the second time. Jimmy Carter in his second try seemed to take the same path, walking a tightrope between appealing to the Wallace voter and actually embracing Wallace's ideas. But Carter was not just a sophisticated, scrubbed-up Wallace. Liberals, like Reg Murphy, who saw only overweening ambition and ruthlessness were seeing only a part of the character, not all of it.

Carter has, over time, developed authentic commitments, intrinsic to his character—as far as we can know it—and not to be discarded at convenience. Though he has his faults, he's not a hollow man. He's not a phony. In 1976, talking about the Georgia years, Carter remembered: "When I ran for governor in 1966 and 1970, I told people that conservatism did not mean racism. But if I had gone in and said, 'All of you are wrong. You shouldn't have done what you did. I'm better than you are,' . . . I wouldn't have been elected. I wouldn't have gotten more than 10 percent of the votes. The point I'm making is that the South, including Georgia, has moved forward primarily because it hasn't been put into the position of having to renounce itself. You've got to give people credit for the progress they make and the change in their attitudes."

His background led him to this position. Complex himself, he believed racial justice could not simply be classified black or white. In his own character, he comprehended both sides, and tried to reach out to as many voters as possible, the poor whites *and* the pro-Sanders blacks. By his lights he wanted to give everyone better leadership, starting from where *they* were. His critics could correctly point out that an Ellis Arnall and a Carl Sanders had been elected without red-neck appeals. But that avenue in 1970 was closed to a hungering Jimmy Carter. Critics can argue that Carter didn't *have* to win; a Sanders would have done just as well or better for the people of Georgia. But that, most emphatically, could not be an argument available for Jimmy Carter, so intent on winning. He had been born again, in part to drive out gnawing feelings of pride and selfishness. He could now, he said, take defeat without suffering a loss of self-esteem. But his new faith in his own goodness had given him another powerful spur. He had a mission, political and religious, and a zeal to match. He *had* to win now because he was good. He could tell himself that he was a better man after the born-again experience, and therefore even better qualified to govern with love and compassion. In this man of paradox, defeat had become both more acceptable and completely *un*acceptable at the same time. The paradox lives on in his Presidency.

IV

CARTER HAD RUN a coldly effective campaign against Sanders, based on a theme of Sanders' being in the pay of the Establishment, while he, Carter, was its enemy. He made a virtue of his outsider's role, where possible goading the Establishment, and especially the Atlanta *Journal* and *Constitution,* into attacking him. "We loved all their scurrilous cartoons," a Carter campaign manager said. In rural Georgia, Atlanta meant Sodom and Gomorrah, liberal *and* wealthy. Atlanta's opposition to Jimmy Carter helped elect him, so he went along with the red-neck image. But it bothered him. He knew himself to be a worldly, well-read, serious-minded man. He wanted the liberals to vote for him, just as he wanted the support of the blacks. Unlike more experienced politicians, who learn not to expect enemies to love them, Carter wanted it both ways. He made a personal attack on the editor Reg Murphy before, of all audiences, the Georgia Press Association—and with Murphy and his young daughter in the room. Too late he realized his mistake: "These attacks had a serious effect on some of our tentatively committed liberal and idealistic supporters who did not know me personally."

They didn't know him personally. If they had, they would have understood, since Carter believed—knew—that to know him personally would convince people of his goodness and high intentions. Anyone who had spent some time with him would realize that his implicitly racist campaign was only a realistic means to an idealistic end. The company of his supporters, and their reasons for supporting him, demonstrated this personal principle.

Some of his personal supporters, after all, *belonged* to the Atlanta Establishment. Philip Alston and his wife believed that Carter could end racial discrimination and strife in Georgia. Charles Kirbo, as a partner in King and Spalding, also belonged whenever he wished to. Personal qualities rather than policies attracted him to Carter: "I've just got absolute confidence in his ability, and I know that whatever the situation is he wouldn't back out of it; he'll hang in there and he wouldn't ever embarrass you . . . trying to make some money out of something, or being rude to people, being inconsiderate of people, things like that."

Other, younger men had been working up the professional ladder when they met Carter and felt both attraction and opportunity. Stuart Eizenstat, the son of an Atlanta shoe wholesaler, was twenty-seven when he met Carter in early 1970. After graduating in 1967 from Harvard Law, he became a researcher and speechwriter for Lyndon Johnson. Then he served as candidate research director for Hubert Humphrey in the 1968 campaign. He had returned to Georgia and joined the law firm of Powell, Goldstein, Frazer and Murphy, after clerking for a federal judge. Eizenstat sought out Carter in the candidate's modest offices in Atlanta. "He was informally dressed, and I talked to him I suppose for an hour and a half," Eizenstat remembers. "Then he called me back up and I talked to him again, and finally decided I would work for him. The thing that most interested me, as I look back upon it, was that this seemed to me a person who would be able to bridge the traditional rural-urban gap in the state of Georgia."

English-born Peter Bourne came to Georgia with his parents; his father was a doctor, and Bourne himself went to Emory University and Emory Medical School. Trained as a psychiatrist, he never practiced privately. During the civil rights period of the 1960s, he became a political activist and sat in at Rich's Department Store. Then he went off to Vietnam (where he did medical research on the problems of mental stress and use of drugs) and came home to join Vietnam Veterans Against the War and Vietnam Veterans for Eugene McCarthy. He marched in the streets of Chicago outside the Democratic National Convention in 1968 and vowed to be inside in 1972. In late 1969, he first met Jimmy Carter. Bourne remembers most of all "the intensity of Carter's interpersonal relations. He had an ability to fix on you, to look you in the eye, to make you the center of attention, to show you he was aware of you." Most politicians, Bourne noted, look around the room when they talk to you, looking over your shoulder, seeing who else might be there, ready to "trade up." Carter's concentration, that thirty seconds of individual attention he gives the person he's meeting, had a very powerful effect. Bourne also thought Carter could win in 1970. He impressed Bourne as the sort of man who could maintain relations with both black and white people. He could say to the blacks, "I understand your anxieties and your frustrations. I want to do justice." Face to face, blacks believed him. Then he could say to the whites, "Segregation is wrong. We have been guilty of injustice. But the past no longer matters. You are good people, and we now have to move ahead." Face to face with whites, Carter seemed to be able both to stimulate guilt and to give absolution.

Jody Powell and Hamilton Jordan got involved with Carter early in his political career, and in their own lives. They have had no other career but his. Hamilton Jordan came from Albany, Georgia. His grandfather, Hamilton McWhorter, had been president of the Georgia state senate, and an ally of Senator Richard Russell. Jordan went to the University of Georgia, majoring in political science. In the summer after his first year, he interned for Russell. In 1966, he heard candidate Jimmy Carter speak at an Elks Club. The speech, he thought, was mediocre—Carter mumbled and ran over his best lines. Still, Jordan remembered a certain strength of personality. He gave up his summer work spraying mosquitoes—a state political-patronage job—to work for Carter at fifty dollars a week. A foot soldier, really, he didn't get very close to the candidate during that short campaign, but the two stayed in touch. At the age of twenty-four, Jordan became the full-time manager of Carter's gubernatorial campaign. He later explained to a friend, "This is a man who goes to church on Sunday and believes it."

Jody Powell came from Vienna, Georgia, not too far from Plains. His father farmed, his mother taught school. He went to the Air Force Academy, where in 1964, in his senior year, he cheated on a history exam, stupidly and unnecessarily. The Air Force dismissed him. He came home—on Christmas Day—and, trying to pull his life together, studied political science at Georgia State University, then shifted to Emory University, and began to write a thesis on independent parties. He wrote Carter to get information about the thesis; Carter invited him to Plains, and then hired him to be his driver during the 1970 campaign. "My part of the state had turned out a lot of bombastic, racist politicians," he says, "and I felt Jimmy Carter might be able to change that."

Each man, in his turn, testifies to Carter's personal qualities. One-on-one, he made a lasting impression on his immediate supporters far beyond the ordinary, and generally at first exposure. Naturally, as supporters talking to interviewers, they can't be expected to put down their candidate—and, in some cases, their meal ticket. But unless they had joined in a group rehearsal, in which everyone learned a written part, his supporters, individually, offer a common picture that registers true. Carter reconciles opposites. Eizenstat talked about Carter's bridging the gap between rural and urban; Bourne spoke of bringing together the two races. Kirbo favored winning in Vietnam, no matter what it took; Bourne joined

Vietnam Veterans Against the War—and both men supported
Carter. Complex himself, possessed of his own contradictory nature, Jimmy Carter could serve as a common point for complex
and opposing goals.

V

THE FACT THAT Carter as campaigner or as President does
not qualify as "populist," using the strictest definition of the term,
ought not to close off understanding of what he has in mind. Strict
populism involved a radical criticism of finance capitalism and, at
certain times and with certain advocates, the desire to overthrow
that system. Carter patently does not have "pure" populism in
mind when he speaks of being a populist. It would be extremely
hypocritical, if not impossible, for Carter to advocate any such
program; Carters have been credit merchants and among the biggest landowners in Sumter County since Mr. Earl's prime. As
Lawrence Goodwyn, a leading student of populism in America,
has argued, from the traditional populist perspective, the Carters
"are part of the problem, and not part of the solution."

But Carter's use of populist symbolism—his expressed concerns for the workingman, his attacks on the citified Sanders or
Big Oil, his appeals to anti-Establishment feelings—make him
what can be called a "stylistic populist." During his 1970 campaigns, and at critical points in his Presidency, Carter embraced
the style of populism, rather than its content. In place of an economic program for change, Carter, to many listeners, seems to be
venting a generalized *resentment* about the power structures of
Atlanta and Washington. Some of the traditional populists knew
resentment, too, with disastrous consequences.

Populism started as a protest movement in the 1870s and
1880s, sparked by desperate times, especially the farm depression.
The severe drop in agricultural prices put thousands of farmers
into debt bondage—the infamous lien system that forced them to
mortgage their produce to merchants and bankers before planting
time. Gradually, a Farmers Alliance took shape. The Alliance sent
out "lecturers" to convert others, started newspapers, and conducted a grass roots campaign in the Southwest and the South. It

soon claimed a quarter million members. Populists advocated a "free" silver currency—cheap money. By 1892, the populists, now organized politically, ran James B. Weaver for President; he won more than a million popular votes and twenty-two electoral votes.

In 1896, populists joined with the Democratic Party and backed William Jennings Bryan. His "cross of gold" campaign, and the advocacy of free silver, nailed the populists to a hopeless plank. With the election of Cleveland, the populist movement faded as an effective political force. Populism survived mainly as a myth, and a generalized inspiration that defied the normal categories of political description. Jimmy Carter also defied the usual political categories. In 1970s Georgia, stylistic populism could strike a resonant chord; its vagueness, bypassing the usual liberal-conservative split, appealed to groups otherwise divided in attitude or interest. It evoked values held in common by groups that are otherwise apart.

The other, *resenting* side of populists allowed opposition to Eastern domination to slide into strident anti–Wall Street rhetoric and then into anti-Semitism (because the Jews supposedly controlled the big international banks). Anti-black feelings inevitably grew, out of frustrations, and because the blacks, everyone knew, were part of a Jewish plot to pollute the white race. One man, as much as anybody, embodied all these emotionally charged attitudes; he came from Georgia, professed populism and then became a virulent hater. That man, Tom Watson, claimed the friendship of Jimmy Carter's revered grandfather, the redoubtable Jim Jack Gordy. Populism, as myth and inspiration, was part of Carter's background. Once Carter emerged on the national scene, the fear that he might be, or become, the stereotypical Southern Baptist small-town bigot haunted non-Southerners who may never have heard of Watson or read a word about populism. Tom Watson, however, hovers ghostlike behind Jimmy Carter.

VI

WATSON, BORN IN 1856, saw the destruction visited on the Old South by the Civil War. His family's agrarian life—based on slaves—ended at the hands of Yankee capitalism. Watson's father could not restore the family fortunes. His mother read to him and inspired him to the life of the mind. A shy child, he learned to cover over his shyness with determination. He studied law, earned a reputation as a trial orator, sympathized with the poor and oppressed, and grew wealthy in his practice. He attacked the railroads, corrupt politicians, and the Establishment, as well as industrial visions of the "New South." Watson looked back to agrarian communitarianism, to the Jeffersonian vision of democracy. His enemies accused him of being "communist." He in turn denounced racism as a device to subvert yeoman democracy. Although he opposed the excesses and monopolistic growth of capitalism, he accepted the basic capitalistic system. "Keep the avenues of honor free," Watson declared. "Close no entrance to the poorest, the weakest, the humblest. Say to ambition everywhere, 'The field is clear, the contest fair; come and win your share if you can!' "

He ran for Congress in 1890 and won; in Washington, the committee system frustrated him. He did manage to put through Rural Free Delivery mail service (Jim Jack Gordy's favorite idea). In 1892, running for a second term, he lost in a flagrantly fraudulent election. With the right effort, he might have been able to overturn the result; instead, he stood on his idealism, wrapping himself in self-righteousness, and went down in defeat. In 1896, he opposed the affiliation of the populists with Bryan, and watched his political base disintegrate around him.

He had just turned forty. For several years he remained a political recluse. Frustrated and depressed, he began to see himself betrayed everywhere. On his re-entrance to public life, he seemed a changed man. He could find no effective therapy for his distress except in virulent hatred. He started a journal called *Tom Watson's Magazine,* and became a power again in Georgia. This time his oratory contained the message of hate—hatred of the Negro, hatred of the Jew, hatred of capitalism—as well as sympathy for the poor. He defended the lynching of Negroes; his words sent hundreds of Georgians into the streets of Macon, outside the trial of Leo Frank, a Jewish businessman accused of seducing and killing a Christian employee. The mob lynched Frank, and the story, told and retold in novels and motion pictures, made Watson the model demagogue of the South.

Carter, not surprisingly, doesn't see Tom Watson when he looks in his mirror. He told a reporter that he could be counted "a populist in the tradition of Richard Russell." Running for governor in 1970, it would be natural for Carter to evoke the name of Georgia's longtime United States Senator, a distinguished (as he was invariably called) figure and one of the five or six men who ran the Senate. But five years later, Carter repeated his admiration for the "populism" of Russell, and cited the Senator's sponsorship of the 1946 School Lunch Act.

Russell's courtly manners, personal wealth, and enormous power as chairman of the Senate Armed Services Committee made him an unlikely populist figure. He was a staunch segregationist, but in his grandee's manner. As governor of Georgia in the early 1930s, he had reorganized the administration. In 1948, opponents of a pro–civil rights plank at the Democratic Party convention rallied behind Russell and nominated him for President. He won all of the votes of all of the Confederate states (except a part of the North Carolina delegation) and lost to Harry Truman. In 1952, he began running for President early, with the same result, losing to the liberal Adlai E. Stevenson.

Hamilton Jordan, who had interned with Russell, remembered him as the "best of the Old South—a great man." Carter had long cultivated Russell's patronage, ever since the Senator helped him get out of the Navy when Mr. Earl died. According to Carter, the two met frequently during the 1970 race, and Russell advised him how to run a frugal campaign. "He told me one time that he spent $4800 on his whole gubernatorial campaign in 1930," Carter recalled. Although the Republican candidate in the general election, Hal Suit, eulogized Russell and courted his support, Russell endorsed Carter and the straight Democratic ticket.

A "populism" so flexible that it can be applied to the careers of Richard Russell and Tom Watson cannot have much meaning. If anything, Carter brings Watson and Russell up to date, and in line with contemporary political realities. Watson's South—and Russell's—no longer exists, practically speaking; black voters, in close statewide elections, may hold the balance of electoral power, and Carter prudently campaigned to pick up whatever black votes he could. Practically, too, gubernatorial and senatorial campaigns now require large cash outlays for television time and staff organization; "radical" candidates scare off the big-money contributors needed to mount a modern media campaign. Quiet prudence paid off here, too. The Atlanta Establishment, the "target" of Carter's populist rhetoric in 1970, felt itself far enough removed from any real bull's-eye to invest in a Carter victory. Hedging political bets has always been a good business practice: support both sides so that whoever wins will be indebted to you. If some of the Establishment, willingly or grudgingly, gave to Carter, he swallowed his slogans and received what they gave, though in deep secrecy. Not until six years later, under intense pressure, did Carter make public his 1970 contributors list.

The question of who helped Carter came up during the 1970 campaign partly because Carter had accused Sanders of accepting large corporate contributions. A reporter asked Carter if he had received any large corporate contributions. Carter acknowledged that he had; but the man who campaigned on openness in government refused to say how much they amounted to or whom they were from. Legally, he didn't have to, because Georgia law in effect at the time did not require disclosure. During the 1976 campaign, when Carter was asked about the contribution list, he said that because there was no disclosure law in Georgia "nobody ever made a report of contributors and we didn't maintain those records." Journalist Phil Stanford checked with two accountants who worked for Carter's campaign in 1970; both told him that the campaign organization kept records of all contributions. One of them, Richard Harden, a C.P.A. whom Governor Carter later appointed to a position in his administration, said that the contribution lists were kept by computer, and that Carter's campaign managers received a monthly printout of all contributors.

When the "missing tapes" were produced in October 1976, they showed that some 4800 contributors had given a total of about $690,000. Philip Alston and his wife contributed $7276; David Gambrell, his wife, and his father gave $5000; Robert Lipshutz, who served as Carter's campaign treasurer, gave $6000. Bert and LaBelle Lance gave $1500. The largest single contribution came from Ann Cox Chambers, chairman of the board of the Cox Broadcasting Company, and her husband, Robert (the Cox newspapers, the Atlanta *Constitution* and *Journal*, had editorially opposed Carter). Also, $4995 came from Delta Airlines, and $4000 from the

Coca-Cola board chairman, J. Paul Austin. Most of the contributions over $500 came in late in the campaign, when Carter looked like the winner. ("You are sort of buying equal treatment," one Georgian told the New York *Times*.) However, others in the Atlanta Establishment, including Richard B. Rich, the department store magnate, and Mills Lane, the flamboyant banker, gave Carter nothing. His populism didn't bother them. They just didn't believe Carter had a chance against Sanders.

As in Carter's Quitman County fight eight years before, his 1970 campaign did not pit the "pure" outsiders against the insiders in storybook fashion. As with much of American electoral politics, one group of insiders opposed another group of insiders who were *in a little more*. Lawyers, corporations, and "big shots" helped make Jimmy Carter a big man. But he didn't forget he had been one of the little people. In politics, style can become substance; a leader leads as much from the impressions he creates in the minds of his followers as from formal authority. Political style, in turn, reflects character, emotions, habits of mind, personal demeanor. Emotionally, Jimmy Carter's identification with the underdog exists, right alongside the reality of his wealth and position. As governor and as President, he has the power to act about matters of substance as well as style.

13

"A Great Urge
to Govern"

"THE TIME FOR racial discrimination is past," Jimmy Carter declared when he was inaugurated governor of Georgia. The year was 1971, hardly a time when such a declaration would sound revolutionary. Coming from Carter, who had moved so effectively to the right in order to win the governorship, the words startled many people. Some Carter supporters thought that he had been slightly ashamed of the way his campaign had been conducted and that he wanted to start his term on a higher plane. They argued that his race-politics tactics had been just that to him, a means to get elected in a "sinful world." In office, he could convert the people to good ends.

Carter's years as governor and President test his goodness as a *governor*—a justification for hardball campaigns—and his conviction that he could lead the people forward. The task of governing demands other attributes besides goodness of intentions—the qualities, for example, of the lion and the fox and the serpent, as Carter has been finding out.

II

RACIAL MODERATION, once in office, made sense for Carter and the other New South Democratic governors elected in the late 1960s and early 1970s. The Republican Party, pursuing the Southern strategy of Goldwater in 1964 and Nixon in 1968 and 1972, had staked out the reactionary-right ground in the states of the old Confederacy. The long-term trends ran toward enlightenment for Democrats. After the 1964 Voting Rights Act, black registration in the South went from 2 million voters to 3.5 million (though still only about 50 percent of the potential). Lyndon Johnson had shown the path to the new order. Though not a Southerner, strictly speaking, a part of him, as his biographer Eric Goldman noted, "belonged to Dixie." Once President, Johnson sent his own persistent message to the South, both publicly and still more privately, telling it to let up on "nigra nigra" and concentrate on economic and social advancement. In the end, the message got through and the South was ready to join the nation's political mainstream.

Now, a deep Southerner could think about running for, and winning, the Presidency. Paradoxically, this began to happen when Southern control of the Congress through the party seniority system had begun to crumble. Senators like Richard Russell or J. William Fulbright with narrow Old South bases couldn't realistically run to win. But a new crop of moderate Southern governors were now perceived as qualified national candidates. Bumpers of Arkansas, Askew of Florida, Carter of Georgia, among others, represented the new politicians of the New South; and *Time* magazine put Carter's face on its cover in 1971 to tell the nation of the exciting new breed.

Did the governor of Georgia stand head and shoulders above the governor of Florida or the governor of Arkansas? Or was it partly that *Time* had a major news bureau in Atlanta, convenient to Carter? It was perhaps as much geography as anything else, for in many ways the new breed all resembled one another—attractive black-eyed peas in a Southern pod.

III

THE BUSINESS and industrial boom came to Arkansas in the 1950s, a little later and with less force than it had hit Georgia and other Sun Belt states. The transitional figure in Arkansas, Orval Faubus, had become governor in 1954. Faubus' country-hick name concealed a go-getter's personality; he spent money on schools and industrial development programs, and acquired a reputation as a governor "close to the people," who knew what people were thinking. He was also one of the first governors to use public opinion research to track his legislative programs. At Little Rock in 1957, Faubus defied a federal court order to integrate the high school and lost in the facedown with President Eisenhower. He could win three more terms as governor but go no further beyond Arkansas.

In 1966, Republican Winthrop Rockefeller succeeded Faubus, getting elected by a coalition of blacks and moderate Democrats. Rockefeller had no legislative support and a severe drinking problem; he slowly declined in popularity. By 1970, polls showed that almost any moderate Democrat could best him. Enter handsome Dale Bumpers with the backing of Senator Fulbright. Bumpers came from a town of 2000, where he was the sole practicing attorney. He had served as school board chairman, taught Sunday school, and directed the choir at the Methodist Church. He also had run for state legislator and lost. Against Rockefeller, he won by a two-to-one margin. Governor Bumpers pushed a government reorganization plan that, he claimed, consolidated sixty-five state agencies into thirteen. A poll in 1974 showed him with a 91 percent approval rating among voters, and he ran for the U.S. Senate, winning against his old patron Fulbright. The national commentators noted his "soft-spoken effectiveness and winning smile" and counted him perhaps the most promising new political figure to emerge nationally from the South.

Reubin Askew of Florida won similar notices. Florida is both Old South and New South, with hundreds of thousands of migrants and retired people from the North. Though Floridians rejected

Goldwater in 1964—he appeared to threaten Social Security—they supported both Eisenhower and Nixon. In 1966, the state elected a Republican, Claude Kirk, as governor. (A high school student from Jacksonville named Pat Caddell did some polling for television and later wrote his senior honors thesis at Harvard about the election.) Kirk pushed for change and a favorable climate for industrial development, but, like Rockefeller, he blundered and ended up alienating voters. In 1970, the forty-two-year-old Askew led a reorganized Democratic Party to victory with 57 percent of the vote. Georgia had abolished its county-unit system in 1966. Florida's similar "one man, one vote" reapportionment in 1967 gave additional power to the growing urban areas and broke the hold of the rural counties. Askew impressed voters as extremely hardworking and ascetic; a non-drinking, non-smoking Presbyterian elder, he brought his religious beliefs to politics. He favored racial harmony and integration for reasons of religious conviction: "I think that your faith has to be at the center of your life, and from it must emanate all of your decisions." Once governor, he appointed blacks to his administration at all levels. "Reubin Who?" the newspapers had scoffed at first. He had campaigned for tax reform, complete public financial disclosure for candidates, and opposition to the special interests. He had appealed to the "Wallace vote" with a different pitch, introducing a corporate income tax and repealing repressive sales taxes. He took the progressive position on the environment, talked up administrative efficiency, and supported sunshine laws to open up government processes. He could smile a New South smile. His fellow governors liked him as well as did liberals in general.

Neither Askew nor Bumpers went anyplace. In Bumpers' case, Arkansas seemed too rural a state; only Little Rock has a population of over 100,000. Supposedly he lacked bold leadership qualities. A standing joke in Little Rock went: If you ask Dale Bumpers if he is wishy-washy, he'll reply, "Maybe I am and maybe I'm not."

Askew, apparently, didn't want to be President badly enough. While politics, he said, "is very much a part of my life . . . I don't have to be in it." When he keynoted the 1972 Democratic National Convention, he sent word to George McGovern that he was not interested in the vice presidential nomination. Friends say his wife didn't want him to run.

IV

GOVERNOR JIMMY CARTER of Georgia talked the same language of government reorganization, tax reform, open government, environment, racial harmony, and opposition to the special interests. By all objective accounts, he made a good New South governor, perhaps no better than any other of the new breed but certainly better than his predecessor Maddox. If Lester Maddox, the restaurant owner who passed out pick handles to his customers to keep blacks out, proved that anybody could be elected governor of Georgia, he also showed that the governor didn't have all that much to do. One of Maddox's major campaigns as governor took aim at street-vending boxes for the Atlanta newspapers; Maddox attempted to ban the machines from the capitol grounds. The Georgia legislature also didn't suffer from overwork, meeting in session forty-five days a year. Half of that time—the first two or three weeks—involved the budget hearings. Frank Moore, who worked on legislative liaison for Governor Carter (and later for President Carter in Washington), remembered how casually the Georgia lawmakers worked: "Things just happened, just compressed, in the Georgia legislature. . . . I've seen bills drafted, introduced, passed, and signed into law in three days there. Scratched, I mean, off the back of an envelope."

The business they conducted tended to be cozy. Officials deposited state funds at favored banks around Georgia. Department heads ran state agencies like personal fiefdoms, with jobs to pass out to the politically faithful. For state employees, recalls Don Young, a radio news director who covered the Carter Administration, "there wasn't too much to do, and fortunately, not too much money to spend." When Governor Jimmy Carter came into office sounding the New South doctrines about government reorganization, skeptics around the state house took that to mean the traditional political reorganization—throwing *their* rascals out and throwing *our* rascals in.

Jimmy Carter carried special burdens in office in addition to the governor's normal lot. The Georgia legislature was a predominantly conservative body—Maddox people—whose leaders had tasted power in 1966 when they chose between Maddox and Callaway in the election. The liberals, in turn, could be counted Sanders people, with no initial love for Carter. The handful of black legislators, such as Julian Bond, retained their skepticism of Carter from the campaign. And presiding as president of the state senate sat Lester Maddox, Carter's lieutenant governor. In the primaries, Carter had praised Maddox for bringing a "high standard of forthright expression and personal honesty to the governor's office." Maddox, he said, was "the essence of the Democratic party. . . . He has compassion for the ordinary man." The words represented the least attractive consequences of wanting to win and of positive thinking—Carter's expediency and his proneness to exaggeration.

In the campaign, he had needed Maddox supporters; as governor, his major opponent would be Maddox. Lester Maddox never had to dissemble about Jimmy Carter. Maddox disliked Carter from their first encounter in 1966. As Maddox told us, "He impressed me as trying to mislead the voters as to what he believed and where he stood on issues . . . if he hadn't lied to get elected governor, he never would have been elected." Carter, Maddox confessed, did have some good points: "I think he's a master of politics; he exceeds all the others that I've known." But, added Maddox, Carter is driven by "madness for power . . . if you oppose him, he'll crush or destroy anything or anybody that gets in his path." This was the man with whom Jimmy Carter would have to work as governor.

Carter's way of dealing with Lt. Gov. Maddox was, characteristically, to hold in his anger. Carter controlled his temper, worked directly with some legislators, and tried to use his intelligence and his state senator's knowledge of the structure of Georgia government to outwit Maddox and his supporters. In his first move as governor, he asked for power to reorganize the administration. He really meant reorganization and not shaking loose some jobs to reward campaign workers. Bypassing the usual politicians and lawyers, Carter also set up study groups made up of business executives, professional consultants, and men and women from various state agencies. He worked his study groups hard, setting seemingly impossible deadlines and digging into the niggling details of the bureaucracy himself.

Reorganization became the most publicized of Carter's

claimed achievements as governor. He proclaimed successes in reducing the number of state agencies, in saving money, and increasing efficiency. In his speeches and autobiography he said he found 300 state agencies, "and we abolished 278 of them!" According to Carter, every major department had its own independent computer system; his administration created just one central system. Each large or small agency had its own printing system; his administration merged forty-three of them into one system. All of this happened, he said, without one merit system employee being discharged because of government reorganization. Instead, he filled only a portion of the vacancies when they occurred through normal attrition.

All public officials cherish such statistical achievements. In 1803, Napoleon of France combined three hundred of the independent principalities of the Holy Roman Empire into about one hundred. In the eyes of Carter's critics, his accomplishments resemble less Napoleon's than those of Czarist Russia's Potemkin —a facade of words behind which business went on as usual. There were only sixty-five budgeted agencies when he began. The number of state employees increased from 34,322 to 42,000 during Carter's gubernatorial term. Most of the agencies abolished were small, or else they were not actually abolished but placed as subagencies in one of the new departments. These departments, according to Carter's critics, were monsters of inefficiency, impressive only on an organizational chart. Budget reductions, when looked at closely, turn out to be paper reductions, with the actual amounts spent increasing.

In fact, almost two dozen states since 1965 have been reorganized. Most specialists point out that the results do not turn up in the balance sheets. Reorganization has been primarily a management tool for gaining control of bureaucracies. When states regroup existing agencies under a smaller number of department heads, they intend to increase accountability to the chief executive. They do not intend to eliminate government employees.

Carter also claimed a 50 percent saving in administrative costs and a budget surplus of $116 million. When Phil Stanford asked Carter's campaign staff for something to substantiate the 50 percent saving, he was told that "no such statistics are available." No one in the Georgia state government has such statistics, either, according to Stanford. Carter did indeed leave office with a surplus of $116 million—$13 million more than when he took office; but during Carter's term in office the state debt increased $205 million.

The figures, good *and* bad, actually have little real meaning, since they all have to take into account normal inflation and increasing costs on one side and an expanding economy and increasing revenues on the other side.

Some of Carter's actions have worked better than others. He put the state's cash balances up for competitive bank bidding in time deposits, rather than letting them sit uselessly in a few favored banks; and as a result he increased annual state revenues by some $2 million. While this sort of management of the state's cash balances had been developing when Carter came into office, nevertheless he got it done. He also did a good job of improving Georgia's crony-ridden judicial system, though it got less attention than other changes. Carter relied on expert advice and assistance and created a Governor's Commission on Judicial Processes. Its chairman had a good deal of autonomy, unlike other study groups, where Carter ran the show. The commission produced a judicial nominating system in which the governor selects judicial appointees from a list supplied by members of the state bar instead of appointing them through the old buddy system.

Carter, of course, didn't forget his friends and supporters. He appointed Bert Lance as commissioner of transportation. The job carried great potential political power, since the commissioner makes decisions on where roads will be built, who builds them, and who gets employed in their building. A memo, marked "Personal and Confidential," and coming "From the Desk of Jimmy Carter, May 26, 1972," shows how the governor and Lance played the political game of rewards for service. Carter's cousin Hugh, the state senator and proprietor of the worm farm in Plains, faced re-election:

Bert: Hugh Carter has contacted me regarding a highway project in his district. Hugh would like to see the Lee County end of the Americus–Lee Street Road resurfaced as soon as possible. This road runs from Leesburg to Americus—parallel to Highway 19.

Hugh would like to be involved in the announcement when a definite decision has been made as to when a contract will be sent to the county. The portion of the road in Lee County is what Hugh is particularly interested in as that is where Hugh's opponent is living. Jimmy.

V

JIMMY CARTER'S HELP for Cousin Hugh with road repairing demonstrates merely that New South governors also understood how state funds, judiciously and legally applied, can smooth over possible chafing by voters before a local election. The big effort, however, involved Thomas Bertram Lance, the associate Carter called his closest friend in the world, though they had known each other only since 1966.

Carter wanted his friend Lance to succeed him as governor. Physically, they seemed like opposites: Lance, a bear of a man weighing well over 200 pounds, expansive, a glad-hander ("I never met a man I didn't like"); Carter, small, contained, careful. But Lance also came from rural Georgia. His father, president of Young Harris College, a tiny Methodist school in the northeast of the state, had also been an important personage, a big man in his small community. Lance, too, had wanted to get away from home. He had boyhood dreams of going to sea, his wife, LaBelle, reports in her inspirational Christian book, *This Too Shall Pass.* Lance, too, possessed that contrary combination of defensiveness and pride in his small-town origins. He, too, had been a born-again Christian. He took his Methodism seriously, and the Carters and the Lances often went to each other's churches. Lance, too, had an awesome drive for success. "I've always tried to set some goal," he once told an interviewer. "I wanted to be better than anybody in the banking business." His religious experience gave him a strong sense of righteousness, the optimistic conviction that everything always works out if "pertinaciously pursued." He combined his religious piety with business, as Carter had combined his religious piety with politics. But Lance had no time for Niebuhr or dour philosophy; every day in every way did seem to get better and better for him.

Lance married LaBelle David, a bank president's daughter, in

1951, and started as a teller in the family bank. He mastered the intricacies of banking, as Carter had mastered nuclear submarines. Leveraging loans and pyramiding holdings, he eventually created the National Bank of Georgia, which grew to become the fifth-largest bank in the state. By the time he left Atlanta in 1976 to go to Washington with Carter, he was earning $450,000 a year and could afford a mansion outside of Atlanta worth a reputed $2 million. LaBelle Lance called the place "Butterfly Manna." The butterfly, she explained, was her symbol, and manna acknowledged that the Lord had sent fortune to the Lances.

The Lord also takes away. Like many another family, including the children of Lillian and James Earl Carter, the Lances' optimism-piety has been sorely tested by personal tragedy. LaBelle Lance's brother, Beverly Banks David, who had been involved with Bert Lance in the National Bank of Georgia, committed suicide in 1975. Even earlier, the Lances and their family of four children suffered; her life has been touched, as LaBelle Lance wrote in her book, "by such human afflictions as alcoholism, drugs, broken homes, death, violence, serious illness, car accidents, jailing, homosexuality, murder, adultery, and runaway children."

While Carter and Lance had much in common personally, Lance took these qualities to extremes. What worked for Carter in the governor's race in 1970 couldn't work for Lance in 1974. The banks, the newspapers, and the rest of the Atlanta business establishment supported Lance as they hadn't Carter; but George Busbee, his opponent, got the rural and red-neck vote. Just as Carter had hung the label "Cuff Links Carl" on his rival Sanders, so, too, Busbee had hit upon the catchy "Loophole Lance." Loose, free-wheeling Lance had opened two accounts at his Calhoun bank to finance his campaign. The bank also paid bills for Lance's campaign activities totaling $78,000 and listed them as "bank expenses." Later, these practices came under scrutiny of the Comptroller of the Currency and were found to be so serious a matter that they were referred to the Justice Department for possible prosecution. The same Comptroller's report confirmed that the Calhoun bank permitted, routinely, large overdrafts by bank officers and their relatives. In May 1979, Lance was indicted on thirty-three counts by a Federal grand jury for violation of banking laws.

Lance could reply that he repaid the bank for his campaign funds in installments—though it took him months to do so. Perhaps he had been a little more expansive than fussy bank examiners might want. He knew he was right, a country slicker from the mountains of northern Georgia beating the big-city boys at the money game by bending the rules just a bit (as Carter had beaten Sanders in 1970 by playing hardball).

In the campaign, Busbee beat Lance by outslickering him. Busbee got Lance to disclose his net worth. Lance proudly reported assets over $3 million, though some people suspected he padded the figure. Kited or not, the disclosure didn't help Lance with the voters that Carter had courted; as the commentator Garry Wills shrewdly observed, "It says something about a political figure when he claims more wealth than is good for his campaign." Busbee won, narrowly.

VI

As CARTER'S COMMISSIONER of transportation, Lance had run a department free of scandal and he won the praise of the Reg Murphys and the Maddoxites alike. The major controversy of the Carter gubernatorial administration—generating more disagreement than the general reorganization plan—centered on the Department of Human Resources. Tedious as these matters may be to the non-expert, Human Resources reflected a central part of Carter's emerging ideas of running government. He had always seemed open to the complaint that he had concerned himself solely with winning and working and had no serious political ideas. James Fallows, leaving Carter's employ after two years, would repeat that charge about the Carter White House. Carter's Department of Human Resources, at least, pleased political scientists; it had a philosophy—the concept of the "troubled Georgian." Carter wanted one central agency where a troubled person could go. Previously, the sick troubled Georgian went to the Department of Public Health; the unemployed troubled Georgian went to the Department of Labor for unemployment compensation and help in finding a job and to the Manpower Training Program for job training; the disabled troubled Georgian or the single-parent troubled

Georgian went to the Department of Family and Children Services. Each had been set up not to help people in trouble but to deal with specific kinds of trouble. Carter wanted to help the whole person. It was a *personal* matter for him.

The department foundered immediately. District health directors fought county health departments; mental health workers fought social workers; doctors fought administrators. No one had figured out how the new mammoth agency related to local agencies.

Carter's own version holds that "Naturally, there was intense opposition from the bureaucrats who thrived on confusion, from special interests who preferred to work in the dark, and from a few legislative leaders who did not want to see their fiefdoms endangered. But the people insisted on the changes, and they were made." To be entirely accurate, it was Jimmy Carter, in the name of the people, who insisted on the changes; ordinary people—the social workers, not high-level bureaucrats—opposed his plan. Differences of opinion existed among good professional people, and not just special interests, about what exactly to do and how to do it. The same situation reappears in his Presidency, as when he blames "special interests" for opposing energy conservation. Excoriating the enemies of the people, exaggerating his own gains, Jimmy Carter stays in character. He needs to keep up his own spirits; only if he believes that he really is succeeding can he continue to put out the work and energy necessary to produce change. In the best positive-think manner, he confuses wish with accomplishment. Carter declares, "When I was governor of Georgia, I cut government costs by fifty percent." In "translation," he means, "I ordered that the government be cut fifty percent." Yet, on balance, Georgia state government benefited from reorganization, as other Deep South states did, when brought into the second half of the twentieth century by the new breed of governors.

Jerry Rafshoon calls Carter a "softie" with a special compassion for children. Former speechwriter Pat Anderson remembers a visit to a home for retarded children that was so painful to Anderson that he had to turn away, while Carter talked intently with the children.

Some associates give a pragmatic explanation for Carter's concern about the troubled and poor. "It's an area in Georgia that has been grossly neglected, so it was natural for him to be interested," says Stuart Eizenstat. Back home in Plains, Georgia, the "afflicted child" had to go to Atlanta for psychotherapy. Plains had no psychiatric services, no mental health facilities—not even a pharmacist, Carter declared during his presidential campaign. "I can go two hundred yards from my house, where people are so poor when they get sick, it's almost impossible for them to get a doctor."

Carter didn't have to go that far. He knew of sister Gloria's boy, of sister Ruth's breakdown; of brother Billy's demons; and of his own depression. Jimmy Carter's family, too, had personal experiences with drugs. His son Jack, a Navy enlisted man, had been forced to resign when caught smoking marijuana. Carter's policies, then, do not take shape in a political, social, or cultural vacuum, or on a reorganization chart. They involve real people, with all their feelings and quirkiness. Through the successes and failures, Jimmy Carter's governor's characteristics reoccur—his intelligence and his dedication to managerial techniques, as well as his exaggerations and his fixation on control; his drive to win and his compassion for poor and afflicted people. Staying in character, the man who can't stand to lose worries about the "losers" in the competitive society.

VII

GOVERNORS MUST WORK with others to achieve goals; Governor Carter's record in this regard contains few successes. He wouldn't horse-trade. His critics said this showed he was overly proud and stiff-necked; his supporters thought it meant he was incorruptible. His biggest difficulties came when working—rather, not working—with the Maddox-minded legislature. According to Neal R. Peirce, a specialist on local and state governments, "Carter drove most of his priority programs through the Georgia Legislature in a high-handed manner. He resorted to the media to ridicule the lawmaking branch, creating many lasting antagonisms in the process. He often went over the legislators' heads—to the 'people'—to generate public support for his proposals."

His liaison with the legislature ranged from bad to poor. Julian Bond, the Georgia state senator and former civil rights leader, remembers one time when Carter wanted a bill passed. The black legislators could have been the key, "so he had us all down in his office. But while we were down there talking to him, the speaker called it up and it lost while he had the notes necessary to pass it down in his office." Bond, no fan of Carter, thought the probable reason for the bad liaison lay in Carter's personality, his inability to be really "in" with his legislative leaders.

Peirce, and other students of the governor years, found Carter's cabinet and staff appointments disappointing generally, with the notable exception of his judiciary choices. One explanation might have been that Georgia state salaries were so low that it was hard to recruit top talent. But, Maddox excepted, other recent Georgia governors were thought to have done better, although even Carter's severest critics credit him with a consumer-oriented administration and for making historic advances in appointing blacks to state positions.

In another area, the environment, he offered something for both the conservationists and the developers. For the conservationists, he rode rivers in rafts, canoes, and kayaks; he and his wife studied wildlife programs at game preserves and inspected virgin cypress groves on the Altamaha River. He worked to preserve the scenic Chattahoochee River from developers. At the same time, he also posed as a friend of business and of industrial developers; and they, in turn, treated him as a friend. Banker Mills B. Lane—Mr. Atlanta—lent Governor Carter his yacht as a floating hotel suite during the 1972 Democratic National Convention in Miami Beach, though he hadn't voted for him. In mid-November 1972, Carter traveled to a hunting lodge as a guest of the Brunswick Pulp and Paper Company, a corporation very much involved in environmental regulations. He also accepted a free hunting outfit made by "Game Winner," a Georgia sports clothing firm.

Most of these perquisites came to Carter before the Nixon Watergate revelations and various congressional scandals caused public officials to be more sensitive to possible conflicts of interest. From Carter's point of view, he felt secure in his belief that he acted in the public good. On a South American trip in a Lockheed Corporation aircraft, for example, he talked up the virtues of the made-in-Georgia Lockheed C-130, hoping to create more jobs for Georgians by selling more planes.

He didn't feed at the public trough or live ostentatiously, as some officials have been known to do. Carter saw himself not only as a "no deal" man, but as a man of simple, even spartan, tastes. He and his wife permitted few trappings of power in the governor's mansion. He neither accepted the gaudier invitations of Atlanta society—one source of the Establishment's disdain for him—nor invited society to state parties. His aide Landon Butler regarded it as a matter of cultural tastes. Though Carter is "a businessman himself," Butler told us, "he just didn't pal around with the country club set."

Though a businessman, Carter as governor is more than another managerial-minded New South businessman in politics. He minds the store, but is also mindful of poverty and injustice. This contrary combination disturbs his fellow entrepreneurs and puzzles political observers. Carter is a Christianlike "governor" as well as a businesslike administrator and must be understood in those terms.

VIII

HIS FRIEND Philip Alston understood this fundamental point. "Jimmy Carter is a student of history, and he reads prolifically," he told us. "He's got a very retentive mind, and with that background it has come to him—it probably doesn't come to everybody with those qualities—but it has come to him a great urge to govern. . . . He thinks in the process of governing he can improve the quality of life around him. 'Thinks' is a great understatement; he knows he can. He hasn't got any doubt about it." Carter's confidence in his self-confidence seemed confirmed by his governorship; his success, as he saw it, encouraged him to think about governing the United States. "I'm persuaded that Jimmy simply likes the process of governing," Alston concludes.

We are persuaded, as well. Jimmy Carter, too, sees himself as a "governor," rather than a politician. "When elected governor of Georgia," he once said, "I went to Atlanta not as a politician—

although I like the word and am not trying to avoid it—but as an engineer, a planner, a scientist, and a businessman." He now enjoys politics, but mostly as a means to another end—"a fine avenue for the utilization of what talent and ability I have."

As State Senator Carter, he had a limited power, over a limited constituency; as Governor Carter, he presided over an enlarged, though still limited, dominion. His basic character stayed the same as he moved to higher office, but the scope of power and the number of people he could affect did change. "When I was on the Sumter County school board," Carter said to us, "the only people I was concerned about was the schoolchildren in Sumter County. Later, I got to be a state senator; I had seven counties. Later, I got to be governor; I had 159 counties. And you obviously grow in your sense of a broader range of responsibility on your shoulders, and you have to accommodate more wider adverse viewpoints when you have to find a conclusion on a public matter." The more people Carter serves, the more he accommodates. As President, he has been so accommodating to other views that he has been judged without vision of his own. The Carter Administration, as ex-speech writer Fallows has complained, wants to do fifty things but no one thing.

Governor Carter had tested himself on a middle level of power and accommodation. He wanted more power to help a bigger flock. Personally, of course, by helping others—the poor and oppressed with whom a side of him identifies—he is helping himself, dealing with his own feelings about authority. "The President," he once said, "had a lot more authority than a state governor, and at the same time a lot more responsibility . . . the President can speak with a much clearer voice than can a governor. The President can go directly to the people." His friend and associate Bert Lance sent Carter a gift about this time. He presented Carter with a small set of medals of all the states. You have dominion over one now, Lance said. Someday, Lance hoped, you will have dominion over all.

Lance and Alston together help sum up a part of the "Jimmy Carter Story" that appears so puzzling to so many in his dominion. What makes Jimmy run? His need to govern. What gives him the will to make the necessary effort? His absolute self-confidence. Over a decade ago, as a result of his born-again experience, Carter said he believed he could govern his own passions and could be a governor over others. If he has, indeed, succeeded in his own interior life—and the evidence is that he has—then his outward pursuit of power need not be a means to allay any sense of insufficiency—a familiar compensatory mechanism of behavior. His pursuit of power can, in fact, be a way, as he says, of sharing his great strength with those less strong.

Did he *need* power? interviewer Bill Moyers asked presidential candidate Carter, putting a question that reflected some of the apprehensions about the candidate. Carter answered that he didn't have "an unfulfilled, all-obsessive hunger." He added, "I feel powerful enough now. And secure enough now. Wealthy enough now. . . . But I like to have a chance to change things that I don't like and to correct the inequities as I discern them and to be a strong spokesman for those that are not strong. And I guess that's power. So, I can't deny that one of the purposes that I want to be President is to have power, yes."

Carter's answer left another question to be asked. His born-again experience almost certainly made him a good governor of his own emotions. He doesn't need power as simple "compensation." But does that necessarily qualify him as a good—much less great —governor of the people? When he summoned guests to his retreat at Camp David in July 1979, he characteristically took careful notes of their criticisms and advice. One piece of sharp criticism he remembered and repeated publicly: You're not leading the country, a Deep South politician had told him, you're just managing the government.

On our reading of the Georgia record, Carter made a good governor, but not a great one. In a life of testing, his toughest test has been in a Presidency that has become one continuing series of trials. He has become a contemporary Sisyphus, laboriously pushing his legislative proposals up the hostile Hill, and learning that governing is not the same as leading.

14
Running

IT IS A COMMONPLACE POLITICAL OBSERVATION that running *for* office and running *the* office often require different talents, and that the man who succeeds at campaigning for President may not be a success as President. For much of his first term, Carter seemed to confirm the commonplace.

At the start of Jimmy Carter's 1976 presidential campaign, the personal qualities of the man and the task before him matched perfectly; campaigning required a ceaseless effort directed toward the single consuming goal of winning, the talent that Jimmy Carter had been developing ever since his father first called him "Hot Shot." But campaigning also requires that the candidate offer certain themes to the voters along with his talents. Carter presented himself as the fresh new outsider—which indeed he was—and also as the leader who combined in his own person the best of the old values and the new, the candidate who could restore the country's spirit and self-esteem. He offered himself as a planner and a hard worker. He accented his differences, his Southernness. He could be trusted; he was pure; he wouldn't lie or play politics. He was dedicated, even ascetic, and above faction and party (the same pose De Gaulle had assumed in a divided and embittered France). His talents and his themes worked in the early primaries. Then they began to sour, and his campaign as well. He almost lost the election, and once in office, he steadily lost a good deal of his popular support and credibility.

The only surprise is that anyone should be surprised. To come out of Archery, Georgia, young Jimmy Carter had set high expectations for himself. To come out of nowhere politically, candidate Jimmy Carter had created unrealistically high expectations in the electorate about himself personally, about his above-politics politics, and about the "new spirit" that would sweep the land. He couldn't possibly deliver on these expectations. The outsider had to become the insider; the man above the party had to play the old politics. For most people, nothing much did seem to change, and the conviction grew that "he's just like the rest of them." But, of course, he's not just like the others. If he had been, he never would have won the race in the first place, or created the conditions for inevitable disappointment and disillusion during his first years in office.

II

BECAUSE JIMMY CARTER traveled so far so fast, his political abilities impressed many commentators as nothing less than brilliant. One of the more tough-minded political reporters, Richard Reeves, thought that Carter stood "head and shoulders above" most politicians. Along with almost everyone else who had been taken by Carter's initial political success, Reeves later revised, downward, his assessment as Carter appeared to stumble in the general election campaign and in his first year in the White House. Actually, Jimmy Carter moved in just about the same dogged way through media-certified success and media-certified failure. He was never quite as good as his first press notices, or quite as bad as his later ones. As political campaigns go, the "brilliance" of the early Carter campaign that so dazzled so many people came from an alloy of precious and common elements, and more of the latter than the former.

The major valuable element was Carter's ability to make long-range plans. As early as 1972, both Hamilton Jordan and Peter Bourne prepared memoranda to Carter on how they saw the 1976 campaign taking form. Bourne, the M.D. and psychiatrist, wrote in his memo that Carter should "capitalize on your greatest asset—

your personal charm." Bourne, too, believed in the power of positive thinking: "What is critical is the psychological and emotional decision to take the risk and to run for the Presidency to win, whatever the outcome." Jordan, then twenty-seven years old and Carter's chief political manager, argued the need to get national attention. Jordan worried about winning the Wallace vote, as Carter had in 1970. Although crippled in an assassination attempt, Wallace could "pre-empt" a Carter candidacy, Jordan wrote. Jordan advised Carter that he should "encompass and expand upon the Wallace constituency and populist philosophy by being a better qualified and more responsible alternative." Jordan listed the reasons why Senator Edward Kennedy would be a formidable opponent for Carter in the primaries but probably could not win the general election ("the unanswered questions of Chappaquiddick run contrary to the national desire for trust and morality in government").

Carter achieved his strategic goals in 1976, an impressively solid accomplishment. But as he himself had concluded after meeting the other presidential hopefuls, no one had to be superman to win. On the level of campaign strategy, his national efforts reflected the kind of practical wisdom that could be distilled from Theodore H. White's quadrennial accounts of the presidential elections, or from any number of other campaign books.

Later, after the 1976 election, Jerry Rafshoon would remember that "as far as our knowledge of campaigns and national politics were concerned, we knew what we read, what was in the newspapers and what was on TV." Also, the new federal campaign laws had changed the rules of fund-raising and the ways of financing campaigns. The law rewarded early campaigning, and the Carter people read and mastered the new rules of the game. Similarly, Democratic Party reforms, aimed at "opening up" the party to more local participation in 1976, had made the Iowa state caucuses important, and the Carter people understood that, too. They also knew the importance of New Hampshire, where fewer than 100,000 registered Democrats, most of them in three or four small cities, made the state a model of a "one-on-one" political campaign, the kind Carter had done before.

The mechanics of the new campaign finance law and all the other new rules and old truisms were also known to Birch Bayh,

Henry Jackson, Fred Harris, Morris Udall, and the rest of the Democratic candidates. The other candidates had the same charts available to them and had read the same books on presidential politics. Why did Carter win and not the others? Most analyses credit the combination of personal drive and political chance for giving Carter his victories in the primaries and then against Gerald Ford. Jimmy Carter did work harder than any other Democratic candidate; he did benefit from luck, the accidents of weather, the timing of certain primaries, and the bad luck of others. He may have even benefited from the availability of Lance's bank money when other candidates were struggling for funds. But something else beyond his marathon efforts and luck and guile also worked for him. He benefited from that confusing, complex, contrary, contradictory mass of opinions, hopes, anxieties, convictions, intellect, and emotions known as "the national mood." By 1974, Jimmy Carter believed himself ready to lead America. America, for its part, seemed ready for Carter to lead it; that is, enough voters stood ready to cast their lot for the leadership of someone very much like the image that Carter projected. Certain qualities in Jimmy Carter appealed to the voters—and certain qualities in them responded to him. The race for the American Presidency involves matters of feeling as much as matters of issues, more so in 1976 than in the previous three or four elections.

III

BY LATE 1974 and early 1975, the public opinion polls reflected a great crisis of public confidence: Americans had profound doubts, not just about specific national politicians but about national politics itself, and the entire process that had produced, in the shorthand of our contemporary communications, Vietnam, Civil Disorder, Watergate, CIA-FBI Abuses, and Corporate Bribery. Whatever the actual performances of past administrations had been, most Americans until the early 1970s held to a basic trust in governmental institutions, in the office of the Presidency—which could exalt even its mean-spirited occupants—and in the system's capacity to work and respond. "All the beliefs of the past," Pat

Caddell was to say in 1975, "were summed up in one central belief: America was a special place . . . Americans were a chosen people, different from others." Public opinion polls had over the last decades consistently reflected the idea of progress, so rooted in the American mythology of an ever-expanding land and nation. In 1965, three out of four Americans polled could be classified as "optimistic," that is, they believed things were better today than yesterday and would be better tomorrow. In 1975, answering the same question, only one American in five was classifying himself as optimistic.

Caddell found two instincts—his term—at war in the national psyche. One was "the desire for change," born out of the public's sense that nothing was working. The other was "the desire for a restoration of basic values," for a return to the idealistic goals and visions that, people believed, had made America great. Most people, Caddell suggested, saw the only chances for change and restoration outside the normal political categories of party and ideology. *They didn't want liberals, and they didn't want conservatives; they wanted something else.* Caddell presented his material at a Democratic Party conference in November 1975 in Louisville. He concluded his talk with the observation that the public seems "almost ready for a nationwide roll of the political dice." Jimmy Carter, who attended the Louisville meeting, thought so too. In late May 1976, nearing victory in the primaries, Carter used almost the same words to describe his strategy: "We figured the odds as best we could and then we rolled the dice." In politics, he does not flinch from high-stakes gambling. Three years later, in early 1979, when his Middle East policies appeared to be coming apart, he made another high-stakes gamble—his personal-diplomacy shuttle to Jerusalem and Cairo.

IV

CONVENTIONAL POLITICS, the Carter campaign strategists had concluded very early, would not be important in 1976. In presidential elections, issues perhaps have always been less important to voters than most of the experts imagined. Carter's close associate Jody Powell once explained that most of "the people" only think of national politics "once every four years for fifteen minutes or so." In his same direct way, Powell also put the pollsters' discovery of the great "national yearning" in sharp perspective. Many of those who said they yearned for the good old days of the American past, he offered, were ethnics and young working people from the big cities of the Northeast who had never seen a small town and had never known the old days—but that did not stop them from wanting the restoration of this mythic past.

Carter went forth talking about the goodness of the past and of the people, not only because the people wanted to hear it but because, as a born-again Christian and a Baptist lay preacher, he believed his words. As it happened, millions of people *did* want to hear, and believe, those words as well. Who could object to the particular likeness of the American people in the mirror held up by Jimmy Carter? Carter found that saying what he believed proved to be good politics in 1976. Therein lay the secret of Jimmy Carter's early success.

Carter pursued a number of strategies, some contradictory. He needed to be both the candidate of the South—his real origin and base—and to transcend that local identification and be seen as a national figure. He pictured himself as the outsider, the man who stood free of the Washington Establishment; he even claimed to stand free of the Democratic Party itself, while seeking to capture it. Once secure in the party's nomination, however, he had to appeal to party loyalties. Consequently, he had to mount one sort of campaign for the primaries and then shift to another sort of appeal, presenting another side of himself, once he had captured the nomination.

The Southern outsider's image worked well at first. Carter early established his appeal to fundamentalist Christians—white and black—a major gain; the Southern Baptist Convention, the largest single evangelical church, has some 13 million members and the black Baptist Church claims another 12 million. Later, he began to soften the religious notes, but they never wholly disappeared. Evangelical pietists, as Garry Wills points out, tend to support "persons of distinct moral character: and to ignore intellectual issues." Coming from this religious tradition, Carter kept making his "character" a central "issue" and playing down or waffling on the political issues. Like Carter himself, the pietistic tradition could be at once "conservative" and "progressive" (evangelicals like the Quakers, for example, fought the slave trade). Certainly his own polls instructed Carter to talk character rather than policies. But that was a beautiful bonus, matching his religious beliefs.

He infused his campaign with a spiritualistic fervor. His emphasis on achieving justice for the victims of injustice was not something he had copied out of a civics text or a pollster's questionnaire. He had learned a hunger for justice at his father's knee —more accurately, at his father's hands. At a reception for him arranged by the actor Warren Beatty at the lush Beverly Wilshire Hotel in Los Angeles, Carter chose to sermonize his audience—all of them wealthy, successful people from the entertainment business—on the obligations of the wealthy and successful. Public officials, he said, "have a special responsibility to bypass the big shots, including you and people like you, and like I was, and to make a concerted effort to understand people who are poor, black, speak a foreign language, who are not well educated, who are inarticulate, who are timid, who have some monumental problem."

His openness was disarming. When he traveled, he lived with the people. He could even say, "I don't know . . ." and "We don't have all the answers." He asked others to come to know and trust him personally. He used overtly religious symbols. By walking through his peanut fields and picking up the plants by their roots, and then recultivating them, he affirmed his own roots and traditional values of love, honesty, hard work, and decency. By emphasizing his own technical background—"I am a nuclear physicist"—he also sought to link the older values to the new world "a-bornin'." Periodically, he returned to Plains and took a hand in draining the dammed-up pond next to his mother's weekend house. Pond draining involves opening a sluiceway to lower the water level, and then thinning out the stock by catching or trapping enough fish for a fry. To the casual eye, it looked like just another, though admittedly exotic, press photo opportunity. Yet, as symbolism it combined in one image the hardworking country man, the environmental conservationist, the dutiful son, and the fisherman after other people's souls.

V

AN ANTHROPOLOGIST looking at the early Carter campaign at the deeper levels of its appeal to an electorate beset by doubt and a sense of disillusion would see the familiar pattern of a revitalization movement. These movements arise in times of unusual stress, when the values of the society have been threatened, generally as a result of some great natural disaster or man-made breakdown in social relations. The revitalization leader has himself usually undergone a profound spiritual crisis, often signaled in his own physical or mental breakdown, which he has overcome by some intense personal change, or rebirth. On the basis of his own experience, he offers his followers social as well as personal salvation. He goes back to the old values of the society, reinterpreting and connecting them to new values and ways required by changed social conditions.

The cultural anthropologist Anthony F. C. Wallace tells how, at the end of the eighteenth century, Handsome Lake, a Seneca Indian, found his people demoralized and scattered, languishing on the white man's reservations. Handsome Lake had a series of religious revelations that instructed him to become a leader of his people. He told them they had to take on a new life purged of the sins of the past, such as drinking and quarreling. They were to become new men, leading pure and austere lives. He also urged them to revive the old Indian values, while not rejecting those worthy innovations of the white culture.

The revitalization leader brings both political and religious sustenance to those in need; he converts his own profound religious experience to political purposes. In his mission of bringing spiritual rebirth, such a leader necessarily deals in symbols; he often derives his power from the ability to communicate with supernatural agents. He talks directly with God, often through prayer. An "outsider," he stands apart from the existing authority structure, and against the Establishment, deriving his powers from personal qualities—the mesmeric appeal that many of his supporters feel on first meeting him—and from his experience with the supernatural.

The parallels can be pushed only so far, although Jimmy Carter himself often uses the word "revitalization" in his speeches (and has talked of being a missionary after his service as President). Such leaders, in any case, can't lead on personal qualities alone over extended periods, as Carter has learned.

VI

THE SPIRITUAL QUALITY of the Carter campaign did not hinder it from making some shrewd political decisions. Carter understood, perhaps better than any other Democratic candidate, how both the national press and likely campaign contributors would respond to the candidate who achieved early primary victories and "front runner" status. Carter, accordingly, pushed hard to do well in the Iowa precinct caucuses, which came in January, well before the so-called first-in-the-nation New Hampshire primary. Well-organized Carter forces produced a sizable turnout of supporters in the Maine caucuses, largely overlooked by his major rivals, a few days later. Carter's Iowa win was intended to show how a Southern Baptist could do well among Midwestern Catholics and professional people. The Maine win demonstrated the same appeal among Yankees, and just at the time when the national press was turning its attention from Iowa to Maine's neighbor, New Hampshire. Carter grasped the importance of victories in the "caucus states" like Iowa and Maine, where the trick was not to get voters to the polls but to get Democrats who were committed to Carter to party caucus meetings. The other candidates, by and large, did not. "It wasn't because we were so smart," Hamilton Jordan would later say, in his forthright way, "but because they were so dumb." Similarly, chance, as much as planning, produced an ideal situation for Carter in New Hampshire. Morris Udall, Birch Bayh, Fred Harris, and Sargent Shriver competed for the liberal vote, while Carter and Henry Jackson had the right and center to themselves.

But Democratic primary voters still weren't sure they wanted Carter as their presidential candidate. Expected to win the Massachusetts primary, he finished fourth. It snowed that day, and

Carter voters, it seemed, were less likely to go to the polls when it was inconvenient.

The Carter campaign regarded Florida as its make-or-break state. At the start of the year, George Wallace had been elevated in the minds of the Carter people as their chief opponent, replacing the "threats" of Teddy Kennedy and Jay Rockefeller in the earlier analyses. Wallace had run as an "outsider" in national politics throughout the late 1960s and 1970s; well before Carter, Wallace represented a new kind of protest candidate, a voice of the blue-collar and white-collar worker who felt squeezed between the upper monied classes and the undeserving poor, mainly black and brown. He had transcended "regional" policies. Wallace would say he was speaking out on behalf of the working man and woman, the little people in the beauty shops and bowling alleys and service stations—lines later echoed by Jimmy Carter. Still, despite attempts to scrub up his candidacy, Wallace remained a one-issue race politician (insofar as he believed in any issue at all, other than his own continued stay in office). Probably millions supported his race message but chose to back the more conventionally respectable version offered by Richard Nixon.

In hindsight, just about everyone in 1976 overestimated the strength of the Wallace candidacy—another bit of Carter luck. Worried liberals saw in Carter a way to block Wallace. The stop-Wallace strategy gave Carter some unexpected dividends when liberals, not so much pro-Carter as anti-Wallace, joined his campaign. Thus, by this time, Patrick Caddell had agreed to do polling work for Carter. Another winter soldier, Atlanta Congressman Andrew Young, joined the campaign "through Florida."

Caddell brought national experience to Carter. At the ripe young age of twenty-six, Caddell was in his second presidential campaign. Andy Young brought the appearance, if not the reality, of major black leadership support to Carter at a time when Carter sought to establish himself as something more than a regional candidate. Like other prominent liberals and black leaders, Young stayed on with Carter when neither of the well-known and "inevitable" liberal Democrats—Hubert Humphrey and Teddy Kennedy—came forward in strength to "claim" the nomination. While Young in particular has often been described by Carter as his close friend, actually the two were never close, or very friendly, during the Georgia years.

Support for Carter, white and black, ebbed and flowed. In Florida, the first Caddell polls showed "a stereotype of Carter as just another Southern politician," especially among the more recent migrants to the state. To counter this impression, Jerry Rafshoon, the Carter media expert, concentrated on buying radio-TV spots in central Florida, where many ex-Northerners live, and in the Miami area to reach the Cuban and Jewish communities. Playing off the old George Wallace slogan—"Send them a message" —and playing off Carter's victories in Iowa and New Hampshire, the Carter media campaign in Florida found its theme: "Send them a President." When Carter won in Florida, he all but finished off the Wallace candidacy.

VII

Just as Carter, and his opinion sampler Caddell, tried to read the "psychology" of the voters, so too did voters try to read his "psychology."

Carter the man earned excellent initial notices. Journalists generally judged him by far the most "intelligent" and "serious" of all the candidates. Carter was as nimble as most politicians, yet always with a studied, decent politeness, that level of manners many Southerners exhibit. Carter was also admired for his powers of concentration and his awesome "will." He got up earlier than anyone else and worked longer, he didn't smoke, he drank only a glass of Scotch on rare occasions, and he never chased women. He impressed those who got reasonably close to him as self-absorbed and humorless, or else seemed to have a sarcastic humor. But a presidential campaign is a grueling, self-absorbing, brutal, humorless process for any candidate, especially for a candidate running a campaign the way Carter did. His mother, Lillian Carter, said to us that Morris Udall, Carter's chief rival in the primaries, was something of a "clown" because he cracked jokes and bantered during what was supposed to be a serious endeavor. For Carter, campaigning was grim.

As an outsider—"Not from Washington"—Carter campaigned on the fact that he was different from the others. Some voters began to feel that he was, in his behavior, perhaps *too* different. His "aloofness" and "strangeness" began to worry some people. Political campaigning is the most public of activities, yet Carter appeared to be standoffish. He opened himself for inspection, but he seemed nevertheless remote. He shook hands, grabbed elbows, squeezed shoulders, hugged and kissed women, picked up babies, beamed his smile at everyone, and did personal campaigning with as much style as any other successful politician.

At the same time, however, it was obvious that Carter was not one of the boys. He made no small talk; he may have professed his love of The People, but as far as anyone could see during the campaign, he didn't care much for any specific people beyond the small circle of his immediate family and personal staff. One Washington journalist maintained that Jimmy Carter had made no close friends, and "I don't know anyone who would want him for a friend." The spiritual fervor that attracted many voters repelled others. The bluntest reading came from those who worried that Carter was "some kind of religious nut." A journalist who had covered the candidate worried about Carter's emotional "stability," given his obvious intensity and drive. Would he have a "messianic strain" in his dealings with other world leaders? One disadvantage of having a Janus-like personality may be that it presents a face for everyone to hate as well as love.

Carter's appeal in most of the primary races had been undeniably broad. He attracted Democratic voters of every kind—self-described liberals, moderates, and conservatives. A headline in the newspaper *Newsday* over its analysis of the Florida vote declared, "Carter's Appeal as Broad as His Grin." It was an arresting image, for a smile can be superficial, transitory, and not necessarily revealing of underlying emotions. Another problem with offering something for everybody—with fusing contradiction—may be that broad support doesn't go very deep.

In the late primaries and in the general election, voters confessed to interviewers that they were "uncertain" about Carter; they said that they "didn't know him very well," they thought he was "fuzzy on the issues." They were beginning to see the wrong side of the tapestry, to be puzzled by what we have identified as Carter's fundamental need to fuse contradictions. What seemed to be troubling the voters was not Carter's position on any specific issue but his "different" character. The doubts began to surface in the Massachusetts primary, where Carter had been expected to win handily. By the end of the primaries, as well as in the race against Gerald Ford, Carter's supporters wavered.

After his first primary victories, Jimmy Carter began to say things like "As President, I will . . ." rather than "If elected, I will . . ." The idea of Carter as President began to bother some voters. In Michigan, he won by only 1800 votes; on the same day, he lost Maryland to Governor Edmund G. Brown, Jr. He also lost Nebraska to Senator Frank Church.

Pat Caddell explained that Carter had been running for a time, while Brown and Church appeared as fresh faces—the new challengers against Carter, who now appeared like one of the old established politicians. Carter, Caddell held, suffered from overexposure. Caddell was wrong. The fault lay not principally in the public's flightiness or simple-mindedness; more and more voters had been doing what Carter had been telling them that serious, intelligent voters did—they had been judging his character, and it worried them.

The flagging campaign managed, however, to win primary victories in California, New Jersey, and Ohio, which all but assured him enough delegates to win a first-ballot victory at the party convention.

VIII

THE DEMOCRATIC NATIONAL CONVENTION in July was, everyone agreed, a handsomely mounted coronation. Carter's choice of Walter Mondale as his vice presidential running mate set the general "liberal" tone of the convention, and Carter's acceptance speech offered a vision of social reform: The gospel of love would bring simple justice. On the climactic night of the convention, party chairman Robert Strauss summoned to the platform all the well-known faces of the Democratic Party. Carter and Kennedy, Wallace and Humphrey, Udall and Daley, Muskie and McGovern, Bayh and Brown beamed from the platform and into living-room television sets. The Reverend Martin Luther King, Sr., led the convention in the closing prayer. The Peter Duchin orchestra, following a script worked out by Strauss and Carter, played "We Shall Overcome (Someday)." The cameras dwelled on the faces on the convention floor as black and white, young and old, North and South, men and women, some of the faces tear-streaked, sang the anthem of the civil rights movement of the 1960s. Carter, unifier of opposites, had brought the factions of the party together.

The image of a united Democratic Party contrasted sharply with the opposition party in the summer of 1976. Gerald Ford won his party's nomination, after a divisive fight. Not until the week following the Republican Convention did he meet for the first time with the men who would run his campaign. John Deardourff, one of the major architects of the Ford campaign, recalled that his task in late August seemed quite simple, and all uphill: "We were 32 points down in the polls, and we had 75 days to go."

For the Carter campaign, the seventy-five days should have been simple, and smooth. But Carter's behavior in the race against Gerald Ford followed to a great extent the pattern he had set in the primaries: a skillful beginning, early successes against indifferent opposition, and then a series of setbacks and near disaster. On paper, Carter should have had no difficulty beating Gerald Ford. Registered Democrats outnumbered registered Republicans by two to one. While traditional Democratic voters had deserted McGovern in 1972 to elect Nixon, the 1974 congressional elections had clearly reflected the swing back to the Democratic Party after Watergate.

IX

IN AUGUST, Jimmy Carter rested in Plains, getting to know his running mate, Walter Mondale, planning the fall campaign, making appointments to his staff, giving interviews to journalists. He also pitched in the softball games between his Secret Service escort and the press, helped drain Lillian Carter's pond, and served up the catch at a Saturday night fish fry. He had to build a national campaign, recruiting workers beyond the ranks of his Georgia cadre. A non-Georgian involved in this effort likened the 1976 summer transition to the 1940s experience of the Chinese Communists —a band of comrades from the Long March who had to transform themselves into a national organization. Demanding as this effort was for the comrade Georgians, their task was made more complicated by the need to reach out to Democratic Party leaders and the traditional Democratic interest groups that Carter had earlier run against. He had to make overtures to the Washington Establishment, to show them he was neither a parochial figure nor a complete amateur unsuited to walk in the traditional corridors of power. Running for President, Carter had to try to straddle both the popular outsider's track and the potential insider's track. Even in his contradiction-fusing character, the strain wore through.

Carter started out as the anti-Establishment preacher of morality in politics. He finished as a Democrat supporting traditional Democratic social programs and traditional Democratic solutions through government activity. Carter did keep to his special vision of justice, competence, and a politics beyond party. He combined in his speeches the rhetoric of help for the poor with the rhetoric of hard work. He combined in his policies both the liberal and conservative positions. He could talk about the need for a strong defense—and for support of Israel—while arguing that $2 billion in "fat" could be cut from the military budget. Both positions were tenable, and both accommodated wide audiences.

Carter had succeeded in the first stages of his efforts in part because of an extraordinary coming together of the man and the moment; his post-politics stance seemed in accord with the feelings of a majority of Americans. In the general election, he had to change themes and run as a traditional Democrat. Carter opened his campaign with a Labor Day speech on September 6, talking of Roosevelt and Kennedy; Carter was telling Democrats he was part of the Democratic Party they knew.

After the election, Carter acknowledged that one of his major difficulties was deciding "how to deal with the President." During the primaries, Carter had criticized his opponents, such as Birch Bayh and Henry Jackson, for resorting to personal attacks. During the fall campaign, Carter also started out with a strategy of being above politics and avoiding personal attacks on Ford; but as the polls disclosed Carter's steady drop in his ratings, Carter turned to direct criticism of Ford. He did not handle this very well. By his own frank admission, he had not lost his awe of other rivals or his concern about measuring up as much as he thought he had.

The attacks on Ford occurred during the last weeks of September, a period Hamilton Jordan remembered as the "low point of the campaign" for Carter. Another associate, former speechwriter James Fallows, recalled the same period as the time when everyone had a "sinking ship" feeling. The tide that almost swept Carter away began to rise on Monday, September 20, when the contents of a *Playboy* magazine article were disclosed. In his willingness—or compulsion—to reveal himself and his thoughts to his listeners, Carter had invited discussions with writer Robert Scheer of his family, his religion, and his personal life. As the last interview ended, Carter was asked about his rigid Baptist faith. Carter responded by asking if the *Playboy* interviewers had attended any of his Sunday school lessons at the Plains church, and went on to say that it was a good way to learn something about the Baptist religion. Then came the now famous passage about lust in the heart and the Biblical injunction against adultery.

It was all innocuous enough, and more Niebuhr than Eros. At worst, he could be accused of using the calculatedly with-it—in Carter's mind—word "screw" to impress 10 million *Playboy* readers and potential voters. But clergymen and Republicans denounced his words without ever reading them. Carter's openness had opened him up to ridicule. His ratings dropped sharply in the polls. According to Hamilton Jordan, the *Playboy* interview increased many voters' concerns about Carter's character—"the weirdo factor," he called it, talking to us.

Four days later, Carter and Ford met in their first televised debate. By the common agreement of the polls and the political commentators, Carter lost the first debate to Ford. Actually, the three meetings between the candidates were not debates at all, but side-by-side news conferences. The two men stood at lecterns set several feet apart, an arrangement the Carter side wanted so that the five-foot-seven Carter would not be seen standing too close to the six-foot-one Ford. Looking back on the first meeting, Carter agreed he did not do well. He attributed this to, as he put it, "what I subjectively analyzed as an overly deferential attitude" toward Ford. A Gallup poll, taken before the first debate and before all the

Playboy publicity, showed Carter ahead of Ford by 54 to 34; after the debate and the interview, the figures were Carter 50 and Ford 42.

Carter by himself could not arrest his campaign slide at the end of September. For that task he got help—from Gerald Ford. The Ford campaign began to sputter. In the days between the first and second televised meetings, Ford was dogged by a reported investigation of his personal finances and by continuing stories of a "deal" to pardon Richard Nixon. Then Ford's Secretary of Agriculture, Earl Butz, and his incredibly tasteless racist jokes finally drove the *Playboy* interview off the front pages and television news programs. Next, in the second debate, Ford got deeper into trouble with his "Eastern Europe" remark ("There is no Soviet domination of Eastern Europe, and there never will be under a Ford Administration").

From that point on into the next week, Ford began getting the unfavorable newspaper and television stories. The best position Carter could take would be to stand aside and let the press chide Ford. But Carter went on the attack himself. He compared Ford —unfavorably—to Richard Nixon, and he suggested Ford couldn't tell a Russian tank from a Polish tank. His campaign managers said they were appalled at this "new" Jimmy. Carter admitted later he had been, in his own words, "overly aggressive, overly strident."

The intensity of Carter's reaction all but canceled out the gains that came his way as a result of Ford's inept campaign. Why did he get so angry? One explanation has nothing to do with Eastern Europe or any campaign issue. In this interpretation, Carter got mad in early October, with four weeks to go in the race, when rumors about him and alleged affairs with "other women" were circulated among journalists and others in Washington, apparently by Republican Party sources. Jody Powell told Carter of the rumors shortly after the second debate, and Carter's response took the form of attacks on Ford. No one had any evidence that Ford knew about the role of Republican officials in keeping the gossip in circulation. Still, Carter grew more strident.

Carter doesn't like being ridiculed; for that matter, who does? More important, Carter felt angry with himself for being on the point of losing the campaign. He was angry at having allowed himself the weakness of being awed by Ford, the President. He now turned this anger not inward but outward. It was one of the few times that he lost a bit of public control over his angry feelings.

X

BY THE THIRD and final televised meeting in Williamsburg, Virginia, on October 23, the level of both campaigns had disintegrated into a demeaning, negative name-calling contest. The setting of Colonial Williamsburg gave a dignity to the last meeting, and Carter finished with a vision of America that recalled his earliest appearances as the fresh, open leader.

By then, however, the campaign had contributed to voter dissatisfaction rather than relieving it. Some 81 million Americans voted on election day, 53 percent of the electorate. The figure was somewhat higher than expected; still, 72 million registered voters chose not to vote for either man. In the end, Carter won a traditional party victory. The haves voted for Ford, the have-lesses for Carter, and the have-nots didn't vote at all. If some 8000 people in Ohio and Hawaii had voted for Ford instead, Ford would have been President.

Carter's victory had been narrower than anyone suspected it would be. At one point in the final weekend of the campaign, some polls showed Ford ahead for the first time. That may have been his undoing; the question before the wavering voter no longer was "Do I want Carter?" The question was "Do I want Ford for four more years?" The waverers swung back to Carter by Tuesday morning. Carter had talked of the need for trust, but in the end the voters were moved more by distrust of Ford's abilities and of the party of Watergate. The voters regarded Carter warily. Still, he had, more than Ford or his earlier rivals, given the promise of something fresh, new, and different, perhaps a better day.

15

A President in the Middle

By THEIR NATURE, revitalization leaders do not look like promising administrators. When a leader who regards politics as a process of inner change comes forward, he can exert powerful effects on the public. Such a leader can move men and women, as Gandhi did in India. Once having powerfully moved the populace, however, the shaman–spiritual leader often has an inability to deal with specific political issues (in Gandhi's case, the level of workers' wages and the threat of partition).

Jimmy Carter, too, exerted a powerful attraction in 1976 by stressing the possibility of inward change. His own new life as a born-again Christian could serve, so he thought, as a model for a national rebirth in the bicentennial year. With key groups of voters, like churchgoing blacks and white Southerners, who exerted a disproportionate influence in a half-dozen early primaries, Carter succeeded so well that he built a near-unassailable lead.

In his passage from outsider to *the* insider—the President of the United States—he necessarily disappointed some of his followers, and reinforced the skepticism of those who had long nursed their misgivings about him. Within nine months of taking office, his Administration appeared to be in disarray: his energy program stalled, tax reform and welfare overhaul delayed, inflation rampant, his close friend Lance disgraced, his White House staff judged ineffective and amateurish, the SALT II talks at an impasse, a Middle East settlement seemingly further away than ever.

"Carter's Woes—Any Way Out?" *U.S. News & World Report* asked, and explained that while perhaps there was a way out, it would be a while in coming as the inexperienced White House strugged against a stubborn Congress in full view of a dubious public. The same words could have been used to describe the Administration of his predecessor, Ford. Carter's election, in short, hadn't made much difference.

Of course, the country was not the same with Carter in the White House, any more than Carter the man was just like all the others. First of all, certain political "crises" never go away; they are part of the institution of the Presidency. In the first formal study of the American Presidency, written over 150 years ago, Augustus B. Woodward found the same "crises" that have bothered every President since Andrew Jackson: strained relations with Congress; poor presidential staff work (important documents were being lost, and the President should have an official secretary); government leaks; contested presidential leadership in foreign policy; the need for government reorganization; and managing the President's time (there should be less pomp and official entertainment, but the President's personal contact with the public should be maintained by continuing the traditional right of any citizen to drop in on the President).

Secondly, some things *have* changed in Washington since Carter took office. Carter has tried to promote justice—as well as equity and charity—in this sinful world. In Carter's Washington, more blacks and more women have been appointed to more positions of genuine authority than in any previous administration. However, since the expectations of what could be done had been pitched so high, inevitable disappointment—and skepticism—followed. He appointed two women to Cabinet posts; in the previous 200 years of American history, there had been only three other women of Cabinet status. Of the top presidential appointments, more than one in ten were women; in the Ford Administration, the figure stood at one in twenty. He had pledged in July 1976, "I am going to do for women what Lyndon B. Johnson did for blacks." Some women's groups looked at other figures—for example, only one woman in his first fifteen appointments to Federal District Court positions, and none in his first ten appointments to the U.S. Circuit Court of Appeals—and thought he had reneged on the promise. To make matters worse, the fact that blacks and women have key roles in the Carter Administration has done nothing to lower the rates of black teenage unemployment, or speed the passage of the Equal Rights Amendment.

Finally, all too many things remain unchanged because some things may not be changeable. Since presidential power lies largely in persuasion rather than command, the initiatives a President can take, say, "to deal with inflation" have limits; when multinational corporations and powerful trade unions force price or wage increases, the President can deplore or jawbone or attempt to dissuade. But some issues may themselves be supra-personal, resistant to suasion, and indeed intractable. Which school of economists truly knows how to exorcise inflation, or its more virulent late-1970s strain, stagflation? Economic solutions—and solutions to other issues like welfare, defense, urban decay, and racism—involve not so much the heart as the head: Do we know what to do?

The test, then, of Jimmy Carter and his Administration turns not on his goodness and sincerity—we are convinced of both, and he convinced enough voters to win in 1976. No one, moreover, worries about his capacity for hard work or purposeful activity. James David Barber, the political scientist Carter most admires, has already told us that Carter appears to be an active/positive President, full of zest for the job and its possibilities. But the real test of a President turns on the qualities of mind and habit he brings to the matters about which Presidents must be active and positive (or passive and negative). A President can be active and *ineffective;* he can be positive in the pursuit of bad policies. The test for Carter turns on his abilities as a leader, a manager, and a planner —abilities he keeps telling us, and himself, he has.

Carter confessed, in his open way, his own inexperience in his first months in office. He did not know the rituals, shortcuts, and safe passages around the corridors of Washington. (How could he? No one had codified them.) Running the government of Georgia did not necessarily prepare him for running the federal government. His record, personal and political, over the first fifty-three years of his life has shown a capacity for learning—as well as a capacity for blind spots. The record of the first years of the Carter Presidency reflected this play between his abilities and liabilities.

230

II

THE DAY OF HIS INAUGURATION, Carter immediately accomplished one impressive long-range achievement without lifting a finger. His Presidency reintegrated the South with the nation, as John Kennedy's election brought Roman Catholics into full symbolic citizenship. In his own life, Carter lived with the pulls of union and separation. He is the ideal figure to release the South from the burden of its past, bringing it back into the mainstream, while preserving its special nature. He offered a form of identity to the South, an identity which did not require the South to give up one part of its soul in order to affirm the other.

Carter's election fused a second kind of division in the country—or obscured it, depending on the political perspective used. Carter's Presidency confirms the judgment that he cannot usefully be classified as liberal or conservative. Some now see him as a conservative Democrat; others have to call him a liberal Republican—"the best liberal Republican since Theodore Roosevelt," the political scientist Walter Dean Burnham has said. By blurring the lines between liberalism and conservatism in his Presidency, Carter has been true to his own character, with its basic need to embrace contradictions. During the primaries and campaign, of course, his stand proved to be politically shrewd. He recognized that the American people had moved away from the slogans of the liberals. He ran on a platform calling for more government activity but knew people believed government had become a source of problems. Moreover, "liberalism" had been tagged with a lifestyle worrisome to large numbers of Americans. The Nixonites had identified McGovern as the candidate of "acid, abortion, and amnesty." Polls showed a sharp increase in the number of self-described conservatives over, say, a decade ago. By January 1978, one survey reported that 42 percent of Americans described themselves as moderately or very conservative, 23 percent moderately or very liberal, and 27 percent middle of the road (8 percent did not know where they fit).

Upon closer inspection, however, an alert candidate could see that the meaning of the word "conservative" had also changed.

People who called themselves conservatives favored specific government initiatives once thought to be liberal: low cost medical care, standards to protect workers on the job, the principle of full employment. Conservatives did not turn their backs completely on forty years of the New Deal and the accomplishments of big government. The declared "conservatives," like increasing numbers of "liberals," accepted the accomplishments but did not have faith in the power of government to do more—although no one quite explained what institutions other than government would deal with the problems people wanted solved.

"Post-politics politics" made good campaign strategy; governing in these terms became another matter. On specific issues, Carter could be either liberal or conservative; or more likely he would take the *fused* position. He slowed the B-1 bomber, but his ambiguous "one step forward, one step back" orders for the neutron bomb program satisfied neither conservative hawks nor liberal doves. On a particular issue, he would attract a particular kind of support; but his support would be different on different issues. In his first two years of office, Carter governed by a shifting consensus on each proposal he made, but without a solid following, united on the general direction of his policies. He failed in the first instance to "inspire" in the Roosevelt or Kennedy style even those groups on his side on any given issue. His staff people, for their part, did little initially to help; inexperienced themselves, they failed to work effectively with interest groups. For example, consumer organizations were never properly mobilized for the President's "must" energy legislation.

Carter did not, and perhaps cannot, establish a constant coalition. Washington columnist James Reston had been somewhat disdainful of Carter when he first appeared as a candidate (Reston called him "wee Jimmy"). But Reston proved to be one of the more astute Carter watchers during the first years of the Administration, catching the unified ambiguities (and ambiguous unities) of the man and his policies. "The hardest things for this city to handle these days are the blurry lines between one policy and another at home and abroad," Reston wrote in the New York *Times* in late June 1978.

Washington wants a clear sharp line from President Carter between high property taxes and adequate public services, between inflation and unemployment, the Israelis and the Arabs, the Soviets and the Chinese, but there are no clear lines, and Mr. Carter refused to choose up sides. His latest press conference illustrates the point. Confronted with a series of complicated and ambiguous questions, he simply refused to give simple answers. He agreed that taxes were too high but rejected the Steiger-Jones tax reforms he thought would favor the very rich. He criticized the Israeli Government's answers to his questions about the future of the West Bank, the Gaza Strip and the Palestinians, but insisted that the peace negotiations should go on anyway. He condemned the Soviet violations of human rights under the Helsinki agreement, the Soviet-Cuban aggressions in Africa and agreed that this competition between Washington and Moscow would probably go on for almost a generation; but meanwhile he thought it was in everybody's interest to keep trying for control of the arms race.

Carter's harsher critics, and many voters, took the ambiguities of policy as just one more disillusioning example of the waffling they had seen in the campaign—a man without a center, waiting upon the guidance of Pat Caddell's latest polls. More reflective critics considered Carter's "fuzziness" the result of his too-simple —though at least honest—approach to governing. They saw him as a technician of process, who decides case by case on each issue using procedural standards, rather than a statesman with any political goal in mind. Commentators repeated the story of how President Carter arrived at major policy decisions, drawing up twin lists of pros and cons, and assigning weight to them, engineer's style, just as he "scientifically" diagrammed Dylan Thomas' poems. Where, his critics asked, was the column for emotion? One answer is that Carter, characteristically, was keeping his feelings contained.

The political scientists Jack Knott and Aaron Wildavsky argue that Carter's "coherent philosophy," such as it is, centers on "how government ought to work," not on the ends of government: "Carter's basic beliefs are about procedures for making policy. . . .[His] concern is less with particular goals than with the need for goals, less with the content of policies than with their ideal form—simplicity, uniformity, predictability, hierarchy, and comprehensiveness." These procedural guides are "individually contradictory and mutually incompatible," they conclude; consequently, "we are all in for hard times."

Knott and Wildavsky rightly point up Carter's technician side, as other critics have. They omit, as others have, too, the other sides of Jimmy Carter: the pietistic idealism that exists within him, the hard-won commitment to living with contradictions that characterizes his personality, the smoldering feelings, shading into resentments, about the injustices of the sinful world. They overlook that he has read, and absorbed, the realistic idealist Niebuhr as well as U.S. Navy manuals and managerial casebooks about zero-based budgeting. They also underestimate the extent of the convergence of old-time liberal and old-time conservative goals, and the development of liberal-conservative fusion as a goal in itself. All the sides must be put together to understand the man and his Presidency.

III

CARTER'S LIFE until he came to Washington had been a successful balancing act. His Presidency, not surprisingly, has continued the act, on the highest wire. He has tried to stand separate from the Democratic Party, yet depend on its supporting net. (Before the election, he thought the "people" would be that supporting net.) Few maneuvers demand more skill, and he has alternated between slipping and maintaining his balance.

He had expediently embraced the traditions and goals of the Democratic Party in his campaign speeches. Once in office, however, he tried to stand above party again, like a De Gaulle. This stand seemed to fit the reality of his shifting, joining, and unjoining constituency with its changing consensus on particular bills, and coalitions that last, if he's lucky, as long as the vote on a bill. The above-party stand made sense initially, given the general decline in voter loyalty to the established parties. Further, the breakdown of strong party discipline within Congress itself discouraged strategies of working with party regulars; the results wouldn't be worth the effort. Carter's own experiences in Georgia politics reaffirmed this attitude. The party, after all, seemed to him to be simply another one of the special-interest groups, an obstacle to the public interest rather than a means of reaching it. Aloof from legislators,

Carter initially preferred to reach out directly to the abstraction, the people, seeking the ideal unity. That suited his character. De Gaulle had done it; but he in fact stood head and shoulders above everyone else in France—and had to start his own party as well. President Carter couldn't go over the heads of the legislators; he found out he needed his party and the Congress.

At the very beginning of his term, for example, he announced his opposition to the construction of a number of Corps of Engineers dam projects, including the Senator Richard B. Russell dam in his home state of Georgia. The outcry from Congress, especially from Democrats, helped set the level of Carter's relations with the Hill for the rest of his first year. Eventually, the White House and the Democratic leadership achieved a compromise on the dams, based on mutual distrust rather than a harmonious deal. By his second year, his tenacity had gotten him the victory he wanted. Initially, his inexperience as well as his inclinations caused other troubles. Texas Democrats had backed Carter's candidacy on his promise that he would support deregulation of natural gas controls; they cried betrayal after his call for increased federal regulation of natural gas. When he finally came out for gas decontrol, it hardly earned him any support. His opposition to logrolling and pork barrel, in theory, deserves applause; in practice, however, it earned him a reputation for naïveté and called into question his ability to lead, to govern as a politician.

A feeling grew that he couldn't keep up on the fast track of Washington. Representative Thomas P. "Tip" O'Neill, the Speaker of the House and the embodiment of traditional interest-group Democratic politics, recalled his first conversation with Carter: "He told me how he had handled the Georgia legislators, by going over their heads directly to the people. I said, 'Hey, wait a minute, you have 289 guys up there [the House Democrats] who know their districts pretty well. They ran against the Administration [Ford], and they wouldn't hesitate to run against you.' He said, 'Oh, really?' " Tip O'Neill, Carter discovered, believed himself as concerned with the people as Carter. Congressmen and Congresswomen also often knew in detail about the bills coming up for vote.

Carter learned, as much as he could, from these experiences. With the openness and self-scrutiny that so uniquely co-exist

235

with his self-confidence, he took his own measure of his performance. "I have a substantial lack of experience and knowledge about the history of Government here in Washington, the interrelationship among the agencies, the proper division of authority and responsibility between the Congress and the President," he confessed toward the end of his first year in office. His shortcomings were those of someone who hadn't served in Washington long enough, "who hasn't actually been President. That is a handicap for me and a limitation."

Such an astounding admission, with its implied promise to reform and learn, could come only from someone accustomed to self-appraisal and the confessional mode. In much the same repentant's way, Carter belatedly converted to the orthodoxy of the Democrats in his dealings with the party. He agreed to support Democrats where he could, and to play the political game according to the established back-scratching rules. Since he saw himself as a politician in a sinful world, he learned to accept a little more of the sin that inhabits it. It was not as if he were a complete innocent; he had dealt in the patronage game in Georgia and the giving and taking of favors. Niebuhr would have understood. After the first year of bruised relations with Congress, Carter quietly summoned a group of Democrats—lawyers, lobbyists, and veterans of previous Democratic administrations—to meet every ten days or so at the White House to discuss ways the Administration could broaden its political base and improve its record on Capitol Hill. The New York *Times* called the advisers "charter members of Permanent Washington." Characteristically, Carter tried to accommodate his behavior to circumstances.

IV

CHARACTERISTICALLY, too, the White House had invited critics to take the measure of its performance when it published a "promises book"—a list of more than 600 pledges Carter had made during the campaign. Taking up the offer, the Washington *Post* selected a sample of ninety-five items and concluded that Carter had fulfilled almost half of them in less than a year in office, either by taking action as President or gaining passage of legislation embodying the essentials of his program. On the other side, almost one fourth of the promises had been broken, "either by Carter changing his mind or by government action in the opposite direction." About one third of the list remained undecided. Most of the promises involved straightforward though hardly nation-shaking matters. Carter, for example, delivered on his promise to bring Walter Mondale into the center of presidential activities, not just vice presidential chores. Mondale advises on foreign as well as domestic policy, and serves as Carter's principal spokesman on Capitol Hill, assigned the job of avoiding legislative quarrels.

On the other hand, Carter couldn't deliver on his promise to balance the budget by the end of his term. (It's now uncertain if it will be balanced in 1981.) He promised government reorganization; it went ahead slowly, often with the same old activities collected under new headings. He promised to reduce the size of the White House staff; the "reduction" has been accomplished by bringing assistants in under different agency payrolls.

Carter ran on a promise to reduce the defense budget. His first budget included a modest increase in projected spending. While Carter scrapped the B-1 bomber, his subsequent decisions to request funds to study conversion of the F-111, an alternate plane, and to proceed with the development of the cruise missile, acted to counterbalance the loss of the B-1. He has tried to fulfill his promise to cut back arms sales while still using weapons transfers in the interests of specific foreign policies. The SALT agreements hung on Senate approval, but Carter earlier cleared the way by winning the Senate vote on the Panama Canal treaties. In the Middle East, Carter tried to be both an impartial mediator and a participant with a plan. Steering between these two contradictory roles, he also tried to steer between the demands of the Arabs and the Israelis, and the risks of alienating American Jews and the risks of alienating American companies eager to do business with the oil sheikdoms. At Camp David, the policy of fusing contradictions began to pay off. His personal diplomacy was rewarded with the Egyptian–Israeli peace treaty, signed on March 26, 1979. To win that gamble, he turned to his strongest suits—his enormous confidence in his own abilities, and his effectiveness as a one-on-one persuader.

Carter's conduct of foreign policy reflected, like so much in his life, his deep-seated reluctance to draw lines. For the formal, intellectual structure to support these personal traits in his policy dealings, he depended on the counsel of Zbigniew Brzezinski, his national security adviser. While Secretary of State Vance was the public spokesman for Administration policy, each morning Carter began his White House work day by listening to Brzezinski's thirty-minute review of current intelligence information from around the world; often they met two or three times again during the day. When Jody Powell explained that the two "agree on most of the fundamentals," he touched only the surface of an extraordinary relationship. Bert Lance and Jimmy Carter shared a certain optimistic-pietistic approach to the affairs of business and politics; Brzezinski and Carter shared a distinct optimistic-technocratic approach to global matters.

The two men first met at a session of the Trilateral Commission, the love child of banker David Rockefeller. Rockefeller provided the initial funding for the commission, a private group intended to explore the common interests of three major capitalist centers—the United States, Japan, and Western Europe. Brzezinski, then a professor at Columbia University, took a leave to become the commission's director. The commission set up working groups where businessmen, civil servants, government officials, and academics discussed the world monetary systems, energy, world trade, the future of the seas, and other appropriately weighty subjects. One of the business members, J. Paul Austin, chairman of the Coca-Cola Company, sponsored for membership the young governor of Georgia, Jimmy Carter. As a member for four years, Carter apparently never missed a meeting, though he had no real role. He treated it as a kind of graduate seminar in international affairs, and read all the working papers studiously. "Membership on this commission has provided me with a splendid learning opportunity," Carter later noted.

The commission also provided Carter with his major advisers on foreign affairs when he decided to run for President, including Brzezinski, Henry Owen, and Richard Gardner. For eight years Henry Kissinger had dominated the conduct of American foreign policy, with his distinct personal style, his pessimism about Western power, and his preoccupation (shared with Nixon) with power blocs. When Carter became President, he appointed Brzezinski National Security Council adviser, and Brzezinski came in with other trilateralists.

A manifesto for the trilateralists can be found in Brzezinski's study *Between Two Ages*. Brzezinski plays professor to Carter's student, filling out the curriculum after Niebuhr's work in religion and politics. *Between Two Ages* contains the basic philosophical tenets of the Carter-Brzezinski foreign policy; from it, Brzezinski, with Carter's approval, drew up a four-year plan outlining Carter's future policies in the international arena.

According to Brzezinski, the world has entered the Technetronic Era (the subtitle of his work), in which society is shaped "culturally, psychologically, socially, and economically by the impact of technology and electronics." Issues and institutions have become transnational rather than national; we live in a world of multinational corporations and territorial vulnerability (as a result of atomic weapons). Consequently, the division between domestic and international politics has become blurred. Brzezinski's predecessor, Kissinger, became absorbed in American-Soviet relations. For him, the central problem of foreign affairs concerned the two superpowers. Brzezinski stresses instead the global nature of relations, involving first the United States, Western European nations, and Japan, and next the third-world nations. Instead of Spenglerian assessments, Brzezinski looks ahead with optimism. Kissinger focused on nineteenth-century European models of power politics; Brzezinski on twentieth- or twenty-first-century possibilities of technical developments, and economic and social groupings rather than political alliances—a global society. The transformation to the global society, for America and eventually other nations, involves the paradox of increased togetherness (the global community) and increased fragmentation (the dissolution of traditional loyalties).

Like Niebuhr, Brzezinski praises the ideals of Marxism as a new universal vision, lifting man's aspirations and broadening his concerns. But, again like Niebuhr, Brzezinski deplores the reality of Soviet dogma and dictatorship. He is optimistic about the development of Christian-Marxist dialogues, and foresees the humanizing of communism in both Eastern and Western Europe. Brzezinski does not expect too much from the Soviet leadership, since the

Soviet leadership does not believe in the end of ideology, but rather in the intensification of ideology. Brzezinski also recognizes that there will be continuing U.S.A.–U.S.S.R. rivalry and that the Soviet Union will offer little cooperation on global problems, though its own technological concerns lead to a certain convergence with American interests. On occasion, operating viscerally, Brzezinski can lapse into an anti-Soviet posture, undercutting his own well-thought-out emphasis on global society.

Domestically, Brzezinski argues, the two-party system does not seem a promising agency to alleviate problems. Government is inefficient, meaningless. Conventional liberalism, Brzezinski tells us, has become dogmatic and outdated; it believes it can solve problems by creating agencies, but other than this it has no solutions. Against dogmatic liberalism, Brzezinski advances a kind of pragmatic liberalism. Such a position recognizes the "complexity" of problems—Brzezinski uses the word almost as frequently as Carter—and holds that there are no predetermined, simple solutions. The planner will eventually displace the lawyer "as the key social legislator and manipulator." The problem is how to reconcile the need for planning with personal freedom. Brzezinski urges defined goals and "more self-conscious preoccupation with social ends."

"Rational humanism" is the phrase Brzezinski uses to describe his desired philosophical position. (The phrase echoes the description of Carter used by his friend Warren Fortson in Georgia some twenty years ago.) There are no once-and-for-all solutions, for Brzezinski, in domestic or international politics. We must restrict ourselves to realistic aspirations, humanistically inspired.

Brzezinski has been criticized for advocating a technocracy, for writing off ideology too soon, and for giving pompous names to too-simple ideas. Western Europe and Japan, for example, have only the most tenuous ties to one another. Western Europe is not really an entity, but a collection of states without a common voice; with some issues, like oil and energy, the interests of the three parties may not always be the same. Nevertheless, Brzezinski has attempted a synthesis, political and philosophical, of new developments. He provides a world view on which to base a foreign policy, since he articulates values as well as problems, links domestic and international concerns, and gives a long-range basis for day-to-day decisions. He offered Carter intellectual ideas in an area where he was weakest; equally important, the ideas would appeal to his technocratic planning side, as well as his Christian "humanist" side.

The two seemed made for each other, and Brzezinski had the additional virtue of being connected with the foreign policy establishment and yet having partly set himself outside it. He would bring the trilateral group along with him, while leaving behind Kissinger.

Personally, the two men had certain affinities. Brzezinski in his own life and thought added religion to the mix of conservatism and liberalism. A Roman Catholic, Brzezinski once described himself in a phrase echoing Tillich as "religious in a searching way." Brzezinski, like Carter, perhaps for similar religious reasons, impresses everyone as a supremely self-confident individual. He can be independent to the point of arrogance. Like Carter, he also feels himself something of the outsider. He was born in Poland, a non-American, who though successful and with many of the Establishment trappings, recognizes his essential difference. Like Carter, too, he is an ardent achiever. "He was always fairly intense, with a will power to be best at anything he did," his younger brother once said. He used to sleep on the floor in Poland when he was seven or eight "to develop character." He never missed Mass. Once when the family went on a trip outside Montreal and everyone was thirsty, he said, "I'll keep my mouth dry because I must build my character." Carter could recognize a soul brother in Brzezinski, as well as a philosophical compatriot.

V

IN HIS FIRST three years in office, Carter demonstrated his capacity to learn—whatever the judgment on the results—from instructors like Brzezinski, as he had learned from Niebuhr. He had more trouble learning how to manage his time and energy. He proved to be glaringly weak where his strength supposedly lay—in organizing, in managing, and in procedure.

By his own admission he tried to do too much too fast in his first year, presenting more initiatives than either an independent-minded Congress or his inexperienced staff could handle. In part, this wheel-spinning followed from his enormous and, in this case, overinflated, self-confidence. His expectations for himself and his expectations for all the alter egos he had assembled on his staff exceeded everyone's abilities. His errors also followed from his distinct operating style. Jimmy Carter needs to remain in control, the center that holds together all the parts. The Presidency became an arena much like Jimmy Carter's own interior life: a place where warring forces had to be reconciled and kept from flying apart. The Carter White House itself, in an arresting choice of images, likened its organization to the spokes of a wheel. Carter engaged himself, much like his hero Rickover with "the pinks," in all details, important and trivial. He prided himself, at first anyway, on reading thick briefing books. (Dwight D. Eisenhower, at the other extreme, wanted summaries of no more than a page or two.) He personally administered the White House tennis court schedule, so no one could play without his permission. He chose to get along without a chief of staff to coordinate White House activities, to control the flow of paper and people in the Oval Office, and to take initiatives in the "President's name."

Liberal critics in the press and Democrats in the Congress deplored the "loose," "uncontrolled," "amateurish," "uncoordinated" White House staff—showing just how short Washington memories can be. Professor Richard E. Neustadt, one of the steadiest analysts of the American Presidency, points out that ever since "serious" presidential staffing started under FDR, no Democratic President has wanted a number-one man with authority. The strong chiefs of staff have been Republicans: Rumsfeld in the Ford Administration, Haldeman in Nixon's, and Sherman Adams under Eisenhower. Roosevelt, Truman, Kennedy, and Johnson all preferred, and usually tried, to do by themselves such things as chairing staff meetings, handing out assignments, and vetoing initiatives. Neustadt believes Democratic Presidents have good reasons for being their own number-one men: "Republican administrations, relative to Democratic ones, have pressed less controversial social legislation on reluctant Congresses, and to them, White House 'coordination' seems a relatively simple thing, a matter more of process than of substance." Neustadt, however, sees a major difference between Carter and his Democratic predecessors: they all presided over White Houses far smaller than Carter's. Carter is the first Democrat to work in a Republican-sized White House. Republicans who tried it quickly got themselves staff chiefs. Carter did not, despite the fact that, in Neustadt's opinion, he has been less accessible to his staff as a whole than his Democratic predecessors.

Carter straddled the worst of both worlds, administratively; he tried to do more than even activist Democratic Presidents did, with less of the orderly hierarchical organization that Republican Presidents have depended on. When the results slowed his staff performance, some changes did occur. Carter, for example, gave up control of the tennis schedules. The Carter White House attempted better coordination in the early planning stages of long-range policies. But the chief coordinating job remained unfilled through thirty months of his Administration. Finally, in the tumultuous changes of July 1979, Carter did appoint a staff chief, naming the politically astute Hamilton Jordan. In the past, Jordan had let it be known that he had no inclination to do administrative work and lacked organizing ability. But Carter, faced with criticism of his "disorganized" White House, gambled again—characteristically—counting on Jordan to do the job.

Carter had no trouble delegating responsibility, as opposed to power. Indeed, some of his staff think he delegates too much. His style appears to be to give responsibility to a Cabinet officer or staff person and then not to interfere, except to demand final results. As an agribusiness man, he was used to telling one of his employees or sons, "Fix the tractor." He did not tell them how to do it, confident that they could. The habit became ingrained, though White House policies proved infinitely more complex than a tractor motor. Unlike a Johnson or a Nixon, Carter tends to stay clear of the details in areas where he has delegated authority. He often prefers staff memos to talk—the spokes all converge on the hub, Carter. He expects absolutely knowledgeable and "authoritative" recommendations from his staff. He refuses to allow his staff to jockey for position or authority—he gets very upset at even the hint of infighting by his people. Jimmy Carter wants to keep the level of anger—of potential violent outbreaks—down. His White House office style remains in step with his deepest personal needs. The parts of the operation should not be at war with one another. He holds them all together, and he makes the decisions. He wields the power. Yet it is a curiously gentle power. Error-prone staffers never seem to be disciplined. Carter put up with free-wheeling cabinet officers, like Joseph Califano, for thirty months before exerting authority. To Mr. Earl's son and the born-again Christian, forgiveness is more prized than punishment. Unfortunately, the White House is not one big family, or Sunday school.

Surrounded in his 1970 campaign and then in the governor's mansion largely by inexperienced assistants, Carter controlled them completely. In the White House, they had grown more experienced perhaps, but as an economist who conducted briefings for Carter told us, "They all took their cue from Carter." In this man's view, one of Carter's difficulties is that "no one makes decisions but he."

Some of these decisions and the ways they were reached have been debatable. The Panama Canal treaties had never been a central issue in the campaign. With many of Carter's domestic initiatives stalled because of poor planning—his energy program and his farm program had been developed without consultation with key Congress people or powerful outside constituencies—Carter decided to make the approval of the treaties a rehearsal for any SALT talk agreements and a test of his political leadership. The Panama Canal fight consumed enormous amounts of White House time and political capital. As far as the public was concerned, the victory was so long in coming and so painfully executed that the Administration looked at the end more grateful than triumphant.

In his handling of Bert Lance, Carter also expended valued time, energy, and political capital—and in a fight not only unwinnable but not worthy of winning. The Canal treaties fight, once joined, had to be finished in the national interest as well as in Carter's personal interests. The Lance affair got out of hand a few weeks after the election, when sloppy work by Carter's closest advisers permitted Lance's nomination as director of the Office of Management and Budget to go forward with no attention to the warning flags, prominently displayed in the record, about Lance's loose banking practices and his own campaign irregularities. Carter would have declared such evidence overwhelming if it had been assembled against, say, one of Gerald Ford's close associates.

The drawn-out defense of the indefensible Lance exhibited some of the worst sides of Carter style—including his stubborn pride and his need to see the best in himself and in the loyalists he picked around him. Some critics, perplexed by the way the Lance affair dragged on, darkly wondered "what Carter owes Lance." Perhaps the Lance defense was necessary to ensure Lance's loyalty when the grand jury probe got into Carter's finances. Still, a bond existed beyond money and intrigue. For all his down-home diligence, bright optimism, and religious faith, Lance turned out not to be so smart after all. Jimmy Carter kept his eyes closed in the Lance matter for so long because with his eyes open he would have seen some of himself in Bert Lance. When Carter rashly said to the beleaguered Lance at one point, "Bert, I'm proud of you," he was expressing pride in himself, too.

The Lance case marked the end of Carter's era of good feelings with the Washington press corps. When Lance continued to hang tough as the evidence mounted, the Carter White House developed a bunker mentality, an us-against-them attitude reminiscent of the last Nixon year. In the Carterite view, if the Lance case stayed in the headlines and on the evening news day after day, then it had to do less with new details of his wheeling and dealing than with a voracious press pack in full cry (and with an anti-Southern strain as well). For the longest time, Carter and his loyalists failed to connect the messy little realities of Lance with the lofty expressions of Carter's presidential campaign. When he asked, "Why not the best?"—or the most decent? or the most honest? or the most competent?—he left himself open to trouble when the public perceived less than the best, or most honest, or most competent.

VI

THE SYMBOLISM he had used so magically during the campaign also returned to spook him. Carter rose to the Presidency in part as a plain hardworking figure whose religious appeal promised spiritual regeneration; an unassuming man, he would set aside material trappings. His Inauguration Day walk down Pennsylvania Avenue symbolized his wish to be one with ordinary Americans. He carried his own suit bag off airplanes; his fireside chat in a cardigan sweater signaled the new President's unpretentiousness. After the Johnson and the Nixon years, Carter correctly understood that large numbers of Americans had become disaffected with the powers and perquisites of the Imperial Presidency. They wanted—or *thought* they wanted—an austere, low-key, demystified President, a figure dressed in blue jeans and open-collar shirts rather than a morning suit. The idea of a stripped-down Presidency, as it happened, matched Carter's own style. Physically small, mild-looking, unassuming and careful in his tastes, feeling himself a soul mate of society's victims, Carter had no difficulty fitting the part of the non-Imperial Presidency.

Such an appeal can wear thin after a while; it seems contrived. Worse, it runs up against the deep-rooted desire of a good part of the electorate for a strong leader, for a father figure of sorts. In the campaign, a candidate can say, "I don't know." When a President makes the same statement, commentators spin out columns about the "crisis of leadership." The non-experts—ordinary men and women—also look for a "higher" level of conduct from the President and his First Family. The office supposedly elevates the occupants; if they act like "regular people," it worries other regular people—an *aura* of authority seems missing.

Carter, then, found himself at the center of contradictory American images of the President—one of us, but one who is stronger, wiser, tougher, more vigorous. One of Carter's familiar campaign themes held America needed a government as good as the people. But people, as Carl Rowan observed, "seem to be saying that they want a President wiser, more frugal and braver than the people." We must feel secure that our President can protect us, and can represent us effectively in contests with other strong national leaders. When Carter had difficulty clothing himself in the trappings of power, many people worried whether he was "big" enough for the job. In one popular assessment, he was seen as "an undersized man in an oversized job."

This fear, of course, mirrors the old childhood fear in Carter's own mind. By settled middle age, he had assuaged these fears satisfactorily enough for himself. Winning the Presidency, he did not need further outer signs to confirm his inner security. But the symbolism of presidential leadership demands more: The President must look like the Chief Executive.

VII

ONE OF THE SUPERLATIVES in Carter's vocabulary, his associates say, is the word "adequate." When he tells an associate that he or she did "an adequate job," he intends high praise. A grading sheet of President Carter's performance would rank him *adequate* in his learning abilities and *less than adequate* in his leadership and managerial abilities, including the managing of his public image as a leader.

Honest graders, however, would quickly add how much they don't know about the works of President Jimmy Carter; they would admit epistemological doubts. The common notion holds that the President of the United States performs in a goldfish bowl, with his activities on public display. But the fish bowl only shows the photo opportunities and daily media events that the President's publicity apparatus has arranged. For the clues to important matters—how the President deals with people, how he makes decisions, what he says of issues in private—the public depends upon morsels, impressions, gossip, possible truths—*factoids* rather than facts. These come from the President's men and women and from Congress people, bureaucrats, and other White House visitors. Their accounts must be treated with suspicion, since both the insiders and the outsiders have special interests to push (for example, to make the President look good, or bad). The most valued kind of informer tends to be the insider, like Fallows, who has become an outsider (for reasons of principle, without becoming an embittered turncoat). We "know," then, what a few people tell us directly and what we can find out from them indirectly.

We know that Carter as President has remained true to his most basic traits. He keeps to the same discipline that got him to the office. He still works a long, hard day, getting up at six A.M., reading papers until midnight. He takes pride in being tight with money. Congressional guests at White House breakfasts for a time were being billed $1.25 for their coffee and Danish. At his televised news conferences, he appears lucid, cool, direct, open, intelligent; his sentences and paragraphs all parse. Yet, when pressed on some subjects, he can be evasive, defiant, almost constitutionally unable to concede that he or his associates might have made an error. Questioned about his possible role in the removal of a U.S. Attorney in Philadelphia named Marston—a tangled case whose merits we do not judge—Carter could only repeat, "I see nothing improper in the handling of the case. . . . No, I don't [see any conflict in his public statements on the case]. . . . I do think that our actions are compatible with my campaign statements. . . . If it occurred now, I would do the same."

Good decisions or bad, he makes them, but gives his staff autonomy in carrying them out. He does not second-guess his associates. He maintains his own high-minded moral posture. His commitment to human rights exists as a guiding ideal; in practice, little has been accomplished, mostly because in this sinful world the price of his preachments would come too high. Carter's policy embraces *all* rights proclaimed in the United Nations Universal Declaration of Human Rights, which means not just condemning torture or protecting free speech but trying to meet such "basic human needs" as food, shelter, and health care at home, as well as abroad. As critics have pointed out, words can be cheap, deeds are not. The economic pressure needed to impress a dictator can mean lost business and jobs for Americans. Attention to basic human needs might mean big tax hikes to finance more foreign aid and/or domestic welfare. Such programs suggest a substantial redistribution of income within and away from the United States.

His concern for justice and equity hasn't prevented him from looking the other way at the sometimes smarmy behavior of his family and associates: Billy Carter and his enterprises, the Carter son who tried to sell a book of White House photographs, Jerry Rafshoon's role as manager of the maritime industries' advertising and public relations efforts, Jody Powell's purchase of a $115,000 home without a down payment, the Carter in-law hired as a Washington lobbyist for Coca-Cola, and the unlamented Bert Lance.

Carter hasn't lost any of his reputation for being standoffish and a private person, yet he has seen more Congress people and held more news conferences than any other President. He emerges in the public perception, and in reality, James Reston reported, as "an 'open' President who seems remote." Thus, he remains the contradictory figure.

VIII

AT LEAST ONE PART of the presidential portrait seems odd. Carter's incredible competitive streak nowhere appears in any of the accounts of his White House days. For all outsiders know, he may be seething angrily and tearing briefing books in two; but the Carter we see looks philosophical, unshaken in the face of setbacks. One possible interpretation would be that Carter no longer needs to measure himself against others, because he finally has measured up to his father's perfectionism by becoming the father of his country. His constant need to win has been satisfied. A more likely interpretation suggests that these feelings never go away. Carter didn't face a full-scale national crisis where the need to win could reassert itself until the summer of 1979 brought gasoline shortages. Then he fought doggedly, mindful that his successful handling of this crisis could restore his image as a strong leader.

Some leaders provoke such situations, but crisis thinking runs counter to Carter's instincts for accommodation and balancing. A careful man, he doesn't like surprises. Unlike, say, Nixon, a measure for those who worry about Carter, President Carter seems less likely to create public tests to prove himself. In a serious and unavoidable crisis, Carter's carefully dampened aggressive feelings can surface in a compelling desire to win and to prove his leadership abilities. His energy-inflation broadcast of July 15, 1979, for example, gave him a near-final chance to fight back and measure up.

IX

ONE OF JIMMY CARTER'S parables, passed on to him by his lawyer friend Charles Kirbo, goes like this: A man comes before a judge, accused of being drunk and setting fire to the bed. The judge asks him how he pleads. The man says, "Not guilty," explaining, "I was drunk, but the bed was on fire when I got in it."

At the end of his first year in office, President Carter saw himself a little like that hapless defendant—a man who inherited when he entered the hot spot of the White House a lot of volatile problems, domestic and foreign. As a campaigner, he offered symbols that promised change and solutions; but magic cannot resolve political issues. Once in office, Carter began asserting that the President can do only so much: "Those who govern can sometimes inspire, and we can identify needs and marshal resources, but we cannot be the managers of everything and everybody. . . . We must move away from crisis management." While Carter may be characteristically expressing his lifelong desire for accommodation rather than confrontation, he is also expressing his renewed recognition of the blazing sinfulness of the whole wide world.

With some problems, no one *knows* the solutions; or the best *knowable* solutions may be too politically unpalatable for any President to take—certainly for President Jimmy Carter. The Soviet Union and Cuba, for example, steadily increased their political activities in Africa, supplying arms, training troops, and in general escalating the chances for big-power conflict. Since the Vietnam war disaster, however, the American Congress, firmly controlled by Democrats, has reasserted its power in the conduct of American foreign policy. Largely supine with the Republican Nixon, it now stands up vigilantly against its fellow party man, Carter. The public, or a large part of it, has become understandably gun shy about fresh military ventures in distant parts of the world. We merely want the President, in his brave wisdom and smooth competence, to force the Russians and Cubans to behave—all without the risk of any war, or the dispatch of a single Marine anywhere.

In the absence of a single huge conflagration—an instantly recognizable crisis that commands everyone's attention and support—Carter must struggle against a public tide of widespread, diffuse, free-floating anger and disappointment. Jody Powell had been more profound than perhaps he realized when he said that most voters get interested in presidential politics only once every four years. For the rest of the time, they wish to be left alone, secure in the belief that there's no need to trouble themselves by looking under the hood of the government machine, wanting everything to run smoothly. But the "non-crisis" crises—of the cities and the economy and welfare and the Russians and energy—have been around seemingly for so long that when voters look up, they perceive "nothing has changed." Naturally, they blame Carter.

Given these circumstances, and his own special character, Jimmy Carter has achieved some limited successes; for the rest, he has muddled through, in a kind of postwar British style. The Washington news machine, thriving on action and movement, kept asking "What's the President *doing* today?" The public read, or heard, the answer: "Nothing too much." And Carter's negative job rating dropped ever lower in the polls. When he did act, shaking up his cabinet, the press cried "overreaction."

X

CARTER RECOGNIZED some of his situation in his first State of the Union message, acknowledging the circumstances, not of his own making, of his Presidency. Our time, he declared, has "no single overwhelming crisis," such as the preservation of the Union in Lincoln's day or the preservation of the economy in Franklin Roosevelt's. Instead, he said, we face a series of problems each involving "profound national interests, as in the Presidency of Harry S Truman." Truman, the "little man," measured up to major challenges when they appeared—the atomic bomb decision, civil rights laws, Korea, MacArthur. His style was scrappy; Carter has a different style. Since he needs to see himself in an unbroken relation with the American people, he must merge with them while serving as a "governor." Carter does not impose himself as a leader on the American people, substituting his conception of their destiny for their own. Sensing that the American people have become "conservative liberals," he identifies himself with their perceptions and needs, and then tries to be the "best" leader in these circumstances.

"Each generation of Americans has to face circumstances not of its own choosing, by which its character is measured and its spirit is tested," Carter once observed. The late 1970s, perhaps, are not heroic times. The country, it has been said, had "put behind it" the Vietnam war, the urban riots, and the other divisive issues of the 1960s and early 1970s. But the substantive matters that these dramatic visible events represented—the United States' place in the world, a society of unequal opportunity—endure, and cannot be regarded, in any open-eyed accounting, as "behind" the country. The test of a hero in these circumstances must be to measure up in non-heroic terms to tasks of anti-heroic proportions.

16

Character and Politics

WE HAVE BEEN SEEKING to understand Jimmy Carter, to comprehend the meaning and significance of his life and career. By immersing ourselves in the details while seeking to keep an eye firmly fixed on the broad themes, we have tried to give the reader the conviction of truth that comes only from the immediacy of narrative experience. Now we must step back and seek an overall assessment of Jimmy Carter. For us, however, assessment can only take place within the context of understanding, of true comprehension, involving empathy, of a person's whole life.

Jimmy Carter, of course is more than a person. He is also a President. Therefore, we must try to evaluate both the man and the public official, and to bring the two together in one vision. We have studied Jimmy Carter for over a half century of his life; he has only been President for a few years. Yet the two parts do come together.

Jimmy Carter, the man, has certain features that everyone agrees upon, and which pose little problem of understanding. He is disciplined, hardworking, and orderly; he rises early, is abstemious, and is tight with money, a quality that has a major effect on his policy decisions, and is not to be underestimated. It runs against the grain of Carter's character to spend money unnecessarily. These traits in Carter are related not only to his development within his family, but to the Puritan spirit that prevailed in parts of the South and was part of his heritage. Jimmy Carter also is a man of high intelligence. Even his enemies admit that. His power to absorb briefings has become legendary. He seems to have an almost photographic memory; he is able to say of a Congressman, "Isn't this guy from the Sixth District in Tennessee, whose brother lives in Georgia and voted for me in 1966?"

Judgments become harder once analysis goes deeper into Carter's character. His self-confidence sits in odd conjunction with his shyness. In the words of his Georgia friend, Warren Fortson, all the Carters have a "self-imposed competence." "Ego" is another term that could be used. The reporter Elizabeth Drew once worried about Carter: "Too much self-doubt can be paralyzing, but just a little can be healthy." Most of Carter's aides place the trait in a favorable light. Jim Fallows told us that Carter has "a healthy arrogance of character and self." Carter has himself told us that he emerged from his religious experiences without "doubts," and with a sense of utter security. Out of this confidence and security, Carter claims that he can admit mistakes and move on in a changed fashion.

Carter's sense of self-confidence draws upon religious convictions as much as upon heritage. Carter quotes the Bible: "If the trumpet gives an uncertain sound, who shall prepare himself for the battle?" Carter sounds his own trumpet in no uncertain fashion. His statements then tend to become self-fulfilling prophecies, in large part because of his incredible exertions. A large number of Carter's past successes came because he believed he would succeed. For a small, timid, shy boy, this has been the best way—and the only way—to measure up.

In politics, however, positive thinking works only up to a point. The problem is that it can also become a dangerous illusion. Governor Carter believed he achieved a 50 percent reduction in a budget because he ordered it, not because his order got carried out. President Carter speaks to his foreign policy advisers and says, "The Russians have agreed to x and y." In fact, as they have to correct him, the Russians only agreed to negotiate x and y.

Another side of Carter's self-confidence is that, basically, he has a secure sense of self. He knows who he is. Many secure people don't feel the need to be assertive. Not Carter. As a result, he comes through in some personal encounters as a man of steel. Yet, in other encounters, Carter appears as gentle, soft, shy; he seems like a man who is seeking to know himself. Sometimes he actually "steels" himself, throws back his shoulders, on entering a public gathering.

This is part of the complexity of Jimmy Carter. To say that he is self-confident gives us little real understanding unless we immediately add that it is connected to heritage, religion, and mind-cure philosophy, that it lapses over into exaggerated claims and illusions, and that it sits side by side with shyness. The simple trait of self-confidence in Jimmy Carter becomes entwined in complexity. Not surprisingly, then, Carter's critics worry that his self-confidence leads him into self-deception. Carter has been compared to Queen Victoria's moralizing Prime Minister, William Gladstone, who combined "complete sincerity and a seemingly unbounded faculty of self-deception." As we saw, Oliver Cromwell also regarded his own will and desires as being simply those of God.

These same critics also worry about the possibility of Carter's overrigidity. They fear that he walls himself off from criticism, is unwilling to admit mistakes, and is unable to change course. When we asked Stuart Eizenstat about this charge, he said, "I think he [Carter] admits it. Once he makes a decision, he normally doesn't change it unless there is good reason to do so." Another aide, Landon Butler, told us, "I would describe Walter Mondale as firm, but I would describe Jimmy Carter as rigid. The difference probably is that with Walter Mondale you try an idea out on him, and there'll be a little give, and he'll come back to you. With Carter it bounces right off, kind of a 'No, I'm not going to do that.' It's just quicker—he can be quick and impatient."

We believe that Carter's "rigidity" is connected to his other traits of control: disciplined control of time, of mind, and of self. It circles back on self-confidence, because once Carter asserts something positively, he has great difficulty admitting he is wrong; naturally, for it undermines his future power of positive thought. Fortunately, this circle of behavior is not a compulsive pattern, though it is awfully compelling. To take the most spectacular example, after resisting *any* cabinet and staff changes he asked for everyone's resignation.

II

JIMMY CARTER, the man, has a genuine empathy with the little men of the world, those on the bottom rung of society. It comes, we believe, from his own self-image. Carter has overcome his smallness and become a David among Goliaths. Patrick Anderson, Carter's former speechwriter, told us about two of the jokes Carter told and retold during the campaign. Carter does not often repeat jokes, and he tells them rather badly. As Anderson recounted, the first joke goes like this: "A little man goes into a bar and there is a big bully at the bar. The bully knocks him down and says, 'That's a karate chop from Korea.' Then the bully gives him a judo chop and says, 'That's judo from Japan.' And then the bully gives the little guy an aikido chop and says, 'That's from Okinawa.' Finally, the little guy leaves the bar and comes back with a tire tool and hits the big guy over the head and says, 'And that's a tire tool from Western Auto.' "

The second joke goes like this: "A young divinity student goes into a crowded bar and sits down at the last table. He is a very pure and innocent young man, and a beautiful woman comes and sits next to him. Before he has anything to say, she says in a very loud voice, 'I can't go out with you.' He looks at her, very concerned and shocked. And then she says, 'No, you can't come to my room,' again in a very loud voice that makes everyone listen. The young man blushes and is full of consternation at this inexplicable behavior. At this point the woman says in a still louder voice, for all to hear, 'No, I wouldn't spend the night with you.' The young man, humiliated, whispers to her, 'Why are you embarrassing me like this?' And she confides in him that she is a psychology student and this is an experiment that she is conducting. At which point the young man says in a loud voice, 'Fifty dollars?' "

Perhaps we should be grateful that Carter doesn't tell too many jokes. His aim may have been to show that he has a sense of humor, or that he isn't a prude. But as Anderson says, "The point of these two jokes is that the little guy is getting back at the bully or at the system." The jokes show an innocent little man being

subject to unjust harassment; they end with the tormentor's humil-
iation, the tables turned. We hear the echo of some of Carter's
reactions to his father's whippings. But more, we hear with the
third ear the sound of the little man measuring up to the challenge.
By so doing, he himself grows, becomes big.

III

THOSE COMPLICATED IMAGES—of identification with the little
man, of David-like redemption of the ordinary victim—profoundly
influence Carter's conception of the People—the flock he is supposed to lead. The notion of the People is central to Carter's politics; if his presidential leadership in the first few years has been flat
and uninspired, then it may be in part because of this basic political
belief.

Throughout his 1976 campaign he repeated the slogan that the
American people deserved a government as good as themselves.
Reading *War and Peace*, studying the Baptist ecclesiology, serving
in the Georgia legislature, Carter kept extracting the simple lesson
that all good came from the People. The People erred only when
imposed upon by the special interests, like the villainous oil companies in the energy crisis of 1979, or when their leaders failed to
mobilize their rightful instincts. Carter's leader—his governor—
leads by listening to the People and then following their needs and
desires; between the leader and the People there would be no in-
termediaries. Implicit in this notion is that the leader may go directly to the People, over the heads of legislative bodies such as
Congress and bypassing the Washington press.

Changes in the primaries and the electoral process over the
last ten years allowed a Jimmy Carter to emerge from obscurity,
outside the regular party system, without Washington experience;
and by means of personal campaigning, TV, and other "direct"
contacts, candidate Jimmy Carter could see himself at one with the
public and its desires. Once President, however, Jimmy Carter had
to work with the People's representative, the Congress.

An independent, imperious Congress serves as a practical obstacle to Jimmy Carter's view of politics. Equally important, his

view may be seriously flawed in itself, apart from its poor application to current political realities. First of all, Carter's conception of the People may be another example of overly optimistic positive thinking. Are the People always good and always right? In the 1930s, a substantial part of public opinion in the United States opposed the efforts of Franklin Roosevelt to place the United States on the side of Great Britain against Nazi Germany. Today are the People ready to support a strong energy policy? Or a SALT agreement? Carter's conception of the American People may be one-sided and overtrusting.

Secondly, how is the will of the People and the public interest to be known? By public opinion polls or by a leader's intuition? Is it a metaphysical notion? Is there a public interest that can be achieved without sorting through the competing claims of special interest groups? Carter simply slides over a question that has perplexed serious minds for centuries. Quite obviously, while leaders have to listen to their followers, they can't be weather vanes blown this way and that, as Edmund Burke pointed out to the electors of Bristol. Jean-Jacques Rousseau once suggested that what he called the General Will could be arrived at by counting up the Particular Wills, something like a Pat Caddell public opinion poll. But Rousseau later rejected that notion, arguing that the General Will really equalled Virtue, and that one leader could define it. A realization of this Rousseauistic vision was Robespierre and the Reign of Terror.

Third, are special interests always bad? Carter has taken on the oil lobby and doctors and lawyers; but what about other special interests? Consumers, teachers, small businesspeople, blacks, women, Greek-Americans, Chicanos, and other groups have lately come to understand the value of lobbying and forming coalitions for specific legislation. In the past decade, previously powerless groups have gotten together and learned how to push some of the levers of influence in Washington. Organized groups can be seen as a more sophisticated—that is, a more knowledgeable and effective—form of representative democracy.

Moreover, the People is an aggregate whose views on an issue —Do you favor abortion on demand? Are you for the Panama Canal Treaty?—can be polled mechanically. But politically the People never act as an aggregate. What counts is that part of the

People that brings its weight to bear in the political process, the part that functions in a *political* manner. Almost always, this means acting as a special interest group, a lobby, a particular political grouping, and only ultimately, and mostly even then in a localized fashion, acting as a collective.

The People in the abstract, then, may be both an unreliable and a false god. But Carter's difficulties do not come only from his oversimple conceptions of politics. His performance as a politician also raises problems. Carter may like politics, as he has said, but he is not a very good politician. We know he won the Presidency in part because he didn't come from Washington; but we also know that every President since Herbert Hoover had considerable Washington experience before entering the White House—Roosevelt as Secretary of the Navy; Truman, Nixon, Kennedy, and Johnson in the Senate; Eisenhower as a "political" general; Ford in the House of Representatives. Carter had none of that background. The Georgia governorship didn't offer this broad experience.

Worries about Jimmy Carter's inexperience—his "parochialism"—surfaced early in the 1976 campaign. We are all parochial in some senses, of course; even the most sophisticated person moves in relatively limited worlds. Carter's parochialism, however, seems to be reinforced by his appointment as his key aides of a disproportionate number of Georgians, who, bright and capable as they are, were without previous Washington experience. Parochialism also showed up in a lack of knowledge of Congress and the ways of Washington; the king was ignorant of what goes on in the court. At the beginning, feeling beleaguered, Carter and his aides alternately reached out to the "enemy" Establishment for help, or fell back on their own limited experiences. Around the White House, a key Carter aide once explained, "We say three things: 'In Georgia we did . . . ,' 'We promised . . . ,' and 'Jimmy says . . .' "

Carter's Administration, similarly, alternated between successes and failures, between making a difference—for example, on such issues as Middle East peace and human rights policies around the world—and just making an ineffectual noise. His first years in office became a race between his fundamental decency and intelligence and his equally fundamental inexperience and limited talent for mass leadership.

IV

AT THE BEGINNING we said that the "mystery" of Jimmy Carter can be resolved by recognizing both his contradictions and the way he handles these conflicting elements in an act of tight control. Edgar Allan Poe's great detective, Dupin, knew that the best way to hide the sought-after letter in "The Purloined Letter" would be to put it in a highly visible place. Carter's secret has been placed right out in the open in his character of controlled opposites.

We have tried to analyze and interpret that open "secret." With that analysis as background, we can offer a few general observations about his Presidency.

First, we believe that Jimmy Carter has resolved his own private wars—the contradictions within himself—and doesn't need to seek out fights in the Presidency to "prove" himself. The creating and managing of crises is not one of Carter's needs.

Second, his short-term actions will be unpredictable. Because he has so many different traits, when these sides come into contact with one another, the result becomes complexity. Jimmy Carter can go in several directions, without being purely expedient, because each of these directions is Jimmy Carter—one of his sides. The directions of his Presidency has been shaped, day by day, by pressures from other political institutions, like the Congress, and by the accidents of politics and life. While all Presidents must respond to outside forces, Carter will respond *more* than others in his behavior. Jimmy Carter is not compulsive, though he is consistent in his character traits. With the Congress, he came to realize that his actions were counterproductive. With his official family, he saw stagnation. So he switched tactics. His expediency exists as a part of his realism, a settled way of reacting in general to events in a consistent direction that remains true to his complex self.

Third, he will stick to his long-term programs, however shifting or temporizing he may seem. Carter doesn't forget his goals, and his plans for achieving them. If he suffers a setback, he will be back to try again, whether on dams or on human rights. The first phase of his energy plan—his Moral Equivalent Of War—flopped

260

in 1978. In 1979, he was back with the program disparagingly known as MEOW II. He won't give up. We believe that Carter really believes in his own promises, and his desire to bring compassion and justice to the victims of the sinful world.

Fourth, Carter's major accomplishments will be limited in his first term, and not just because the post-modern Presidency struggles against political limits. Carter, while intelligent, is a man of limits, too. We *know* the world is full of sin, and needs more justice; but simply willing it won't make it a better world. The power of positive thinking needs to be translated more effectively than it has been into the power of politics.

Fifth, Carter may not have a second term in which to prove that he can measure up to the role of President. He may be wrong about the end of ideology and politics; the parties may not be over. The country, as we said earlier, may have needed a deflationary Presidency in 1976—almost ten years after it thought it was getting one with Nixon in 1968. But what may have been right in 1976 may not be enough for 1980. The appeal to the old values and to trust may provide us with a share of spiritual comfort. But material and political problems still have to be exorcised, not just the spiritual ones. Other candidates in 1980, and 1984, may offer some fresh ideals for changed times, making ideological appeals frankly from the left or right. The voters may be ready to hear a call to get the country moving again. Unless Carter can change sufficiently so as to offer a more charismatic, and even ideological, leadership, he may find himself out of step with the People, whose needs and yearnings he had previously been able to interpret so well, well enough to get elected in 1976. Carter's fusion of contradictions, if our analysis is correct, is now being put to its major test; he may have to choose from some of the contradictory positions he has tried so hard to fuse, and to reject others; accommodation may no longer be the rule. The strain on Carter's political beliefs and on his personality could be intense. Would this simply be one more contradiction he is able to accommodate within his character? Will Carter's fusion of contradictions finally bring success, or facing the end of his term with a lack of such success, will he be able to make the hard choices and opt for an "ideological" position? In the 1970 Georgia election, he made just such an expedient choice.

The novelist Peter de Vries writes of a character, "Deep

down, he's shallow." With Jimmy Carter we need to turn this around, and say something like "On the surface, he goes deep." He is in fact an extraordinary political figure—a moral, religious man in politics. Whether he will be judged a "good" President is another matter. We believe that his place in the history of the Presidency will depend not so much on his goodness but on the way in which his character is brought into conjunction with events, a matter of political as well as personal development.

The Carter-Begin-Sadat meeting and the Middle East treaty are good examples. Success initially did three things: it reversed Carter's decline at the polls, restored his prestige in facing up to the Congress, and shored up his own self-confidence. It also reflected some of his most characteristic traits: it gave dramatic evidence of his extraordinary ability to fuse contradictions; it drew upon his deepest religious convictions to maximum political advantage; and it exemplified his tenacity and his talents in one-to-one relationships. On the other hand, the continuing inflationary spiral, seemingly uncontrollable by presidential action, all but cancelled out the public gains achieved in the Middle East. By summer, people were thinking about gasoline lines.

People keep asking, "Who is Jimmy Carter?" This simple question, we have tried to show, requires a complex answer. Jimmy Carter will always keep a part of himself separate from us while he merges, mysteriously, with God, the Father, and the People. In the end, as Dylan Thomas tells us, we are left mostly in "Fathering and all humbling darkness."

V

AT THE BEGINNING we said that different people see different Jimmy Carters because he has so many sides—some contradictory, but all Jimmy Carter. We also said that how people respond to Jimmy Carter personally becomes as much a part of "the Jimmy Carter story" as his personality itself. Both these points were driven home to us when we came to the point where we had to draw up some bottom line conclusions about Carter, and his Presidency. The two of us, though different by temperament and training—which places us, literally, at different points of view when looking at the tapestry of Jimmy Carter's life—nevertheless agreed on a great deal of what we saw. Inevitably, however, we also saw, or thought we saw, different parts of the tapestry.

As a result, each of us wants to speak in his own voice; in a sense we are offering "two endings" to this account. First, Mazlish, then Diamond.

MAZLISH: As an historian, I seek the long view. Studying character, I seek to be empathetically understanding, interpretive rather than judgmental. As a practitioner in the field of personality and politics, I seek to align character and political behavior in an historical framework. Our portrait of Jimmy Carter's character necessarily involves many themes: the fusion of contradictions, belonging and being apart, measuring up, winning and losing, thinking positively, depression, control, shyness, and toughness. These themes find resonances in the political world in terms of questions about authority, power, planning, modes of leadership, accommodation, and so forth. In the historical background are the great issues of the South and the nation, caught up in questions of belonging and being apart, of caste and class; of religion, morality, and *Realpolitik;* of populism and conceptions of the nature of the People. Carter's complexity of character mirrors America's character and concerns.

Such an interpretive study carries its own implicit judgments and points of view. They are the ones that I think most meaningful. Still, if forced to stand up and be counted in more explicit terms, I am prepared to state, bluntly, that my evaluation of Jimmy Carter is positive. I believe that history will speak better of Jimmy Carter than do his contemporary judges. In 1972, I published a book on Richard Nixon, analyzing his patterns of behavior. At the time my analysis was not popular; since then, I like to think that my general portrait has been confirmed by events. Now I find myself in a somewhat similar initial position with Jimmy Carter only in reverse. I am reassured, though others are not, by his patterns of behavior, both as to his personal and political qualities, and am willing to wait for more long-range judgments to bear me out.

Carter is an unusual President in a number of ways. One of the most striking is his advocacy of complexity both in his person and in his policies. One can postulate two basic kinds of politicians: simplifiers and "complexifiers," to coin a term. The first tend to reduce issues to either/or, to black/white terms. The second tend to see both "either" and "or" in all issues, to insist on mixing the colors of the rainbow. Most politicians are of the first kind. Made dangerous by the demagogues of the world, the Hitlers of history, the resort to simplification is nevertheless an essential and ordinary part of politics. The "complexifiers" in politics are very rare, for they tend to turn people off with their refusal to advance yes/no propositions. In fact, they rarely enter politics or get elected.

Carter, though he is not above occasional simplifying, is fundamentally a "complexifier," who did enter politics, and who won. He recognizes this trait in himself, as well as its general political liability. As he remarked, "The more simplistic an approach can be, the more the public can be aroused." Nevertheless, he went on to defend his refusal to simplify by saying, "Although this opening up [of the complexity of issues] to the public produces an appearance of confusion, in the long term I think it is good." It is this trait that, whatever the long-term outcome, in the short term gives the image of the "fuzzy" or "waffling" Jimmy Carter, and tends to make our analysis of him, with its emphasis on the many "sides" and on complexity, seem perhaps too "bland."

Complexity aside, I suspect that Jimmy Carter will figure largest in future history books as a truly "religious" American President. Almost all of our Presidents have had religious affiliations (mostly Protestant, of course) of varying strengths; and a number have tried to be moral leaders. Overwhelmingly though, their private religion was subordinated to what has been called the "civil religion" of America: the beliefs enshrined in eighteenth-century Enlightenment thought, held by our Founding Fathers, and embodied in the symbols and ceremonies of our nonsectarian republic. Jimmy Carter is within this tradition, too. But unlike perhaps all our other Presidents, he is, first, a religious figure, and only afterward a political one, practicing his "civil religion." He is closer to the line of Luthers and Gandhis than to Jeffersons and Jacksons. A Richard Nixon constantly appealed to the verdict of history. Jimmy Carter appeals to a different sort of judge: God.

Carter's religious nature makes contemporary judgments of him unusually difficult. He marches to a different drummer than his critics (and I, personally, confess to hearing another sort of music too). Carter is trying to appeal on a truly moral-religious level to this country while performing as a practical politician. In this lofty effort, he often falters, and he may well fail (though, at this writing, a portion of his first term—and a possible second term —still lie before him). If he does, by and large, fail, history will see it as one of the more instructive "failures" of our times.

On a more mundane level, Carter's Presidency is certainly not a failure. He has shown himself a basically good and decent man. His blemishes are also obvious; but then so are, for example, FDR's and JFK's, looked at closely. As James MacGregor Burns shows us, FDR could be dissembling, devious, even cruel, and often inconsistent. Carter, though he appeals to God, is also very human. As for his programs, they are generally on the side of the angels—whether about defense, foreign policy, even inflation— though hemmed in by the "devilish" constraints of Congress, pressure groups, and, it has to be admitted, Carter's own accommodating character as we have tried to portray it.

We are obsessed today with the question of "greatness." Stars are not good enough; we have to have "superstars." To ask whether Carter is a "great" President, or even a "good" one, seems to me the wrong question. The right one is: What kind of President is he, has he been, and perhaps will he be? Given any realistic expectations as to what any President could have done from 1976 on, I believe that he has "measured up" so far surprisingly well.

Great Presidents can emerge only when character and circumstances combine in a special way. Our recent circumstances can hardly be considered a forcing house for greatness. It is no accident that the whole of the Western world today is without great leaders of the stature of an FDR, a Churchill, a De Gaulle, and even a Hitler and a Stalin. Carter's potential to be a great leader has not been tested; let us hope it never will be. One reassuring measure of his character is that he does not seem impelled to create circumstances that would allow him to be great in conventional terms. True, one must take cognizance of the possibility that the public demand for a "hero," or the appearance of a hero, may be such as to make it extremely difficult for a President who refuses to play the role to survive or even to be able to govern effectively. Nevertheless, in his own non-heroic terms Jimmy Carter is, in my book, enough of a hero for present-day and future historians to speak well of him.

DIAMOND: As a journalist, I know that the reward system of my craft places great weight on not being taken in by public figures, on being tough and realistic about them. Yet many journalists are also idealistic, even romantics. We want to believe in the perfectibility of men and women. Why else would we write and publish, rather than sell shoes or insurance, if not to make life a little better or more understandable in some way.

I don't think that Carter, or his staff, took me in or, for that matter, took in the American voters. Jimmy Carter is what he seems to be—an agribusinessman of intelligence, useful talents and enormous needs: to be loved, to be paid attention to, to measure up at all times. His religious conversion is real, and he can thank God for it. Without the sense of security and self-confidence his faith has given him, he would never have achieved what he has achieved; probably he would be doing nothing more demanding than serving as president of, say, the South Georgia Seed Association. People sometimes ask, Is he really any brighter than his predecessor, Gerald Ford? He probably is, but in handling the one "medium" crisis of his Presidency—the economy—he fell back on the uninspired "inflation-fighting" policies of Ford.

Realistically, Jimmy Carter is like thousands of other middle-aged men of middling stature in authority in our society. He is no hero in the remembered mold of John Kennedy. Certainly he is no leader of Franklin Roosevelt's stature. On the other side, Jimmy Carter is not a villain or a cipher; he is no Nixon or Harding. Realistically, Camelot was never as heroic as we thought at the time, and Nixon was not quite as villainous as we like to believe. Carter fits in the middle. He is the man next door—if you live in the nicest neighborhood in a nice small town or a "good" suburb. He has conducted his Presidency the way he conducted his Annapolis years, or his Navy career, or his married life, or his agribusiness. He has set for himself two or three goals—a favorite Carter Administration word is "priority"—and works unceasingly to meet them. But the priorities are conventional—to learn Spanish, or reduce expenditures. And he does not have, as both his critics and friends would agree, the sure practical instincts to get his national priorities, such as they are, accepted by the Congress or by his mythic constituency, the People. Goodwill and Christian caring and divining the People's will aren't enough.

Idealistically, we may wish that Carter had something more to give us as a nation, the Irish Catholic Kennedy's sense of irony and tragedy, the patrician Roosevelt's gallantry and foxiness, even the gut fighter Nixon's tricks and threats (the world, after all, is full of other leaders with larceny in their hearts). But realistically, given the circumstances of the primaries and campaign, and the alternatives, Carter was probably the most we could get in 1976—and probably will be in 1980 as well. He is still a "small team" leader, good at inspiring his submarine's engineering team, or his campaign loyalists. Beyond these intimate circles, he comes across as weak and ineffectual. He doesn't reach the millions as persuasively as the small team. Nothing in his life prepared him for "big team" leadership. His leadership style in part comes from Mr. Earl, who led by personal example. Carter does what he regards as right, which is fine for a patriarch, a church lay preacher, or a community doer. But it is not enough for a national leader, who has to have the political skills to get his policies adopted. He is decent and intelligent and honest enough—*we* can thank God for that—but he has no political vision; his is a moral vision of Sunday school homilies bolstered by his reading of Niebuhr and Tolstoy.

In truth, our modern "reformed" nominating system does not produce the best man or woman, but the candidate with the most time to devote to running, the most money to spend (or his friends' money), and the most desire to win. Campaigns test endurance rather than leadership or vision or understanding of life's limitations and possibilities. Carter is no hero; perhaps the times do not demand one right now. Equally important, perhaps we have grown up enough as a people, after the 1960s, *not* to look to Washington for a Great White Father, or for the Brightest and Best. Of course, there are some issues—for example, the need for national will to address ourselves to urban "priorities," like jobs and housing—where only Washington can supply the necessary leadership and the money.

In Athens in the fourth century B.C., the comic writer Aristophanes took aim at the pretensions of a society with a higher opinion of itself than was justified. In his play *Plutus,* a slave, Cario, meets an important-looking Athenian on the street.

You look well, the slave says. What do you do? Are you a farmer? he asks.

No, the Athenian replies. Lord save us. I'm not.

Are you a merchant?

No, I have sometimes had to take that trade up as an alibi.

What do you do?

I am supervisor general of all things here, public and private too.

Oh, and what are the qualifications for that job?

Well, I wanted it very much.

Aristophanes would have understood Jimmy Carter.

NOTES

1 • The Figure in the Tapestry

page 9

Arthur Schlesinger, Jr., *The New York Times Book Review*, June 5, 1977, p. 1.
The New Yorker, May 8, 1978, p. 31.

page 10

James Fallows, *The Atlantic Monthly*, May and June 1979.

page 13

Our interview with Jimmy Carter, Plains, Georgia, August 6, 1976.

pages 13–14

Our interview with Hamilton Jordan, White House, June 17, 1977.

page 15

Immanuel Kant, *Idea for a Universal History from a Cosmopolitan Point of View* (1784).

page 16

Elliott Levitas, quoted in *Wall Street Journal*, July 10, 1976, p. 1.

2 • Family

page 20

Quoted by William Greider, Washington *Post*, October 24, 1976, p. A16.

page 21

Francis Simkins, *A History of the South* (3rd ed., N.Y., 1963), p. 388, quoted in George B. Tindall, "Beyond the Mainstream: The Ethnic Southerners," *The Journal of Southern History*, Vol. XL, No. 1, February 1974, p. 15.

page 21

Quoted in Paul H. Elovitz, "Three Days in Plains," *The Journal of Psychohistory*, Vol. 5, No. 2, Fall 1977, pp. 194–95.

page 22

Carter quote from *Why Not the Best?* (N.Y., Bantam Books, 1976), p. 13.

page 23ff.

Information about the Carter family can be found in Kenneth H. Thomas, Jr., "Georgia Family Lines: Carter-Gordy," *Georgia Life*, Winter 1976, pp. 40–46, and *Atlanta Journal and Constitution Magazine*, January 16, 1977.

page 24

Our interview with Griffin Bell, Department of Justice, Washington, February 22, 1977.

page 25

Interview with Lillian Carter by Orde Coombs, a writer and our friend, Plains, Georgia, June 1976.

"the best, biggest . . ." from *Miss Lillian and Friends,* as told to Beth Tartan and Rudy Hayes (N.Y., A & W Publishers, 1977), p. 23.

Quote from Jimmy Carter in *Why Not the Best?* p. 85.

3 • Mr. Earl

page 29

"The potatoes . . ." quoted in Tom Collins, *The Search for Jimmy Carter* (Waco, Texas, Word Books, 1976), p. 38.

page 30

"He was just a wizard . . ." quoted in *Atlanta Journal and Constitution Magasine,* January 16, 1977, p. 21.

page 31

George B. Tindall, *The Emergence of the New South: 1913–1945* (Louisiana State University Press, 1967), p. 616.

page 32

Our interview with Lillian Carter, Plains, Georgia, July 8, 1976.

page 33

"I never did hear . . ." quoted by Henry Allen, *Washington Post Potomac Magazine,* August 15, 1976, p. 27.

page 33

"influence touched everyone" from Ruth Carter Stapleton, "Christmas with the Carters," *Ladies' Home Journal,* December 1977, p. 74.

page 34

"big man" from our interview with Hugh Carter, Jr., White House, March 30, 1977.

page 34

Our interview with Gloria Carter Spann, Plains, Georgia, July 8, 1976.

page 35

"Daddy felt . . ." in Lisa Battle, Knight News Service, Boston *Globe,* February 10, 1977, p. 26.

page 36

"That's something . . ." in "U.S.A. People and Politics," July 16, 1976. Washington Educational Telecommunications Association (hereafter referred to as WETA).

Transcript, p. 8.

NOTES

pages 36–37

Our interview with Billy Carter, Plains, Georgia, August 6, 1976.

Quote from Gloria Spann in Lisa Battle, op. cit.

page 38

Our interview with Gloria Carter Spann.

4 • The Legend of Lillian

page 43

"nice, happy . . ." from interview with Lillian Carter by Orde Coombs.

Jimmy Carter's account in *Why Not the Best?* p. 33.

page 45

Orde Coombs, "The Hand That Rocked Carter's Cradle," *New York*, June 14, 1976, p. 40.

page 46

"He was the head . . ." Elovitz, op. cit., p. 177.

page 49

Our interview with Lillian Carter.

page 50

Our interview with Larry Brown, Cambridge, Massachusetts, May 13, 1977.

page 50

"Ethel Barrymore . . ." from Kandy Stroud, *How Jimmy Won* (N.Y., William Morrow, 1977), p. 78.

page 51

"I thought I just had to . . ." in Lillian Carter and Gloria Carter Spann, *Away from Home* (N.Y., Simon & Schuster, 1977), p. 15.

page 53

Our interview with William Gunter, Atlanta, January 6, 1977.

page 56

"She had the courage . . ." Our interview with Gloria Carter Spann.

5 • Gloria, Ruth, and Billy

page 57

Our interview with Billy Carter.

page 59

Our interview with Virginia Williams, Plains, Georgia, March 1977.

page 63

"My father had loved me . . ." in Ruth Carter Stapleton, *The Gift of Inner Healing* (Waco, Texas, Word Books, 1976), p. 16f.

page 64

"the hardest thing . . ." in Jessamyn West, "Jimmy Carter's Sister: 'How Faith Can Heal,' " *McCall's*, April 1977, pp. 32–42.

271

page 110

Our interview with Greg Schneiders, White House, February 22, 1977.

page 110

"An incremental series . . ." from an interview with Dr. Bourne by Adelina Diamond, Oct. 1977

page 112

"He would talk . . ." from interviews on "U.S.A. People and Politics," WETA, July 16, 1976. These Navy officers were also interviewed by assistants of ours for our study.

page 115

For the full account of Carter's meeting with Rickover, see *Why Not the Best?*

9 • "A Man Like My Father"

page 120

"He used that word . . ." WETA, July 16, 1976, p. 16.

page 122

"I'd say a thousand . . ." Winter interview.

page 123

John Pope's recollection in Stroud, op cit., pp. 146–47.

His penny-pinching . . . William L. Miller has written a book, *Yankee from Georgia* (N.Y., Times Books, 1978), in which he depicts the Puritan ethic as a rare commodity in the South. For a contrary view see Edmund S. Morgan, "The Puritan Ethic and the American Revolution," *William and Mary Quarterly*, 3d ser., Vol. XXIV, January 1967; but see also C. Vann Woodward, "The Southern Ethic in a Puritan World," *American Counterpoint* (Boston, Little, Brown, 1971). We take the position that, though not dominant, the Puritan ethic was a notable feature of the South, as well as the North, and especially after the emergence of the New South.

page 124

Our interview with P. J. Wise.

page 125

Our interview with Mary Ann Thomas, Americus, Georgia, March 1977.

page 127

"He was so tiny . . ." quoted in Howard Norton and Bob Slosser, *The Miracle of Jimmy Carter* (Plainfield, N.J., Logos International, 1976), p. 85.

page 129

"It seems hard . . ." in *Why Not the Best?* pp. 72–73.

page 129

His friend Warren Fortson preferred the term "humanist." Our interview with Warren Fortson, Atlanta, January 7, 1977.

page 135

"was particularly against . . ." quoted in James Wooten, *Dasher* (N.Y., Summit Books, 1978), p. 233.

"I went there several times . . ." quoted in Robert Scheer, "Jimmy, We Hardly Know Y'All," *Playboy,* November 1976.

page 136

When we asked the various parties . . . In Wooten, op. cit., Hamilton Jordan is quoted as asking Jimmy Carter whether he knew his uncle Clarence and receiving the answer, "I know who he is, but I don't think I've ever met him" (260). The quote that follows in our text from Mrs. Jordan is from an interview she gave to Orde Coombs.

10 • Winners, Losers

page 143

William Greider, Washington *Post*, October 25, 1976.

page 145

Our interview with Reg Murphy, San Francisco, April 18, 1977. Paul D. Schindler assisted in this interview.

page 146

Our interview with Philip Alston, Jr., Atlanta, January 6, 1977.

11 • Born Again

page 151

Our interview with Charles Kirbo, Atlanta, January 7, 1977.

page 153

On an autumn day . . . A number of versions of what happened during this walk exist. See, for example, Lloyd Shearer, "The President's Kid Sister Speaks Out," *Parade,* May 22, 1977, pp. 7–9, and Gail Sheehy, "Ladies and Gentlemen, the Second President—Sister Rosalynn," *New York,* November 22, 1976, p. 56. Also in Norton and Slosser, op. cit., pp. 34–35.

page 155

In Colonial America . . . This discussion is based partly on an interview conducted for us by Ruth Daniloff with Elizabeth McKeown, Professor of American Religion at Georgetown University, Washington, D.C.

page 159

William James, *The Varieties of Religious Experience* (N.Y., Collier Books, 1961); the quote that follows is on p. 99.

page 161

Richard Shaull's views were brought to our attention by Mary Reynolds, of Wellesley College.

page 163

New York *Times*, June 19, 1977, p. 36. The quote that follows is also from this source.

page 170

"I make one image . . ." in *The Norton Anthology of Modern Poetry*, ed. by Richard Ellman and Robert O'Clair (N.Y., Norton, 1973), p. 902.

page 171

To McGrory's visible shock . . . As reported to us by Don Winter, based on an interview with Jimmy Carter, and confirmed by Mary McGrory.

12 • White Man's Candidate

page 179

"I think so, too." Quoted by Steve Ball, Jr., Atlanta *Journal*, April 7, 1970, p. 2A.

page 180

"these are my folks . . ." quoted by Reg Murphy, Atlanta *Journal*, August 26, 1971.

page 180

Gwinnett County *Daily News*, September 3, 1970, p. 8.

Voters tended to blame . . . See James Clotfelder and William R. Hamilton, "Electing a Governor in the Seventies," in *The American Governor in Behavioral Perspective*, ed. by Thad Boyle and J. Oliver Williams (N.Y., Harper & Row, 1972), especially p. 33.

page 181

"Carter's as good . . ." Our interview with Reg Murphy.

page 185

"He was informally dressed . . ." Our interview with Stuart Eizenstat, Washington, December 30, 1976.

page 188

Watson, born in 1856 . . . The classic work is C. Vann Woodward, *Tom Watson: Agrarian Rebel* (N.Y., Oxford University Press, 1975; first published in 1938).

page 190

Carter's admiration for Russell. Communication from Don Winter to us, December 31, 1976.

page 191

Philip Stanford, *Columbia Journalism Review*, July/August 1976.

13 • "A Great Urge to Govern"

page 194

In the end, the message got through . . . For the changes, see Jack Bass and Walter DeVries, *The Transformation of Southern Politics* (N.Y., Basic Books, 1976).

page 196
"I think that your faith . . ." ibid., p. 128.
page 197
"Things just happened . . ." Our interview with Frank Moore, Washington, March 29, 1977.
page 198
"He impressed me . . ." Our interview with Lester Maddox, Atlanta, January 10, 1977.
page 198ff.
Reorganization became . . . Excellent accounts of Jimmy Carter's administration as governor of Georgia can be found in T. McN. Simpson III, "Georgia State Administration: Jimmy Carter's Contribution," a paper delivered at the 1973 annual meeting of the Southern Political Science Association, Atlanta, November 3 (which has the great advantage of having been written before Jimmy Carter was ever thought of as a presidential candidate), and "The Department of Human Resources" (Chapter 7 of a draft manuscript, dated December 2, 1976), both unpublished but kindly made available to us by Professor Simpson.
page 207
"a businessman himself . . ." Our interview with Landon and Nancy Butler, Atlanta, January 9, 1977. Anne Mazlish assisted with this interview.
page 209
If he has, indeed, succeeded . . . See Alexander L. George, "Power as a Compensatory Value for Political Leaders," *The Journal of Social Issues,* Vol. XXIV, No. 3, July 1968, pp. 29–49.

14 • Running

page 212
Later, after the 1976 election . . . A post-mortem on the 1976 election was held at Harvard University's Institute of Politics, December 1976.
page 215
Garry Wills quote from *New York Review of Books,* August 5, 1976, p. 20.
page 217
An anthropologist looking . . . Anthony F. C. Wallace, "Religious Revitalization," paper presented at the Eighth Institute on Religion in an Age of Science, at Star Island, N.H., July 26, 1961; and "Revitalization Movements," *American Anthropologist,* 58, 1956, pp. 264–281.

15 • A President in the Middle

page 228
Once having powerfully moved . . . See Clifford Geertz's analysis of Gandhi in these terms in *New York Review of Books,* November 20, 1969, p. 4.

NOTES

page 229

In the first formal study . . . See, for an account of Woodward, Hugh Heclo, *Studying the Presidency* (A report to the Ford Foundation), August 1977.

page 233

The political scientists . . . Jack Knott and Aaron Wildavsky, "Jimmy Carter's Theory of Governing," *Wilson Quarterly*, Winter 1977, especially pp. 49–50.

pages 235–236

"He told me how . . ." *The New York Times Magazine*, July 24, 1977, p. 6.

"I have a substantial . . ." quoted in interview by Saul Pett of the Associated Press, carried in the New York *Times*, October 23, 1977, p. 36.

page 236

Taking up the offer . . . Washington *Post*, December 18, 1977, p. C1.

page 241

Brzezinski in his own life . . . For what follows, see the Manchester *Guardian*, February 27, 1977, p. 17.

page 242

Richard E. Neustadt, "Staffing the Presidency: Premature Notes on the New Administration," *Political Science Quarterly*, Spring 1978, Vol. 93, pp. 1–9 and 12–14.

16 • Character and Politics

page 254

"a healthy arrogance . . ." Our interview with James Fallows, Washington, March 30, 1977.

page 256

Our interview with Patrick Anderson, Washington, December 7, 1976.

page 264

"Although this opening up . . ." quoted by James Reston, New York *Times*, December 5, 1977, p. 42.

On America's "civil religion," see especially Robert Bellah, "Civil Religion in America," *Daedalus*, Winter 1967, and *The Broken Covenant* (N.Y., Seabury Press, 1975). In Bellah's presentation, the "civil religion" is a combination of the Puritan and Enlightenment traditions.

page 265

See James MacGregor Burns, *Roosevelt: The Lion and the Fox* (N.Y., Harcourt, Brace, 1956).

INDEX

Blacks
  disfranchisement of, 31
  as C.'s early playmates, 18
  C's "identifying" with, 86
  "Miz" Lillian's attitude toward, 25,
    52
  in present-day Washington, 229
  in Southern "family," 21
Bond, Julian, 198, 206
Bonhoeffer, Dietrich, 163
"Born again" experience, 66, 151–75
Bourne, Peter, 110–11, 151, 173, 211
Brother Billy (Stapleton), 70
Brown, Edmund G., Jr. (Jerry), 222
Brown, Larry, 50–51
Brown, Sandy, 50
Brown vs. Board of Education, 128
Bryan, William Jennings, 188
Brzezinski, Zbigniew, 238–41
Bumpers, Dale, 195–96
Burke, Edmund, 258
Burnham, Walter Dean, 231
Burns, James MacGregor, 265
Busbee, George, 202–3
Busing, C.'s view on, 129
Butler, Landon, 207, 255
Butler, Nancy, 174

Cabinet shake-up, 10, 103, 251, 255
Caddell, Patrick, 173, 214, 219–20,
    233, 258
Califano, Joseph, 244
Callaway, Howard ("Bo"), 145–46,
    149, 198
Camp David meeting, citizens invited
    to, 174, 209
Camp David summit, 10, 237
Carter, Billy (grandfather), 24
Carter, Billy (brother), 21, 30, 57, 69–
    76, 205, 248
  alcoholism of, 76
  fails in college, 73–74
  father and, 37–38
  "fun loving" nature of, 36
  as "good old boy," 69
  as "loser," 75

in Marine Corps, 72–73
  and "Mr. Earl," 38
  as segregationist, 69–70
  unsatisfactory school record of, 71
  violence of, 70
Carter, Donnel Jeffrey (son), 108, 142
Carter, Gloria, *see* Spann, Gloria
    Carter
Carter, Hugh, Jr. (first cousin once
    removed), 24
Carter, Hugh, Sr. (cousin), 24, 34, 129,
    200–1
Carter, James (great-great-great-
    grandfather), 23–24
Carter, James Earl, Jr. ("Jimmy"),
    247
  affection for Rosalynn, 111
  aftermath of 1966 defeat, 151–52
  "aloofness" and "strangeness" of
    in 1976 campaign, 221
  ancestry of, 23
  anger of, 52, 97, 130, 226, 243
  at Annapolis, 90–92, 96–101
  "apart" feelings of, 15, 19, 21, 112,
    221
  appeal of "public life" to, 139–40
  authority identification in, 28
  "belongingness" vs. "apartness"
    conflict in, 15, 19, 112
  Bert Lance and, 74–75, 244–45
  Bible and, 126–27, 254
  birth of, 30, 77
  black "mothers" of, 21
  black problems and, 128–29
  blacks appointed by, 229
  blacks in early childhood of, 18, 25
  Bob Dylan and, 172–75
  bookishness of, 112
  "born again" experience of, 66,
    151–75
  bureaucrats and, 204
  business enterprise of, 78, 121, 124–
    125
  and cabinet shake-up, 10, 103, 251,
    255
  campaign promises of, 236

War and Peace (Tolstoy), 93, 163, 257
Watergate, 213
Watson, Tom, 26, 31, 73, 188, 190
Wesley, John, 159
West, Jessamyn, 65
White, Theodore H., 212
White House staff, criticism of, 242
Why Not the Best? (Carter), 14, 27–28, 33–34, 38, 42, 55, 79–80, 83, 94, 116, 138, 153, 168
Widow (Caine), 47
Wildavsky, Aaron, 233–34
Williams, Roger, 155
Williams, Virginia, 59, 89, 93
Wills, Garry, 174–75, 215

Wise, P. J., 89, 124–25
Wise, Dr. Sam, 29
Wise Sanitorium, 29
Woods, Charles, 112
Woodward, August B., 229
Wooten, James, 156
World War II, 99–100, 122, 128
Wyoming, U.S.S., 101, 107

Young, Andrew, 45, 51
Young, Don, 197
Young Man Luther (Erikson), 56

Zimmerman, Robert, *see* Dylan, Bob